FATAL REMEDIES
The Ironies of Social Intervention

ENVIRONMENT, DEVELOPMENT, AND PUBLIC POLICY
A series of volumes under the general editorship of
Lawrence Susskind, *Massachusetts Institute of Technology, Cambridge, Massachusetts*

PUBLIC POLICY AND SOCIAL SERVICES
Series Editor:
Gary Marx, *Massachusetts Institute of Technology, Cambridge, Massachusetts*

STABILITY AND CHANGE: Innovation in an Educational Context
Sheila Rosenblum and Karen Seashore Louis

FATAL REMEDIES: The Ironies of Social Intervention
Sam D. Sieber

Other subseries:

ENVIRONMENTAL POLICY AND PLANNING
Series Editor:
Lawrence Susskind, *Massachusetts Institute of Technology, Cambridge, Massachusetts*

CITIES AND DEVELOPMENT
Series Editor:
Lloyd Rodwin, *Massachusetts Institute of Technology, Cambridge, Massachusetts*

FATAL REMEDIES

The Ironies of Social Intervention

Sam D. Sieber

PLENUM PRESS • NEW YORK AND LONDON

Library of Congress Cataloging in Publication Data

Sieber, Sam D.
   Fatal remedies.

   (Environment, development, and public policy. Public policy and social services)
   Bibliography: p.
   Includes index.
   1. United States—Social policy. 2. Evaluation research (Social action programs)—
United States. 3. Social action. I. Title. II. Title: Social intervention. III. Series.
HN57.S52   361.6'1'0973   81-13832
ISBN 0-306-40717-5   AACR2

© 1981 Plenum Press, New York
A Division of Plenum Publishing Corporation
233 Spring Street, New York, N. Y. 10013

Printed in the United States of America

In memory of

Paul F. Lazarsfeld

a giant who stood on the
shoulders of pygmies

. . . for what I would that do I not; but what I hate, that I do.

Paul, Romans 7:15

These are old fond paradoxes to make fools laugh i' the alehouse.

Shakespeare, Othello II.i

Foreword
by Ronald G. Corwin

What do the following have in common: regulatory agencies, magnet schools, a declining empire, puritan asceticism, plea bargaining, the recent tax revolt in California, the Boston Tea Party, the Vietnam War, public drinking halls during Prohibition, police entrapment, and Yosemite National Park on Labor Day weekend? If the answer is not readily apparent, read this engaging book. Dr. Sam Sieber makes a convincing case that harbored in a potpourri of such events are countless instances of how well-intentioned social interventions often produce harmful effects. Searching for a general framework that will force us to think of heretofore discrete events in new ways, he has chosen to use the term "intervention" in its broadest sense. His approach is a superb example of how serious scholarship can produce a new creative synthesis from familiar knowledge when the scholar is guided by a lively curiosity. The wide-ranging subject matter of this book provides a refreshing vision of social reform movements and programs. I think that Sieber has succeeded in doing what he set out to do: namely, to develop a general and inclusive typology for classifying and interpreting the perverse effects of all kinds of social interventions.

This is not merely another treatise on the "unintended effects" of purposeful action, however. As Dr. Sieber carefully documents, sociologists have seldom made a conscientious effort to precisely distinguish the *null* effects and *side* effects of interventions from their *reverse* effects. While many interventions are disappointing, it is indeed sobering to admit that good intentions have often made matters worse for the very people for whom the help was intended. How can anyone disagree with Sieber's admonition that the harm caused by interventions constitutes a serious problem which deserves attention? If a well-intended intervention produces regressive effects, what is the responsibility of those persons who designed and implemented it? In particular, what responsibility should be assumed by those social scientists who have played prominent roles in promulgating programs with negative effects? Given what Merton modestly calls the "indeterminacy of behavioral findings," social scientists cannot hope to resolve in the near future many of the problems they are addressing. And yet there are always a few social scientists heroically ready to offer quick solutions to massive social problems. The Equal Educational Opportunity study and subsequent work by James Coleman and others on busing, the Pygmalian study, and the controversial claims of Arthur Jensen are only a few examples of how the work of competent researchers is now being wisely and unwisely used for policy purposes. Social scientists can no longer pretend that their work is only part of an academic puzzle. When they are wrong today, there is more at stake than a null hypothesis.

Rummaging through an impressive array of references, Sieber finds instances of calculated and inadvertent interventions in many fields. He comes upon seven major ways in which well- and ill-intentioned meddling can produce results opposite from that intended. The examples, some of which I list below, are familiar. They read like today's headlines:

- A raise in Old Age Security Insurance benefits makes poor, elderly persons ineligible for Medicaid.
- Generous local welfare program attracts thousands of unemployed persons to the city.
- Magnet schools succeed at the expense of other schools in the district.
- Legislature neglects to appropriate sufficient funds to launch new program.
- Federal Trade Commission neglects the unfair practices of large monopolies in favor of hit/miss attacks on small firms.

What this delightful book contributes to these familiar complaints is a provocative framework for comparing and integrating what would otherwise remain discrete events. As Sieber reports, for example, I encountered a reverse effect in my study of the Teacher Corps: the schools which were assigned the most reform-minded change agents exhibited the least change. This reform strategy backfired because the change agents had posed status threats to the classroom teachers who were in control of the situation. Such threats represent only one of the many intangible "social costs" of change that policymakers routinely pass along to those who are responsible for implementing new programs. Some of these social costs can be calculated, as in the case of the proposed school curriculum change which offers clear advantages and disadvantages for the principal, the classroom teachers, the students, and the like. The proportion of persons at each echelon who stand to gain or lose from various aspects of such an innovation can be computed. But much of the status anxiety rises as a by-product of the participants' uncertainty about what is likely to happen if an innovation is introduced, and this uncertainty is one of the many social costs which are not easy to calculate. This example from my study represents a type of "provocation," or more specifically, an "implicit threat" as it is defined in Sieber's framework. With the exception of my distinction between the known and uncertain social costs, that is the way I had interpreted it, too. But what I did not clearly perceive at the time is that status threat is part of a family of reverse effects which, with the benefit of Sieber's typology, I can now systematically compare and contrast.

It can be readily observed that some innovations require structural changes, shifts in priorities, or reallocation of resources, while others are merely added to existing routines (e.g., new tasks are handled by working overtime). Sieber calls the latter innovations instances of "overload." Other problems result from a "perverse diagnosis," that is, underestimating an organization's capacity. Sometimes innovations are adopted primarily to obtain funds or for other opportunistic reasons, and evaluations are sometimes undertaken for the sole purpose of legitimating an existing practice. These are cases of "exploitation" in Sieber's schema. Innovations ritualistically adopted for symbolic purposes are examples of what he calls "placation."

None of these observations is in itself new, and of course simply inventing different labels for familiar events would be of little advantage. But what Sieber offers is a general framework for comparing different ways that reverse effects can occur. The typology produces some strange bedfellows, but it seems capable of encompassing almost any conceivable type of reverse effect.

My only reservation is that, aside from programmatic shifts, some dynamic aspects of the intervention process are beyond the scope of Sieber's inquiry. I think it would be fruitful to consider the tentative, fluid, evolutionary nature of many interventions when thinking about their adverse effects. For example, in the course of my recent study of the politics of program design in a federal agency, I identified four ways in which new social programs are often shaped and altered:[1]

---

[1]Ronald G. Corwin, *The Entrepreneurial Bureaucracy: Biographies of Two Federal Programs* (Greenwich, Conn.: JAI Press, forthcoming).

1. Two types of planned mutual adaptations
   A. *Progressive specification.* This refers to the deliberate adjustments through which the original, often tentative program design concepts are fleshed out in greater detail during the program.
   B. *Successive approximation.* In this case, the design itself undergoes calculated step-by-step revisions. Revisions are often required to correct errors in the design and to accommodate the fact that the capacity of local projects often has been overestimated.
2. Two forms of inadvertent slippage
   A. *Reconciliation.* This process grows out of the fact that program designs often contain inconsistencies, and that some groups tend to oppose certain features of a design. Because of incompatible demands and group conflict, designs continue to evolve throughout the course of many programs.
   B. *Mutation.* Completely new design concepts and goals also evolve on occasion as the parties involved reinterpret features of the design, change goal priorities, or synthesize previously sovereign ideas and practices.

The presence of any or all of these processes can help predict whether or not reverse effects will occur, and perhaps they even determine the type of reverse effect that occurs.

Although only cautiously optimistic about the possibilities of preventing reverse effects, Sieber believes that it is possible to temper the extreme cases and offers some plausible policy advice toward that end. But his advice presumes that *someone* in power is sufficiently concerned about the adverse effects and sufficiently rational to go through the prescribed steps. It is a charming fantasy, but social intervention is basically a political act, a strategy that one party uses to control another. The outcome is necessarily a set of compromises and bargains.

I suspect that any optimism about eventually being able to control events for the better is more of an expression of the sociological faith than of sociological wisdom. This faith reaches back to the tradition of conservatism and Compte, who saw in sociology a new religion promising salvation for humankind. Sociology would override the human tendency to drift blindly into the apocalypse; the tools of science would overcome the wickedness deemed inherent in the evolution of modern large-scale societies. This seductive image of sociology inspired the radical sociologists as well, who borrowed from the conservatives the assumption that sociologists, when properly armed with knowledge and power, can learn to manipulate society. The radicals became imbued with a flattering estimate of their ability and their mission to transform the world through policy research and political action. Add to these traditions the liberals' resilient insistence that objective social scientists can remain neutral and stand apart from and above the events of the times, and you have a very optimistic view of social reform.

However, this humanistic, liberal slant of the discipline is difficult to reconcile with an essentially conservative idea at the heart of sociology: that society takes precedence over the individuals who comprise it, and that the social forces which rule history are beyond rational control. Alvin Gouldner once said that sociologists have invented a grotesque world made by people but no longer subject to human control. It seems to me that the impressive cases of reverse effects marshaled by Sieber fit Gouldner's grotesque, fatalistic world at least as well as they fit any other model

Even though Sieber's discussions of policy implications are insightful, the ultimate contribution of his book is the guidance it provides for new directions in research. Consequently, one could imagine a study that would inquire into the different conditions associated with each type of reverse effect. For example, in my Teacher Corps study mentioned above, there were a few instances where liberal reform agents did succeed in introducing new practices despite the resistance of classroom teachers; namely, in the least bureaucratized systems where teachers were not unionized and typically did not hold advanced degrees from good universities. Such teachers lacked the structural protections that hierarchy, peer organization, and technical competence can provide. One might then ask whether a condition such as lack of bureaucratization is associated only with status threat situations, or whether comparable conditions can explain the presence or absence of placation or other forms of regressive effects. More generally, is it possible to predict which type of reverse effect a given set of conditions will produce?

While the framework opens up new vistas, some hard work remains. As Sieber takes pains to stress, many conceptual and procedural problems must be worked out. First, the notion of reverse effect itself presumes that there is clear consensus on the ultimate and proximate goals. Sieber addresses most of the problems associated with the identification of goals and that discussion need not be repeated here. However, it is worth noting again that goals can change during the course of an intervention. A new objective can be adopted as a result of the experiences. This possibility raises questions about how to track multiple, shifting goals which are often defined or redefined after the fact.

He alludes to a second issue that deserves further consideration: What is an "intervention"? It is defined here as any sort of deliberate effort to alter the human situation in some desired direction, such as a welfare program, a military expedition, an organizational structure, or a law. The intriguing juxtaposition of human endeavors as diverse as welfare programs and military expeditions accounts for much of the appeal of the book. Intervention is used as a sensitizing concept which casts a very wide net for heuristic purposes. However, the concept is so inclusive that it seems to encompass almost any collective action; I suspect that tack has now served its purpose and that it is time to focus the parameters a bit more.

Third, there can be reverse effects only if the consequences of the intervention can be accurately assessed. Yet the results of social actions are often indeterminate or un-known, or the data so controversial that all sides can confi-dently claim success or failure. In such cases the researcher may easily become a party in ideological wars.

Fourth, the effects of many interventions are often only temporary. For example, although the effects of busing in order to achieve racial balance in the public schools are still disputable (re: the above point), there is a distinct possibility that the backlash responsible for the so-called white flight occurs only during the initial year of busing, after which the effects become less regressive.

Still another complication arises from the fact that the typology itself presumes consensus on criteria for identifying the different types of reverse effects. While I generally agree with the way most of the examples were classified, there are some shady areas. For example, in some cases overload can reflect a mistaken diagnosis, but it might also be a consequence of what Sieber calls "overcommitment." The final point that I will mention is one that Sieber acknowledges, but one that bears repeating: many interventions are so complex and are implemented under such variable conditions that it is a fiction to speak of "the intervention" as though it were a unitary phenomenon.

But in noting these problems I merely want to stress that it will be challenging to use the typology in research, not that it is impossible. While I remain dubious about our willingness as a society to control the reverse effects of interventions, I am totally optimistic about the ability of social scientists to learn more about them. This insightful book now provides a way.

RONALD G. CORWIN

Department of Sociology
Ohio State University
June 1981

Acknowledgments

I wish to express my great appreciation to the following persons for reading earlier versions of this book and offering valuable advice: David Caplovitz, Catherine Bodard Silver, Louis Schneider, and Gary Marx. Professor Marx was especially helpful with the final version by pointing me in the right direction with his acute criticisms. Robert Merton was also kind enough to give encouragement and to supply me with some of his own work in progress and other materials. And above all, my wife Brandy deserves much credit for putting up with my stretches of seclusion and otherwise distracted frame of mind during the many weeks of work on the manuscript and for her unfailing support.

I also wish to thank Academic Press, Inc., for permitting me to use portions of my essay, "Regressive Intervention: The Solution as the Problem," in R. K. Merton (Ed.), *Unanticipated Consequences of Social Action: Variations on a Sociological Theme.*

None is responsible for the shortcomings of this work save myself.

SAM D. SIEBER

Contents

**PART III—Summary and Implications for Theory
and Policy 183**

PART I

Theoretical and Political Perspectives

CHAPTER 1

The Problem in Perspective

One of the most remarkable and sorely lamented patterns of human affairs is also one of the most obscure in origin: the culmination of action in effects directly contrary to those that were intended. Nor can this pattern be attributed to mere want of circumspection, default of planning, or suicidal impulse. For it appears that few institutions, programs, or leaders are immune to the vexatious experience of worsening the condition that they set out so nobly to alleviate. History past and present abounds in examples, and a nearly universal fascination with the topic is manifested by an array of technical and popular terms—counterproductivity, negative results, backlash, boomerang effect, perverse incentive, Pyrrhic victory, Promethean fallacy, two-edged sword, and going to sea in a sieve—as well as by a host of trenchant aphorisms reminding us that man's good intentions are paving stones on the road to hell, the cure is worse than the illness, the solution is the problem, the enemy is us, or, as Hamlet was maliciously aware, the engineer is not secure from being hoist with his own petard.

Nor have the regressive effects of purposive action escaped the purview of classical social theory. Indeed, the phenomenon has served as a springboard for the historical analyses of such diverse thinkers as Karl Marx, Max Weber, and Herbert Spencer. Thus, Marx's version of historical dialectics envisioned the revolution of the working class as a result of the growing power of capitalism. In *Capital*, from *Marx and Engels: Basic Writings on Politics and Philosophy*, we read:

> Centralization of the means of production and socialization of labor at last reach a point where they become incompatible with their capitalist integument. This integument is burst asunder. The knell of capitalist private property sounds. The expropriators are expropriated. (Marx, 1959, p. 166)

In Marx's view, feudalism and mercantilism, as well as capitalism, contained "the seeds of their own destruction," a metaphor that has dramatized the self-defeating nature of certain social actions as no other. That Marx's prediction of capitalism's demise has not been borne out does not invalidate the basic explanatory model *qua* model. As Henshel (1976, p. 75) has noted, "the idea of internal contradictions, sometimes rephrased as internal 'tensions' or structural 'strains,' has ultimately become a key conception in the hands of *non-Marxian* sociologists."

Weber's theory that secularization in general and mammonism in particular were fostered by the religious ethic of Protestantism (via the emphasis on disciplined, selfless, frugal industry or "inner worldly asceticism," as he called it) affords another classical instance of the centrality of reverse effects in sociological theory. And just as Marx referred to the internal contradictions of material conditions, so Weber became interested in "the tragedy of the idea . . . the idea [that] in the end, always and everywhere works against its original meaning and thus destroys itself" (Marianne Weber, cited in Schneider, 1970, p. 104).

Of the three founders of sociology mentioned above, however, it was Spencer who applied the idea of regressive effects to a variety of governmental programs. In Spencer's view, legislative intrusion into natural evolutionary processes almost invariably produces pernicious results: "Acts of Parliament do not simply fail; they frequently make worse. . . . Moreover, when these topical remedies applied by statesmen do not exacerbate the evils they were meant to cure, they constantly induce collateral evils; and these often graver than the original ones" (Spencer, 1946, pp. 131, 133). And so one finds on Spencer's list of interventional taboos public education, sanitary measures, commercial regulations, welfare, improvements of harbor facilities, and even a postal service.

By far the largest portion of pernicious effects cited by Spencer was attributed to "interference with the law of supply and demand." Interspersed in his medley of economic interventions, however, were such "law-made" problems as the enticement effect of censorship, the "tyranny of officialism," and the false sense of security generated by consumer and industrial safety regulations. Keenly alert to the unforeseen consequences of legislation deriving from the presumed "organic" structure of society, he formulated a doctrine of social evolution that called for the dismantling of public administration in deference to private initiative and the survival of the fittest. Thus, Spencer may be viewed as the intellectual father of contemporary conservatism in its distrust of big government, welfare, unions, and regulation of private enterprise—reminding us that the issue of regressive intervention is very much a part of the current debate over the limits and utility of government at all levels.

Spencer was by no means the first social analyst to rest his case for opposition to social reform on the inevitability of unintended consequences. Here, for example, is Burke (1978, p. 152) in the midst of his vituperative "reflections" on the French Revolution:

> The real effects of moral causes are not always immediate; but that which in the first instance is prejudicial may be excellent in its remoter operation; and its excellence may arise even from the ill effects it produces in the beginning. The reverse also happens; and very plausible schemes, with very pleasing commencements, have often shameful and lamentable conclusions.

For these reasons, Burke averred, only the seasoned states-man is qualified to undertake reform:

> The science of constructing a commonwealth, or renovating it, or reforming it, is, like every other experimental science, not to be taught *a priori*. Nor is it a short experience that can instruct us in that practical science.

Here we have one of the main tenets of antiradicalism: Only those with vast experience in the wielding of power can foretell the outcomes of action, a circumstance which renders their role indispensable to the well-ordered state. In short, there are dark paradoxes beyond the comprehension of ordinary mortals that had better be left to their masters.

But despite the recognition of regressive effects by some of the most brilliant minds of the past, the idea has not been subjected to systematic treatment, that is, to a treatment that might yield knowledge of the special features of interventions in interaction with their contexts that promote reverse effects; and that might thereby afford the opportunity to predict and control such effects rather than acquiesce in their occurrence, on the one hand, or renounce all reform, on the other. Weber and Marx devoted their attention to broad historical trends; this inclination rendered their explanations highly complex and, in Marx's case at least, prone to empirical error. And while Spencer focused on a wide array of discrete governmental efforts, he was not attentive to the distinctive features of these efforts which, under certain conditions, were responsible for pernicious results; he was mainly interested in economic intervention ("socialistic meddling"); he often based his argument on speculation rather than on verified cases and overlooked conservative measures that also yield reverse effects. Indeed, since he believed that the "serial genesis of phenomena, and the interaction of each series upon every other series, produces a complexity utterly beyond human grasp" (Spencer, 1946, p. 133), he had little reason to search for those patterns of regressive intervention that would be comprehensible to policy-makers. In this respect he is even more pessimistic than Burke who at least believed that *experienced* legislators possessed some knowledge of the evils they are likely to spawn by good intentions. Further, the strong ideological odor that clings to the works of Spencer and Marx has weakened confidence in the explanatory power of the models of social evolution and the historical dialectic respectively. This reaction is unfortunate because, as I hope to show, both models have roles to play in the systematic study of regressive intervention.

Owing in part to these features of classical social theory, little effort has been made by contemporary social scientists to treat regressive intervention as a distinct social problem; to identify its variants and analyze their dynamics and sources; and in the process to draw implications for a deeper understanding of social structure, contemporary events, and the guidance of social policy. In a society that has become increasingly interventionist as well as progressively complex, these issues assume an importance that is hard to exaggerate. Indeed, it is arguable that reverse effects of purposeful interventions have become a central feature of modern society.

To allay suspicions that the value of investigating the ironical outcomes of social action is restricted to swelling the storehouse of *arcana sociologica*, let us pause to take a small sample of the diverse problems that fall within the compass of my study: the increased segregation of urban schools as whites move to the suburbs in response to initial busing efforts or, alternatively, as parents are permitted to send children to the school of their choice as a consequence of voucher systems; the stigmatization of the mentally ill as a consequence of institutionalization; the promotion of traffic congestion as a result of expressway expansion; the reinforcement of crime as a consequence of incarceration and the barring of ex-convicts from many occupations; the high casualty rates of certain psychotherapeutic techniques; the engendering of defiance and counterviolence by the use of state force that is perceived as illegitimate; and the educational penalization of pupils who are placed in lower ability tracks for special attention. On a broader historical scale, one might mention the devastation of South Vietnam as part of an effort to preserve the life and prosperity of the people; the gradual depletion of natural resources as a result of a high standard of living and its associated technologies; the rise of the early Christian community as a response to martyrdom; and the fall of empires as a consequence of successful expansion.

As these examples suggest, incidentally, self-defeating social action is politically impartial. The conservative programs of a law-and-order administration, a militaristic regime, a crusade for moral rearmament, or a drive toward self-sufficiency or free choice are as vulnerable to the angels of self-destruction as the liberal programs of a Great Society or a European socialist state. This point has been regrettably overlooked in the debate between liberals and neoconservatives that followed the demise of the liberal consensus. Because liberal reformers were put on the defensive by the charge that negative consequences and failures of social programs were rampant, they felt compelled to assert that such effects were not especially troublesome and could be remedied by more experts, more money, and more compassion. In effect, they adopted a double standard of frank acknowledgment of perverse effects and outraged denial of their significance for the future of humanitarian effort. Conservatives who did their homework had a rather easy time undermining this position, thereby reinforcing their ostensibly do-nothing posture. Overlooked in the fray were the negative consequences of projects that are historically associated with conservatism itself and, even more important, *the need to formulate a theory of unanticipated consequences that will apply to radical, liberal, and conservative programs alike.* We have witnessed instead a great deal of ideological recrimination, with an occasional fresh look at the *few* instances cited by neoconservatives as generating reverse outcomes of social policy. (See, for example, the collection of essays edited by Coser and Howe, 1977.) All sides have diverted attention from the need for an objective, wide-ranging, systematic study of unanticipated consequences.

This point will become clearer when I proceed to examine

the ways in which regressive outcomes are typically underestimated by neoconservatives, liberals, and radicals and then
later analyze a number of concrete instances of reverse outcomes that range far beyond those cited by neoconservatives.
First, however, it is necessary to pause for a definition of the
major terms of my inquiry. Precisely because of the appeal of
the subject to the ironist and neoconservative debunker and its
seeming repulsiveness to many liberal reformers, it is important to circumscribe sharply the phenomenon I have in mind.
And it should become obvious from my effort to stake out the
territory that I am far from being concerned solely with the
social improvement projects of the overly maligned 1960s.

SOME CONCEPTUAL GUIDELINES

In the first place, the term *social intervention* denotes any
sort of deliberate effort to alter a human situation in some
desired direction, such as a welfare program, a military expedition, an organizational structure, or a law. The parable of the
bank panic that Merton (1957, pp. 422–423) employed to
exemplify the self-fulfilling prophecy is, to be sure, an instance
of self-defeating social action, but it is not an intervention.
Instead, it falls into the category of collective behavior. If a
self-defeating belief is spawned or nurtured by a particular
intervention, however, then the effect can be attributed to the
intervention itself. A classical example is the Maginot Line,
which lulled the French into a false sense of security and
consequent immobilization of military resources that contributed to their defeat by the German army in 1940.

Further, my use of the term *intervention* is not restricted to
the alleviation or prevention of social problems, as shown by
my inclusion of such interventions as warfare, revolution,
propaganda, and so on. Moreover, the scale of the intervention might range from guided historical transformations, such
as the Reformation, to interpersonal relationships, such as
parental punishment for bed-wetting.

A second major point is that by *regressive* I mean that the intervention rendered the original end-in-view less attainable, or, to state it somewhat differently, caused a deterioration in the condition that it was supposed to alleviate. A finding of no-effect (or simple failure) would not qualify as a regressive outcome. Thus, the "boomerang effect" of propaganda would not be considered regressive unless the message was understood in a manner that ran counter to the original intent, or unless the public's level of resistance to subsequent messages was increased by the confusion or impatience created by the message. A mere discounting of the message because of its sponsorship or the fears that it arouses is not a reverse effect. Similarly, the term *negative effect* as used in evaluation research is often applied to both null effects and reverse effects (as I will demonstrate in a later chapter), while here I am concerned with only the latter. The popular term *self-defeating behavior* suffers the same ambiguity.

Third, I am concerned ultimately with the influence of the interventions on conditions or goals to which they were originally addressed and not simply with what are conventionally called side effects, second- or third-order consequences, externalities, or Spencer's "collateral evils." Only if a side effect rebounds in such manner as to worsen the condition that was originally addressed, that is, to render the goal even more difficult of achievement, can it be said to play a role in the production of regressive outcomes. As we shall have occasion to see, it appears that regressive outcomes can occur without the mediation of side effects external to the trajectory of an intervention.

The side effects of *technological* innovations have long commanded our attention, of course, but only recently have methods been developed for predicting such effects in a highly systematic fashion. Because of these new techniques, Bell (1973, p. 27), among others, is sanguine about the prospects of alleviating the negative side effects of technological change:

> As a number of studies by a panel of the National Academy of Science has shown, if these technologies had been "assessed"

> before they were introduced, alternative technologies or ar-
> rangement could have been considered. . . . Technology as-
> sessment is feasible. What it requires is a political mechanism
> that will allow such studies to be made and set up criteria for the
> regulation of new technologies.

Indeed, the congressional Office of Technology Assessment was created in 1972 with precisely this mandate. It seems that the emphasis of technology assessment is on side effects with little attention to reverse consequences; this tendency is perhaps not surprising in view of the firm scientific basis for the success of a new technology in meeting strictly technical goals. This is not to say, however, that reverse effects are not possible in the realm of technological innovation. For example, the construction of an atomic power plant in a region that is highly resistant to technological change, or where possible malfunctions pose a threat to a large population, might serve as a rallying point for protest that would *set back* the develop- ment of atomic power throughout the nation. In general, how- ever, regressive consequences of this sort are neglected by TA in deference to a concern with negative side effects on proxi- mate physical and social environments.

Today there is also a certain alertness to the possibly negative side effects of *social* programs—an alertness, in fact, that has fanned the embers of a neo-Spencerian revolt against government intervention of any sort. But those who are favor- ably disposed to programs of the kind that were launched in the Great Society era tend to discount the magnitude of these effects. Levitan and Taggart (1976, p. 9), for example, argue that negative consequences were far exceeded by the benefits precisely because they were detected and efficaciously han- dled. ''The negative spillovers of social welfare efforts were too frequently overstated and were usually the unavoidable con- comitants of the desired changes. Examples are legion. . . . Every program generates problems but these have usually been manageable.'' This view reminds us of a critical feature of side effects that is not shared with reverse effects: their susceptibility to being traded off against the intended beneficial outcomes of action. In short, negative side effects can be accepted as being worth the benefits. This argument cannot be applied to regressive intervention because not only is the original goal unachieved, but the situation is made worse. Not only is the initial investment lost, but the harm that is done must often be undone, and this requires further investment. Furthermore, because remedial measures require the shocking admission that problems have been confounded, they are seldom applied. Reverse effects, then, require special attention because of their far greater potential for harm.

Even if the burden of negative side effects outweighs the positive effects on the originally designated feature (assuming that some such calculation could be made), this would not necessarily be regarded as regressive for my purposes. Only if the side effect impairs the future achievement of an original goal, either directly or indirectly, is it appropriate to speak of regressive action. An educational innovation that seeks to give students the chance to pace themselves but which incurs the hostility of disciplinarian parents would not be regressive unless the parents forced the school to close its doors or to be more authoritarian than it had been before. The loss of rights as a result of therapeutic institutionalization would not be regressive unless such loss undermined the achievement of therapeutic goals. A new drug designed to reduce maternal morbidity might be found to induce blindness, epilepsy, or mental deficiencies in children, in which case it would be "counterindicated"; but it would not be regarded as regressive unless it *increased* the chances of maternal morbidity. Regressive consequences, then, are not synonymous with a "net balance of negative consequences" unless this net balance has adverse effects with regard to one's original intentions.

What constitutes one's original intentions is not always transparently clear, of course. Goals are often left quite vague, either consciously or unconsciously, so as to afford leeway in action or to gain consensus among key participants and supporters. Consequently, in my selection of examples of regressive intervention for analysis, I have applied the rule that the end-in-view should not be subject to serious dispute. In other words, there must be little reason to doubt the true purpose of an intervention held by its instigators. This criterion caused the rejection of a number of candidates for inclusion in my study. For example, in the past fifteen years there have been massive transfers of mentally ill elderly persons from mental hospitals back to the community. Since the rationale given for this policy was that the mentally ill fared better in noninstitutional settings, the fact that transplantation of older persons is associated with increased illness and death (Butler, 1975, p. 241) would seem to make this intervention a perfect instance of regressive action. But it is not clear that improved mental health was the real purpose of this policy. The prospect of incurring savings in state and local funds by manipulating a dependent population that lacked the power to resist, and that could simply be placed on tranquilizers when shifted to the community, is also believed to have been a powerful incentive. This goal, of course, was amply fulfilled. In the absence of agreement as to the real nature of the goal, this intervention was reluctantly excluded from further consideration.

Another difficulty in identifying the goal of an intervention arises from the fact that the mediate goal may differ from the terminal goal. Thus, the mediate goal might be achieved while the terminal goal is confounded. In such cases, I have focused on the terminal goal, even though it might have lower priority to the agents of intervention. Indeed, such "goal displacement" might often account for the condoning of, or at least indifference to, a *terminal* regressive effect. For example, the Drug Enforcement Administration has promoted the spraying of a toxic herbicide on marijuana fields in Mexico, substantial traces of which, according to the National Institute of Drug Abuse, have turned up in samples of confiscated marijuana in Arizona and California (*The New York Times*, December 16, 1977). Spraying achieves the mediate goal of destroying marijuana fields, but at the possible expense of public health. Since the preservation of public health is the long-range goal of measures to suppress consumption of marijuana, and since the scientific consensus has been that marijuana is not harmful when taken in normal dosages (Grinspoon, 1977), the intervention of spraying is decidedly regressive. In short, it is necessary to designate the terminal objective of an intervention in order to assess its negativity, even if the agents seem to have forgotten what it is.

This desideratum is more easily stated than fulfilled, of course. Terminal goals are often taken for granted by program administrators and are therefore seldom subjected to the kind of explicit, precise definition that permits a formulation of operational measures. Their implicitness also means that they might not be truly shared by all concerned with planning and executing a policy. Leaders of underdeveloped countries, for example, might *assume* that the enhancement of dignity, self-fulfillment, and happiness are the ultimate goals of development, while the donor country might be concerned only with accelerating the rate of growth of the national product.

This common situation alerts us to the possibility that *multiple* goals might be pursued by an intervention, and that these goals might be differentially embraced by various sectors of participants or instigators. Accordingly, an intervention can be *partially* regressive if only particular goals are confounded. This is often the case with a discrepancy between the purpose for which the public (or its representative) demands, endorses, or plans an intervention and the purpose for which its executive agents carry it out. When a partial regression becomes visible, incidentally, it is not uncommon for the agent of change to divert attention from negative effects by emphasizing the positive outcomes for other goals. As a rule, then, it is wise to remain especially sensitive to reverse consequences when faced with a program which has multiple goals and outcomes.

An intervention, moreover, can have multiple audiences or types of clients, and the objective might be either uniform or somewhat different for each of these sectors. In either case, a negative impact might be restricted to only a portion of the target system. The following is an example of multiple types of clients with slightly different goals:

> On the basis of the literature, it is possible to conclude . . . that separation into ability groups [in schools] has no clear-cut positive or negative effect on the *average scholastic achievement* of the students involved. There is a slight trend toward improving the achievement of "high ability" groups, but that is offset by substantial losses by the average and low groups. (Persell, 1977, p. 92)

In the field of economic development, it has become clear that the successful transfer of technologies from advanced to underdeveloped areas requires a delineation of the particular goals to be fulfilled precisely because of possible *contradiction* among the diverse goals of development. As a report by the National Research Council (Eckaus, 1977, p. 6) points out:

> Technological change is not necessarily beneficial for all development goals. Depending on the circumstances of their introduction and use, technologies that increase resource productivity may, for example, also increase income inequality or social stratification or urban crowding.

The so-called quality-of-life goals have received special emphasis in recent years, their proponents tending to favor "small-scale activity, self-sufficiency, minimum ecological effects, and equality in income distribution" (Eckaus, 1977, p. 11). Clearly, certain other common objectives of development, such as capital-intensive cost minimization, will need to be sacrificed if such goals are allotted priority. In sum, interventions can be *partially* regressive owing to goal differentiation, target population differentiation, or both.

Here it is worth remarking on the relatively advanced state of thinking in technical assistance fields as contrasted with that in domestic social development. Rarely are the multiple goals of domestic programs assessed in terms of the trade-offs that must be made among mutually contradictory objectives. To do so requires some recognition of possible regressive consequences for particular subgoals or subgroups. This recognition seems more easily admitted while intervening in other people's affairs, perhaps because we are more insulated from the political and social repercussions of misguided ventures in other countries and can therefore be more candid about the hazards.

A fourth major consideration in identifying a regressive intervention is perhaps obvious but might be overlooked in our concentration on a particular end-in-view. If the side effects of the intervention undermine the target system to such a degree that all functioning is subverted, then clearly one's original intention is likewise undermined. Here is an example:

> If we teach mothers to nurse their babies according to schedule, we run the risk of having the baby sleep at a distance from the mother, who cannot then exercise her customary watchfulness against smothering, getting cold, falling into the fire or out of bed. (Mead, 1955, p. 197)

The possibly harmful consequences for the child do not flow from pursuing the nutritional goal of regular breast-feeding. But since the intervention has the potential to destroy the infant, there is some risk that good nutrition will be rendered useless by virtue of sudden death. Here we simply register the point that, leaving irony aside, if the patient dies, then the operation can hardly be called a success.

A final point in circumscribing the issue is that a regressive intervention need not recoil on the agent, as is suggested by the common term *self-defeating*. What is defeated is the end-in-view and not necessarily the agent, for the simple reason that an array of self-protective devices is available to the perpetrator of counterproductive action. And in fact, these self-protective devices might be so effective that a regressive intervention shall have a higher chance of survival than one that is moderately successful. I will return to this point at a later juncture.

Despite the several strictures that I have placed on the identification of reverse effects, their study has important implications for social theory, the future of social policy, and the current assault on the idea of progress. The implications for social theory are suggested in the following chapter and deduced more systematically later on. In the following chapter I will also look at the significance of reverse consequences for the applied fields of planned organizational change, evaluation research, and social problems. The implications for policy research lie, first and most obviously, in the detection and control of the regressive potential that inheres in our social improvement programs, a potential that is more devastating than side effects insofar as the latter can be benignly "traded off." Accordingly, much of my later analysis and recommendations will be devoted to improving the means whereby our detection and control of regressive potential may be enhanced. But there is a second, much broader implication for policy formation: the issue of the general strategy to be adopted toward reform efforts in light of contemporary pessimism regarding the efficacy of rational intervention in human affairs. Before elaborating this issue, it is necessary to provide some background by clarifying the relationship of regressive intervention to the *idea of progress*, an idea that seems to have been driven to the wall in the present century.

THE IDEA OF PROGRESS

It is widely conceded that a plague of pessimism about the chances of rational human improvement has infected many Western intellectuals as well as a large segment of the public. As Henshel (1976, p. 50) has put it:

> It is difficult to characterize Western intellectuals today other than to say that now, more than ever before, they sense an urgent need for drastic change and yet despair of either bringing it about or seeing it occur naturally. Having long ago lost their faith in God, they are losing faith in themselves and human action. The sense of progress is dead among the intelligentsia, and seems, by both objective polling and impressionistic reporting, to be declining with the man on the street as well.

Nisbet (1980), who has analyzed the current malaise in his recent work on the history of the idea of progress, concludes:

"Disbelief, doubt, disillusionment, and despair have taken over—or so it would seem from our literature, art, philosophy, theology, even our scholarship and science" (Nisbet, 1980, p. 318). Major sources of this dismal weltanschauung, according to Nisbet, are a loss of faith in reason and scientific knowledge, an eclipse of the West's sense of possessing a superior civilization, a decline of belief in the value of the past, and a rejection of the inherent worth of economic and technological growth. When one examines what Nisbet considers to be the causes of these transformations, one finds that they share an important attribute: *unanticipated negative consequences* of many of our most self-confident actions and esteemed social institutions. The possibly adverse effects of egalitarian democracy on individualism, sense of status, pride of craft, and ambition; the threatened depletion of natural resources by unlimited economic and technological expansion; the boredom generated by affluence and leisure; the unmanageable effects of scientific discoveries and technological breakthroughs, both past and prospective; the "disastrous 'wars' against poverty, ethnic discrimination, poor housing, slums, and crime"; the despoiling of other peoples of the world by exposure to Western civilization; and the corruption of such values as freedom, popular sovereignty, equality, and justice by totalitarian regimes—all are cited by Nisbet as causative.

Whether or not one agrees fully with Nisbet's formulations, it is obvious that unanticipated consequences have played a critical role in bringing about our current failure of nerve. Especially devastating to our sense of the proper connection between effort and reward is the occurrence of those paradoxical events that I have called the regressive consequences of purposive action. More so than mere side effects or mere failure to achieve goals, reverse effects are demoralizing because they assault the very foundations of our faith in the amelioration of social problems, the efficacy of rational planning, and the good intentions of public agencies and political representatives. In sum, our present sense of disillusionment might be traceable, not only to costly failure to yield that degree of security, freedom, welfare, health, and other features of the American dream that were raised to new heights of expectancy in the Great Society era, but to an even costlier failure to prevent the production of the opposite effects.

The following summation by Banfield (1974, p. ix) gives concise expression to a point of view that has become fashionable among many intellectuals: "My conjecture is that owing to the nature of man and society (more particularly American culture and institutions) we cannot 'solve' our serious problems by rational management. Indeed, by trying we are almost certain to make matters worse." Mass market publications on the reverse outcomes of the health care industry (Illich, 1976), welfare agencies (Piven & Cloward, 1971), education (Kozol, 1967), criminal justice (Clark, 1970; Mitford, 1974), drug control (Epstein, 1977), and government institutions in general (Mintz & Cohen, 1976), as well as scandals involving the highest government officials and political representatives who were presumed to uphold the strictest standards of justice and public service signify that interventions which backfire are by no means alien to the public consciousness. Further, the tendency on the part of agents of regressive intervention to conceal, deny, discount, or exonerate the negative outcomes of their actions poses the spectacle of leaders seeking to legitimize the patently illegitimate.

Our contemporary pessimism is by no means unique, for periods of despair have characterized earlier generations despite the pervasive idea of progress. The Lisbon earthquake, the French Revolution and Napoleonic Wars, the First World War—all fostered a profound sense of pessimism about man's ability to achieve earthly redemption. At a more fundamental level, historicism's renunciation of all theological, biological, or revolutionary views of history's "meaning" contributed to rejection of the idea of progress and launched man on the trackless seas of historical relativism.

But most earlier periods of pessimism have differed from our current mood in a fundamental way: They were not generated by man's accomplishment of evil by his rational efforts to do good, but by natural disasters, military horrors, or the loss of status in the eyes of God or history owing to secularizing tendencies. In fact, not even the term *failure of nerve* as minted by Gilbert Murray in his study of ancient Greek religion is, strictly speaking, applicable to the present situation. The ascension of Fortune, Chance, and Fate as explanatory principles in Hellenistic times was due in large part, according to Murray, to the rise of Macedonian despotism and its related upheavals, not to a tendency toward self-destructiveness. It is instructive to note the difference between this ancient religious shift and the more recent neoorthodox revolt against the *hubris* of the Enlightenment, a revolt that flatly denies that progress can be achieved by rational effort in a world of atomized and despiritualized humanity (cf. Niebuhr, 1949).

This is not to say that a belief in social progress has been altogether abandoned by intellectuals. Indeed, an elaborate sociological version can be found in the evolutionary theory of Parsons (1966, 1971). According to this theory, a set of long-term trends, which Parsons calls differentiation, value generalization, adaptive upgrading, and inclusion, promote the "generalized adaptive capacity" of society. Parsons's theory will be discussed in a later chapter in light of our analysis of many concrete instances of regressive intervention. What needs to be noted here is that his theory differs from the evolutionary theory of Spencer in an essential respect: Interventions are viewed as part and parcel of the process of evolution instead of as exogenous sources of possible interference with that process. In this respect, Parsons is a lineal descendant of L. T. Hobhouse (1911), who took deliberate exception to Spencer by claiming that evolution had become increasingly dependent on rational control by the human mind and that such control would increase in future. Indeed, progress was viewed by Hobhouse as measured by the degree to which such control is developed and dedicated to promoting the harmonious growth of society.

Parsons reaches much the same conclusion in terms of the "functions" performed by various subsystems of society. Thus, the subsystem of the polity performs the function of goal attainment by the "organization and mobilization of resources" (Parsons, 1971, p. 16), with government lying at the core of this subsystem. Also, the legal system is viewed as performing the function of integration (Parsons, 1971, pp. 18–19). But while this conception is certainly more valid than Spencer's sharp differentiation between natural social evolution and unnatural government, Parsons appears to overlook the possibility that interventions can be an *endogenous* source of disruption by virtue of their unanticipated consequences, and in particular their reverse effects. (This point, incidentally, seems not to have escaped Hobhouse, as suggested by his references to undesirable consequences of democratic government.) Thus, it is necessary to subject Parsons's scheme to much the same critique that Spencer applied to the legislative interventions of nineteenth-century England. That the enemy is within rather than without the evolutionary process does not blunt his impact; in fact, it might well strengthen his hand. If so, the end result might be a certain retrograde tendency that neutralizes, and under some conditions reverses, the evolutionary drive toward greater adapative capacity.

This issue will be explored later in some detail after we have had an opportunity to examine a range of regressive interventions and their historical sources and contexts. In effect, a scrutiny of Parsons's theory in the light of my analysis will serve as a rough test of the notion that regressive intervention imposes a major brake on social advancement. If this notion is plausibly sustained, then the idea of progress as a theoretical construct needs considerable revision.

Now let us return to the issue raised earlier: the question of the most appropriate perspective on intervention in a society that has become profoundly skeptical of rational reform.

STRATEGIC POLICY IMPLICATIONS

The idea of regressive intervention helps to clarify the debate among advocates of various positions on the role of government in a skeptical age. In particular, it points to a domain of issues that requires careful study by policy makers and policy analysts alike. To simplify matters, let us consider three alternatives suggested by classical political ideologies: the conservative do-nothing position, the radical revolutionary position, and the liberal position of administrative reform and increased outlays. The following critique of these positions is not intended to be a thoroughgoing analysis of alternative political world views, of course. Many volumes have been written on that subject. Here I am only interested in briefly noting the relevance of the idea of regressive intervention to the analysis of contemporary policy alternatives.

The conservative position claims that rational management as a means of dealing with social problems is frequently, if not invariably, counterproductive. (Elements of this position can be observed in the work of Banfield, 1974; Kristol, 1972; Wilson, 1975; Glazer, 1971; Moynihan, 1973.) There are four major problems with this position: (1) the dismantling of reform can itself be an intervention with regressive potential, for example, the recourse to incapacitation instead of rehabilitative goals in corrections, or the return of the elderly mentally ill to the community; (2) natural drift, or evolution in the Spencerian sense, can be at least as detrimental as rational efforts to control powerful interests and promote social justice, that is, the depredations of Adam Smith's invisible hand, and this is especially true when traditional structures of support have been eroded or destroyed; (3) the evidence of gross inequities and social problems apart from those caused by interventions means that a society with humanitarian values will continue to intervene regardless of any rational arguments or political winds to the contrary, and therefore that interventions with regressive tendencies must be overhauled instead of abandoned; and (4) the decline of ideology and the strengthening of special-interest politics will ensure many new efforts at legislative reform despite their possibly regressive effects.

The radical position would sweep away the system of power and privilege that plays such a large role in the perversities of our social welfare efforts (see, for example, Cloward & Piven, 1975). The difficulties with this position are (1) the system of privilege and power is by no means the only source of regressive effects in modern society, and even the post-revolution society will need to resort to certain power-based mechanisms that produced some reverse outcomes in the pre-revolution society, for example, bureaucracy and technocratic control; (2) radicalism's challenge to authority often provokes a retraction of those benefits that do exist, thereby worsening the situation; and (3) the strong emphasis on ideological consensus among radicals tends to blind them to the occurrence of unanticipated consequences that confound goals, thus impairing their ability to monitor negative effects and to adopt countermeasures.

Finally, the liberal position favoring administrative reform and increased resources (see, e.g., Caplow, 1975; Ginzberg & Solow, 1974; Gans, 1974) suffers from the following defects: (1) a tendency to rely on rational problem solving and expertise as unproblematic and to play down the reverse effects of benevolent interventions; (2) lack of a conceptual framework for calculating the probability of reverse effects so that their prediction and control can be mastered; and (3) insufficient attention to the ways in which the system of privilege and power, including the meritocracy of which liberal policymakers themselves are members, controls the allocation of resources and protects itself from disclosure of the reverse effects of its own policies.

As indicated by my emphasis on the negative aspects of each of these perspectives, each seems to be seriously wanting. While the neo-Spencerian critic of all rational reform effort is correct in pointing to the untoward consequences of many policies, he is incorrect in attributing this tendency to inexorable laws of organic society and social management. And while the liberal reformer and the radical are correct in rejecting do-nothingism and its pseudoscientific grounds for pessimism, their rejection of a strong tendency for interventions to go awry, except insofar as incompetent or self-serving individuals are at the helm, similarly reveals a limited vision. The liberal reformer in particular is inclined to place the onus on simple ineptitude. Thus, in attacking the pessimistic position of the "capitalist–realist" who claims that policies to increase equality have disastrous effects precisely on those who suffer most from inequality, Gans (1974, p. xiv) notes that "the limits are often illustrated by past government policies so underfinanced or faulty in conception that experts, at least, knew from the start that they would fail." Pessimism is rejected, but with the qualification that the agents of reform need only harken to the experts. In the absence of a theory of regressive intervention, one might ask where these experts are to be found. And indeed, expertise itself has been viewed by some observers as a major source of pernicious effects, a point that will be documented later when we turn to a consideration of a number of concrete interventions.

The processes whereby one's intentions produce the opposite effects are complex and often obscure. They are not as yet very predictable by experts because they are not as yet adequately comprehended by them. But neither are they inherently immune to a greater degree of anticipatory diagnosis and control, as implied by conservative pessimists. Let us suppose, for example, that the nineteenth-century physician Lister and his epigone had abandoned medicine when they discovered that their amputees were dying from infection induced by their procedures. Viewed from the vantage point of modern antiseptic surgery, such a consummation would have been impractical, inhumane, and unscientific all at once. In short, it is as reprehensible to renounce efforts to ameliorate social conditions as it is to rush headlong with reformist zeal into the quicksand of unanticipated consequences.

Yet, pessimism does have its virtues. For thinking forlornly can goad us into examining our deepest assumptions about reform, as well as the assumptions of those who are the actual instruments of change and whom we as "experts" might be called upon to assist. Foremost among these assumptions is that which holds that all problems have a solution, when, in fact, we might be doing very well indeed if we can simply prevent the problem from spreading. As Killian (1971, p. 283) has pointed out:

> The unwillingness of the sociologist to be a true pessimist, or realist—his tendency to draw back from predicting that no matter what the members of a society may do things will not turn out all right according to whatever standards he cherishes—restricts his sociological imagination in a number of ways. It restricts his ability to predict catastrophic outcomes even on a limited scale and limits his perception of the negative aspects of present reality.

In the final analysis, as one can never be altogether confident that a society and its reform efforts are sinful by nature, there is always the chance of being spared retribution if the sins of our fathers are acknowledged. It was in this spirit that my investigation of regressive intervention was undertaken, as should become evident when I proceed to analyze those sources of regression that *might* be intractable but which *absolutely* cannot be dealt with unless perceived with neither blinders nor tears.

Having made several references to the deficient treatment of regressive intervention in social theory and to the value for public policy of developing such a theory, I will turn attention in the next chapter to an overview of theory and research in several domains that bear on the issue. In one respect, the fugitive status of regressive intervention in social theory has already been revealed in our brief critique of Parsons's evolutionary theory. For if there were a strong theoretical tradition devoted to the idea, evolutionary schemes would not continue to be formulated without taking fully into account the forces of regression, some of which might well be prompted by those very trends cited by evolutionists as leading to greater adaptation. Clearly, such a tradition has not developed, despite the pronounced interest of classical theory on reverse effects and also the scattered references to the idea in much contemporary theory and research. Much is to be gained from these references, both theoretically and empirically, in building a firmer basis of understanding, as we shall have ample opportunity to see in the following chapters.

After my survey of certain portions of the social science literature, including the fields of planned organizational change, evaluation research, and social problems, I will proceed in the next major section to examine a wide array of cases in which purposive action culminated in effects that ran counter to the intentions of the instigator. Because I want to show that this pattern is of a generalized nature, I have cast my net very wide. Thus, I have necessarily strayed into fields in which I cannot claim any specialized competency. There will naturally, therefore, be latitude for argument about the empirical foundations for some of these cases and the validity of the documentor's own conclusions. But since I am primarily concerned with building theory, the evidential basis of any particular case is not nearly as important as the cumulative plausibility of the evidence and of the mechanisms that are adduced to account for a particular array of regressive effects. Admittedly, then, my approach is exploratory and oriented to the development of theory.

Finally, in the last part of this study, I will summarize my conclusions, apply them to the social evolutionary theory mentioned earlier, and then move into questions of policy and needed research.

Regressive Intervention in Contemporary Theory and Research

In this chapter I will try to show that the idea of regressive intervention has not been accorded the attention by contemporary social science that it deserves. At the same time, I will suggest that research and theory in several domains have, wittingly or not, laid the foundations for a systematic treatment of the idea. In particular, I will be concerned with the place of reverse effects, first, in the writings of Merton and a few other social theorists who have addressed themselves to unanticipated consequences, and second, in the specific fields of planned organizational change, evaluation research, and social problems. By no means is it my intention to cover these fields in depth, but instead to search for certain global clues that indicate the way in which reverse effects have been customarily dealt with. I have relied heavily, therefore, on overviews of these fields and on the work of a few leading exemplars.

MERTON'S PERSPECTIVE

As we have seen, the idea that purposive action may culminate in a state of affairs that is contrary to intentions has a respectable paternity in the history of sociology. This recognition is part of a much wider stream of social thought that has been concerned with the "unanticipated consequences of purposive action," a magisterial phrase coined by Merton (1936) to capture "the definite continuity in its consideration" through centuries of religious, moral, historical, and socioeconomic thought. As Merton (1936, p. 894n) observed in a rather humbling footnote:

> This problem has been related to such heterogeneous subjects as: the problem of evil (theodicy), moral responsibility, free will, predestination, deism, teleology, fatalism, logical, illogical and non-logical behavior, social prediction, planning and control, social cycles, the pleasure and reality principles and historical "accidents."

In essence, Merton's conception of unanticipated consequences denoted all effects of organized or unorganized action that diverge from the presumed purpose (implicit or explicit) of the actor, while the research agenda arising from recognition of this pattern called attention to those objective and subjective conditions that foster such consequences.

Stated thus, the concept obviously covers a sizable portion of the realm of sociological thought. Indeed, Merton (1957, p. 66) later affirmed that "the *distinctive* intellectual contributions of the sociologist are found primarily in the study of unintended consequences . . . of social practices, as well as in the study of anticipated consequences."

While it might seem, therefore, that Merton's original conception was merely a trenchant way of defining the lion's share of the sociological enterprise, several lines of investigation were sketched in his early article that eventually yielded a rich harvest of ideas: the self-fulfilling prophecy, the paradigm of functional analysis, the reconceptualization of anomie, and so forth. This is not the place to trace out all of these lines of thought. My purpose, rather, is to focus on that singular type of unanticipated consequence that runs counter to one's intentions. And it is this particular type of consequence that has been unsatisfactorily addressed in Merton's later work. Since he has been the bellwether of thought regarding unanticipated consequences, this deficiency might help to explain the neglect of the problem of regressive intervention by later theorists. A close examination of those Mertonian ideas that have a near or distant kinship with the problem, however, will give us an opportunity to clarify certain key dimensions and raise specific questions and thereby to lay the groundwork for portions of my later analysis.

The most pertinent concept that Merton later introduced is that of "latent dysfunction" (Merton, 1948, p. 51), or "negative latent function" as Goode (1951, pp. 32–33) called it. This concept quickly became the stock-in-trade of a generation of sociologists. *Dysfunctions* were defined by Merton as "those observed consequences which lessen the adaptation or adjustment of the system," and the adjective *latent* was defined as "neither intended nor recognized." In an essay on functionalism, Goode (1951, p. 33) remarked on the allure of this pattern of events for the "rebels and debunkers among modern economists and historians," which, oddly enough, is where he left the matter. Merton was more instructive, observing that "an item may have both functional and dysfunctional consequences, giving rise to the difficult and important problem of evolving canons for assessing the net balance of the aggregate of consequences. (This is, of course, most important in the use of functional analysis for guiding the formation and enactment of policy.)" But despite the hint that interventions might have negative consequences for the very goal(s) they were intended to serve, Merton wished to focus attention on adverse effects for what he called "functional requirements." As he emphatically pointed out in a subsequent essay on the theory of social problems:

> A social dysfunction refers to a *designated* set of consequences of a *designated* pattern of behavior, belief, or organization that inter-

fere with a *designated* functional requirement of a *designated* social
system. Otherwise, the term social dysfunction becomes little
more than an epithet of disparagement or a largely vacuous
expression of attitude. (Merton, 1961, p. 732)

The example that he offered—the possibly negative impact of
working-class mobility on achievement of working-class goals
by virtue of interference with the requirement of maintaining a
leadership pool—placed this definitional restriction in the
clearest possible light. But what is depreciated by this restriction is the possibility that efforts to promote social mobility will
reduce mobility itself and, further, that such consequences
might ensue without regard to functional requirements.

Merton (1961, p. 720) viewed social disorganization in
general in the same terms:

> The composite of faults in the normative and relational structure
> of a social system described as social disorganization can be
> thought of as inadequacies in meeting one or more of the func-
> tional requirements of the system.

Once again, his examples of negative outcomes—failure to
canalize personal tensions, breakdown of communication,
maladaptation to the environment, decline of social cohesion,
etc.—entail difficulties wholly apart from the aggravation of a
problem that is addressed by purposive action, that is, they
focus attention on side effects and neglect reverse effects on
goals.

One might argue that goal attainment itself is a functional
requirement and that, therefore, all reverse effects entail interference with a functional requirement, constituting a latent
dysfunction pure and simple. But this formulation would
make it difficult to explain reverse effects within a functionalist
framework. For it is tautological, or at the very least unen-
lightening, to say that goals are not achieved because of interference with the need for goal attainment. In order to establish
the operation of a latent dysfunction, one must be able to
specify some functional requirement other than goal attainment that is impaired.

Despite the family resemblance between "latent dysfunction" and "regressive effect," then, the latter's frame of reference is both narrower and broader. It is narrower in that it focuses on consequences for the originally designated purpose or condition, that is, does not stop short at side effects, and broader in that the process is not restricted to interference with requirements. To illustrate, let us take the case of "provocation" as a mechanism of regressive intervention. If an actor seeks to enhance his own security by threatening another actor, his threats might provoke the other to retaliation, thus actually undermining the security of the original actor. It is not easy to discern the operation of a side effect in this process, much less interference with some functional requirement. Even if one could adduce such a requirement, would it not be more heuristically fruitful to avoid the chance of premature theoretical closure by directing attention to a host of possible subjective and objective causes? Thus, one might assert that a norm of mutual trust was violated by the threat, thereby pointing to interference with a system need. But this strategy tends to preclude a search for other factors because it fully satisfies the demand of the functionalist paradigm. Thus, it rules out the alternative hypotheses that the actor who issues the threat (1) makes the other believe that he will presently be assaulted and therefore prompts him to a "preemptive attack", (2) misjudges his own capacity to withstand retaliation, (3) misjudges the capacity of the other to retaliate effectively, (4) is temporarily deranged by fury and therefore oblivious to the possible consequences of his threat, (5) wants to arouse the protection of allies by provoking a known enemy, (6) wants to neutralize the enemy by provoking him to lose self-control but underestimates the unpredictable effects of such loss of control, or (7) has imbibed the values of a culture of violence in which threat and counterthreat are everyday occurrences regardless of the possible outcomes. In short, if one is convinced beforehand that some functional requirement must have been impaired, as dictated by the functionalist canon, then there is the danger that a number of other (alternative, subsidiary, or contingent) causes will be excluded from view.

This example reminds us of one variable in particular that is underplayed in functional theory: the role of human agency. This variable (or domain of variables) includes rationalization of conduct, self-monitoring, goal-setting, and a host of private motives for action, the relationship of which to system requirements seems highly tenuous in the functionalist scheme. While this variable is alluded to by the concept of *manifest function*, it is not given nearly the prominence of *latent function* in Merton's elaboration of the functionalist perspective. As Giddens (1979, p. 211) points out with regard to Merton's model, "society's needs are disclosed as discrepant from (and by strong implication, more important than) the purposes or reasons of the actors engaging in the activity in question."

The purpose of my raising this point of criticism is not to impugn functional analysis as a heuristic. (For a recent overview of the pros and cons of functionalism, see Moore, 1978.) Indeed, the functionalist model is useful for clarifying a number of regressive outcomes, as I will show in the following chapter. But its usefulness is circumscribed. For it does not account for all regressive outcomes, at least in a manner that is not subject to the implicit restriction of the model on alternative or additional causes. This restriction may stem from an omission rather than a commission of the model, inasmuch as it fails to direct attention to alternative hypotheses. But there is also the strong implication of the model that all will be explained when the functional requirement that presumably accounts for the persistence of a sociocultural item has been identified. Thus, theoretic power may be prematurely sought at the expense of grasping the multivariate nature of certain phenomena. Or, to put it more concretely, while impairment of a requirement might be one source of regressive outcomes, in many cases it might not be the most important, let alone the only, source.

The emphasis on features of the social system other than the originally targeted goal, or what is commonly called the side effects of purposive action, reflects only part of Merton's original conception. For in his early essay on unanticipated consequences he referred to Weber's conclusion about the effects of asceticism in the following terms (Merton, 1936, p. 903):

> Active asceticism paradoxically leads to its own decline through the accumulation of wealth and possessions entailed by decreased consumption and intense productive activity.

From this historical case he then derived the generalization that "activities oriented toward certain values release processes which so react as to change the very scale of values which precipitated them," which in turn had implications for the "process of secularization . . . the transformation or breakdown of basic value-systems." And finally: "Here is the essential paradox of social action—the 'realization' of values may lead to their renunciation."

Here it should be emphasized that the magnitude of Merton's subject no doubt precluded more than a passing concern with regressive intervention. Thus, not only did he offer but a single example, but his explanation was limited to absolute value commitments that blind the true believer to the consequences of his action:

> Superficially similar to the factor of immediacy of interest, but differing from it in a highly significant theoretical sense, is that of basic values. This refers to instances where there is no consideration of further consequences because of the felt necessity of certain action enjoined by certain fundamental values. The classical analysis of the influence of this factor is Weber's study of the Protestant ethic and the spirit of capitalism. (Merton, 1936, p. 903)

Not only does this explanation focus exclusively on subjective sources of reverse effects, and thereby deflect interest from features of the objective strategy of action in its objective historical context, but it does not tell us why the end result is counter to one's intentions rather than merely different, that is, a reverse effect rather than a side effect or null effect. Further, attributing the reverse effect to subjective elements does not allow us to understand why many ascetic communities have *not* become wealthy or abandoned their value system. Nor does it help us to understand why actors with absolute value commitments often *do* attain their ends, although sometimes with unanticipated side effects of awful proportions (e.g., American abolitionism). And clearly, since even efforts that are marked by great prudence have fallen prey to reverse consequences, absolute commitment is not an essential factor in the creation of such consequences. In sum, while strong commitment might reduce one's awareness of reverse effects, the actual occurrence of such effects often depends on other factors. At a later point, I will suggest that the case of Protestantism can be understood in terms of a particular feature of interventions in interaction with the situations, terms that have little to do with either functional needs or absolute commitment.

The elevation of means to the status of ends that is occasioned by rational organization, and which Merton (1957, pp. 195–206) called "goal displacement," is still another instance in which the idea of regressive intervention is broached. As he characterizes this pattern at one point: "The very elements which conduce toward efficiency in general produce inefficiency in specific instances." However, inefficiency might not make matters worse but might only fail to serve original ends, for example, the welfare of the public. For this reason, the concept only approximates a reverse effect. Only under certain conditions does goal displacement eventuate in a truly reverse effect (these conditions will be discussed later). Further, to say that an excessive attention to means interferes with a functional requirement of maintaining commitment to goals (providing one applied the functional paradigm to this issue) deflects attention from a variety of factors that force the client into the mold of the organization and increase ritualism independently of either weak or strong goal commitment.

Another occasion on which Merton seemed to refer to regressive intervention was in his study of the "boomerang effect" (Merton, 1957, pp. 517–521; Merton & Kendall, 1944). But despite the provocative title used to designate this effect of propaganda, virtually all of the examples that are offered are not regressive, but only null. That is, they refer to propaganda efforts that, instead of creating a reverse effect, simply fail to achieve their ends. The one rather clear example of a reverse effect is termed, interestingly enough, a "distinct boomerang" (Merton & Kendall, 1944, p. 5), but this case was not repeated in Merton's later and more theoretical treatment of the boomerang effect (Merton, 1957, pp. 509–528). Examples of boomerang effects that might entail regressive consequences will be cited in a later chapter. More important, however, the idea of "discrepant frames of reference" between the agent and target population that serves to elucidate the source of boomerang effects, according to Merton, will be applied to several types of regressive intervention in addition to propaganda.

Finally, we come to the well known pattern that Merton identified as the "self-fulfilling prophecy." His original formulation was as follows (Merton, 1957, p. 423):

> The self-fulfilling prophecy is, in the beginning, a *false* definition of the situation evoking a new behavior which makes the originally false conception come *true*. The specious validity of the self-fulfilling prophecy perpetuates a reign of error. For the prophet will cite the actual course of events as proof that he was right from the beginning. . . . Such are the perversities of social logic.

The pattern was illustrated by a false rumor of bank insolvency (before the Federal Deposit Insurance system) which induced a run on the bank and consequent insolvency, and by racial and ethnic prejudice that produce the very attributes (e.g., joblessness) that are perceived as essential traits of the disesteemed group.

This concept has since been applied to a host of social phenomena, including the reinforcement of deviance by derogatory labeling. Inasmuch as educational tracking or incarceration, for example, fosters self-images or expectations on the part of others that reinforce the undesired behavior, the self-fulfilling prophecy is a regressive intervention. In effect, the negative image that is prompted by treatment may be self-fulfilling and thereby defeat the treatment. This suggests, interestingly enough, that a self-*defeating* belief in the efficacy of certain treatments may be due to a self-*fulfilling* assumption about the situation that one hopes to alter or control. Thus, if one believes that a person who breaks the law has "criminal tendencies," then that person will be imprisoned with career criminals who may well indoctrinate him with the lore and rewards of the underworld.

The idea of self-fulfilling prophecy is by no means limited to consequences that run counter to one's intentions, however, but covers many other types of predictions and beliefs, for example, the bandwagon effect of political polling. Only if a particular image, label, or subliminal expectation is incorporated into an intervention in a manner that creates reverse effects can a self-fulfilling prophecy be called regressive. In order to understand how this comes about, one must direct attention to features of the intervention in interaction with features of the situation, as I mentioned earlier. Because of the fugitive status of regressive intervention in the study of unanticipated consequences, this task has not been undertaken.

There are several additional references to regressive effects in Merton's writings. Here is a hypothetical reverse consequence, for example, that served to illustrate the "self-destroying belief":

> A third pattern of unanticipated consequences, that of the self-destroying belief, is briefly mentioned but not developed at any length in this chapter. . . . Lincoln, for example, was acutely conscious of the pattern. In the dark days of 1862, when McClellan was stalemated and the armies in the west immobilized, Lincoln did not issue a public call for the desperately needed thousands of new troops, explaining, "I would publicly appeal to the country for this new force were it not that I fear a general panic and stampede would follow, so hard it is to have a thing understood as it really is." (Merton, 1957, p. 128)

If one's attention is directed to the pronouncement that might have fostered this collective response, then one is squarely faced with a regressive intervention. Such a shift of interest raises questions about those features of the intervention that interact with the context to produce a reverse effect. But this was not Merton's focus of interest. Instead, he wished to stress the point that collective behavior is sometimes self-destructive as a result of false beliefs, and he chose an example of panic to do so.

There are indications that Merton has moved closer to the view that regressive consequences constitute a distinct type of unanticipated consequences. In a recent paper (1978, p. 27), he refers briefly to the "special paradoxical type" as exemplified by the corrosive effect of eighteenth-century science on the religious faith that partly spawned it. However, he subsumes this special type under the concept of latent dysfunction. In the same paper (Merton, 1978, p. 10A), he refers to "unanticipated consequences as self-amplifying social problems in which 'efforts to do away with one social problem introduce other . . . damaging problems.' " The quotation in this sentence was from his own book on social problems (Merton & Nisbet, 1961), in which the reference is to *side effects* of social programs rather than to reverse effects for the very goals of the programs. Thus, while Merton has been aware that certain interventions under certain conditions might have reverse consequences, he has not systematically distinguished such effects from side effects or from merely self-defeating action. His discussion of self-destroying beliefs, furthermore, was concerned with collective behavior rather than with a perverse feature of interventions in conjunction with particular circumstances. In all these instances, then, we observe a flirtation with the concept that falls tantalizingly short of a proposal of marriage.

To summarize our review of Merton's approach to regressive effects: It appears that he shifted from an early appreciation of a distinct type of regressive consequence, which he explained by absolute value commitment (i.e., Protestant asceticism), to a concept of negative side effects on the fulfillment of system requirements (dysfunctions) and their contribution to side effects. Later, the concept of dysfunction was expanded to include regressive effects on goals (illustrated by the Puritan dedication to scientific inquiry). But as useful as this expanded version may be in explicating certain cases of regression (to be amply documented later), it is too restrictive to account readily for many other such cases. And while other types of reverse effects are alluded to throughout the corpus of his work, they are subsumed under such types as self-fulfilling and self-defeating beliefs and the boomerang effect. Finally, the distinctions between side effects and reverse effects, and between null effects and reverse effects, have not been clearly or consistently drawn, presumably because they have not been viewed as basic dimensions for sorting out cases of unanticipated consequences. This is especially noticeable with regard to interventions that are designed to deal with social problems, which represent one of the most important areas for application of knowledge of the dynamics of regression in contemporary society.

OTHER SOCIOLOGISTS OF UNANTICIPATED CONSEQUENCES

While it is obviously beyond the scope of this essay to trace the immense influence of Merton's ideas on contemporary analyses of unanticipated consequences, it can be asserted with reasonable confidence that the study of regressive effects of interventions has continued to languish at a somewhat primitive level. Three notable students of unanticipated consequences may be cited to support this conclusion.

In a paper delivered at the annual meetings of the Society for the Study of Social Problems in a session on unanticipated consequences, Schneider (1978) applies the "Weberian image" of the maleficent consequences of beneficent intentions to several contemporary interventions, that is, therapeutic medicine, minimum wage legislation, and even, possibly, affirmative action. Further, he acknowledges that the list could be greatly enlarged and expresses apprehension that social reformist inclinations may be "half-frightened and half-persuaded into a do-nothing position on various social problems." The remedy, however, is not broached, namely, intensive analysis of a range of regressive interventions that will enable us to anticipate the heretofore unanticipated. Nor does he undertake any such task himself in the brief compass of his paper. In fact, he closes on a rather do-nothing note:

> There are large and difficult problems here. But I may suggest that it might be exciting to discover again, with a renewed openness to the Smithian image, that there are a few things in the sphere of social action that may safely be left to innocent agents with decidedly limited knowledge and modest aims, who will come out well enough anyway, without outside intervention. And who knows? With the recovery of "optimism" that such openness could bring we might return with a new zest and a new faith to intervention itself, which certainly does not always deserve a bad name.

Such optimism may indeed return of its own accord, but it would be as ill-fated as past optimism unless informed by a far more sophisticated understanding of interventions than we have exhibited in the past.

Henshel (1976) also cites several regressive interventions with special attention to the effects of "labeling" by the criminal justice and mental health systems and of expertise in general. This recital, however, is not accompanied by an effort to formulate a theory of regressive consequences. In fact, when Henshel attempts to identify the sources of unanticipated consequences that flow from efforts to deal with social problems, he seems to neglect regressive effects altogether. Thus, he notes that the consequences of reform may be *better* than anticipated thanks either to an unrecognized problem in the situation that was also solved or to an unrecognized beneficial feature of the reform and that they may be *worse* than anticipated thanks either to an unnoticed good feature in the situation that was eliminated (reminding one of Merton's interference with a functional requirement) or to an unnoticed deleterious feature of the reform itself. Apart from the fact that this scheme does not allow for interaction effects of features of the reform and of the situation, it would seem to allow ample room for regressive consequences with respect to the very goals of reform. But this point is never made explicit and indeed appears to be ruled out. Instead, we are reminded of deleterious *side* effects: "It is entirely possible that reform will not only produce less benefit than expected but produce such harmful side-effects that people would be better off without the reform" (Henshel, 1976, p. 60). This is a restatement of Merton's injunction to calculate the net balance of the aggregate of consequences as a means of arriving at some assessment of overall benefit. Thus, as with Merton, the idea of reverse consequences of intervention is exemplified, but it is denied an explicit and distinctive place in one's main theoretical framework. Furthermore, as a result of such failure to view regression as a generic pattern that cannot be understood simply as a "collateral evil," it is denied the intensive investigation that it deserves and that social policy requires.

Gary Marx (1974), a sociologist with special interest in the ironies of social control, has focused on the reverse effects of control mechanisms over and beyond the labeling process. He points out that deviance may be amplified by *escalation*, (e.g., "preventive violence" or overreaction to a crowd disturbance by police), *nonenforcement* (owing to corruption or principled leniency), and *covert facilitation* (e.g., use of decoys or undercover participants in deviance). In pointing to the neglect of such forms of authority-induced deviance, Marx criticizes the tendency of social theory to draw the line between authority and the criminal too sharply. "Such an image," he argues, "misses the interdependence that may exist between these groups and the extent to which authorities may induce, or help others to break the law, be involved in law breaking themselves, or create false records about others' supposed law breaking." Marx goes on to examine certain societal trends that are conducive to these forms of regressive intervention and speculates that "modern society is increasingly generative of ironic outcomes."

While Marx suggests that his analysis might be applicable

to other areas of contemporary society, he does not specify those features that are generalizable beyond the field of punitive social control. His observations, therefore, are not placed within a general framework for analysis of reverse consequences. For example, Marx cites payoffs to the police as an inducement for nonenforcement but does not treat corruption as a special case of an agent's exploitation of the resources of an intervention, a process that generates reverse effects in many institutional domains. Further, he does not recognize, at least explicitly, that exploitation need not be wholly *illicit*, as with corruption, but may be *semi-licit* (e.g., undercover work by police as agents provocateurs, decoys, etc., which he calls covert facilitation), and even wholly *licit* (e.g., a professional's monopolization of expertise to the detriment of a client's developing skills of personal sufficiency). Recasting observations in this type of framework raises the question of the societal sources of a particular mechanism such as exploitation and the reasons for continual resort to interventions that lend themselves so generously to the operation of regressive processes. These are directions that I will pursue later, when I turn to an analysis of a range of regressive interventions, including those demonstrated by Marx in the field of social control.

In conclusion, if the vision of theorists like Merton is too broad to give adequate attention to regressive intervention, that of specialists is too narrowly focused on a particular field to discern the generic processes at work. Both levels of analysis, however, can be profitably mined for formulating a "middle range" theory of regressive intervention.

The three social theorists examined here by no means exhaust the references in the literature to reverse effects of purposive action. They were selected because of their explicit, theoretical interest in the problem and, therefore, as a means of illustrating some deficiencies of theory that remain. When I proceed in a subsequent section to survey a large number of cases of regressive intervention, the contributions of other social scientists will become obvious. By and large, however, the interest of social theorists and researchers at large in the problem of reverse effects has been notably subordinate to other concerns. This is true even in fields that are preeminently concerned with the practical issues of planned change and its evaluation. Let us now turn to an examination of certain of those fields.

RESEARCH ON PLANNED CHANGE

In studies of organizational change and diffusion of innovations, one would expect to find *some* attention to reverse effects, if not the scrupulous concern that it deserves. But this does not appear to be the case. In a comprehensive review of research and theory on planned organizational change by Zaltman, Duncan, and Holbek (1973), for example, one finds only passing reference to the possibly injurious effects of change efforts in organizations, much less to reverse effects. Thus, at one point they note: "Indirectly, the threat of resistance causes the advocates of change to plan ahead and anticipate possible negative consequences of the innovation" (pp. 102–103). Accordingly, they confess rather weakly, resistance to change might sometimes be beneficial. But just how the advocates of change go about *diagnosing* the possible negative consequences of the innovation, the *dynamics* of the situation that foster such consequences, and the most common *types* is not divulged to the reader. A gesture toward development of types appears in a list of factors called "nature of resistance" (p. 166). These factors are "conflict, occurrence of unintended dysfunctional effects, and disillusionment because of false expectations." Only conflict is discussed in the text. As the authors note, one reason that so little can be said about the "long-range ill effects" of an innovation is the paucity of research on the end result of planned organizational change: "There is very little in the published literature concerning the discontinuance of innovations in organizations or even of innovations intended solely for use by individuals" (p. 92).

Similarly, a review of the voluminous literature on knowledge utilization and innovation by Havelock (1969) only alludes to the idea of reverse consequences by noting the inhibiting effect on information output of the "professed danger to the clients," as in the case of a scientist's reluctance to disseminate information that might be distorted by the public (ch. 6, p. 18). With reference to the client himself, the anticipation of negative effects on the end-in-view is not mentioned as a barrier to adoption.

While some of the deficiencies in the literature on planned change have been partially remedied by more recent studies, such as that of Yin *et al.* (1976), *A Review of Case Studies of Technological Innovations in State and Local Services,* such studies have been sorely lacking in attention to unanticipated consequences, and in particular to reverse effects. With few exceptions, the sole dependent variables in studies of innovation concern the degree of success or failure with reference to formal goals. This is not to say that the qualitative data in these studies do not reveal unanticipated consequences, but these do not enter into the conceptual framework for assessing outcomes. It is as though Merton (1948) had never pointed to the "important problem of evolving canons for assessing the net balance of the aggregate of consequences." To which injunction he wistfully added, "This is, of course, most important in the use of functional analysis for guiding the formation and enactment of policy."

The study of technological change in Third World countries has been more responsive to the need to investigate unintended consequences than have studies on American society, as I noted earlier. Thus, in a review of diffusion research, Rogers and Shoemaker (1971) are able to cite several case studies of innovations that had far reaching, unintended effects on underdeveloped societies, including the classical study by Linton and Kardiner (1952) of the consequences for a tribe in Madagascar of adopting wet rice farming. But even here it appears that the opportunity for examining the "net balance of the aggregate of consequences" is limited. As Rogers and Shoemaker (1971, p. 324) state: "A recent analysis of the diffusion publications indicates that of nearly 1,500 studies, only thirty-eight investigated the consequences of innovations." The reasons that Rogers and Shoemaker give for this low level of attention are three: "change agencies . . . overemphasize adoption *per se*, tacitly assuming that the consequences of innovation decisions will be positive"; "the usual survey research methods are inappropriate for the investigation of innovation consequences"; and "consequences are difficult to measure" because of "cultural norms, personal preferences, and bias." Rogers and Shoemaker go on to offer a "model for studying consequences" that reiterates Merton's functional paradigm of manifest and latent functions and dysfunctions. Accordingly, their model makes no distinction between side effects and regressive effects; in fact, the latter are omitted.

In sum, studies of planned change have been successful in identifying an array of structural factors that inhibit change (centralization, social or geographical distance from cosmopolitan agencies, vulnerability to the environment, goal diffuseness, etc.) and the features of interventions that promote rejection or failure (complexity, cost, low transportability, low visibility, etc.). But because virtually no attention has been directed either to situational features or to features of the strategy of change that produce effects apart from intended consequences, the topic of reverse effects and their sources has been overlooked.

EVALUATION OF SOCIAL PROGRAMS

Evaluation research is another field in which one might expect to find a robust appetite for reverse effects. Surprisingly, however, concern with unanticipated consequences of any sort, despite early observations of their importance in evaluation design (Hyman, Wright, & Hopkins, 1962, pp. 12–17), seems to be a rather grudging exception. Textbooks on evaluation rarely mention the subject, and when they do it is almost entirely in the form of sheer admonition (along with a footnote reference to Merton, perhaps). Concrete guidelines for conceptualizing, detecting, measuring, or assessing a net balance of good and bad effects are not offered (see, for example, Suchman, 1967; Anderson & Ball, 1978). One widely respected text completely disposes of the question of guidelines by informing us that in simple situations "informal observation may be sufficient" to detect exacerbative effects; but "in more remote or complex situations, [the researcher] will want to develop measures and data-gathering instruments to pull in the requisite information" (Weiss, 1972, p. 34). But at least this writer recognizes the *existence* of reverse effects of interventions and gives a few examples. By and large, in spite of a gradually emerging interest among evaluation experts in the study of side effects (see, e.g., Steele, 1977), the field is far from developing a widely acceptable, systematic means of monitoring such effects.

The neglect of side effects and reverse effects in evaluation design is apparently so ingrained that even serious students of unanticipated consequences can ignore such effects when their task is to explicate evaluation research. This dual perspective can be found in Henshel's (1976) survey of the social, political, and scientific aspects of interventions for dealing with social problems. In one chapter of his book he gives an excellent review of the history and current status of the theoretical study of unanticipated consequences and even cites examples of reverse effects, as I noted earlier. But then, in the following chapter, he discusses evaluation designs and their problems without reference to either the need for or the means of measuring unintended consequences. This split perspective is paralleled collectively by, on the one hand, frequent espousal by social scientists of the ubiquity of unanticipated consequences and, on the other, failure to make any provision in evaluation design for the measurement of such consequences. On the whole, then, the indictment issued by John Dewey (1922, pp. 228–229) many years ago has barely been heeded by today's multimillion dollar evaluation industry: "It is willful folly to fasten upon some single end or consequence which is liked, and permit the view of that to blot from perception all other undesired and undesirable consequences"—or, for that matter, other desirable consequences.

Suggestive of the desperate state of affairs regarding the measurement of unintended consequences is a movement in educational evaluation that has sought to compel attention to such consequences by withholding knowledge of program goals. This movement, known as Goal-Free Evaluation (Scriven, 1972), dictates that the goals of program administrators be concealed from the evaluators. Only a vague identification of goals, such as "It is a year-long program to improve reading skills," is permitted. Thus, outcomes are to be judged in terms of a prior needs assessment by the evaluator *independently* of the program's specific goals. This procedure can be criticized on a variety of grounds, for example: the willful neglect of formal goals might encourage a certain laxity on the part of administrators, with the intriguing effect of goal-free intervention; the scope of variables and measurements is very broad, while goals at least provide some foci or even guiding hypotheses; the study of how goals emerge and change in response to program constraints, opportunities, and interim outcomes (including the way in which these matters are monitored by administrators) is neglected; and the study of the functions of goal statements in gaining support, arousing commitment, and mollifying critics is also ignored. (A failure to measure goals on the grounds that they are fuzzy rests on the assumption that measures do not exist for such goals. But see Louis and Sieber, 1979, pp. 34–59; and Sieber, Louis, and Metzger, 1972, Appendix I.) But what is perhaps most striking about this approach is the assumption that evaluators cannot be *trained* to pay attention to the aggregate of consequences in addition to goal attainment or failure, an assumption that seems premature in view of the paucity of effort in the field to give such training.

Not surprisingly, concern with the *regressive* outcomes of

intervention among evaluators languishes in an even more primitive state than concern with side effects. Indeed, the parlance of evaluation research discourages a distinction between reverse effects and null effects by use of the blanket term "negative results." When one is able to discern which type of effect is being referred to, one almost invariably finds that it is a null effect. Carter's (1973) discussion of clients' resistance to "negative" findings is typical: "By negative findings I mean research results and conclusions that are opposed to the expectations of the client for whom the research was conducted." This definition obviously embraces regressive as well as null effects, but all of the cases cited by Carter exemplify null effects only. The employment of the term "negative" is therefore highly misleading. In principle it is all-embracing, while in practice it is applied to cases that are, strictly speaking, not negative at all, but simply null.

The following case appears to be typical of the treatment of genuinely negative results (or *reverse effects* as I call them here to avoid confusion) in the evaluation of social programs. A massive government-funded study of the impact of manpower development programs on 3,598 accused offenders in 9 cities found that one of the major features of the program, counseling, was associated with *higher* recidivism for all types except those with the *briefest* period of unemployment prior to the program. Thus, those who had suffered most from unemployment were not only immune to counseling, but seemed to have been actually harmed by it. Here is how the evaluators interpreted this intriguing outcome (Mullen & Carlson, 1974, p. 155):

> These facts imply that when services are delivered to those who most need them, the effects are rewarding. However, these services appear to have also been delivered to large numbers of participants who neither needed nor responded to them. This undirected distribution of services has weakened the overall impact of counseling services.

And then again in the summary section on program effects:

> Finally, we found a significant decrease in recidivism in response
> to counseling services among those with reasonably stable
> employment histories. However, among those with long-term
> employment problems, no such association was apparent; in
> fact, there seemed to be a higher recidivism rate for those with
> more hours of counseling. (p. 187)

Not only is the first statement erroneous inasmuch as those
who "needed the program most," that is, those with longest
periods of unemployment, were really less likely to benefit
from it, but an indication that counseling might have contributed to recidivism in this group is benignly transformed into
unresponsiveness to counseling. Apparently, being responsive
can mean only one thing: being positively responsive. A
genuinely negative effect is simply ruled out of court.

   When regressive effects *are* fully recognized they are often
relegated to a realm of methodological controversy where they
can be dispatched with little ceremony. The ease with which
such effects can be discounted by pointing to hypothetical
shortcomings in research methods is illustrated by the following excerpts:

> In RAND's examination of a comprehensive youth program
> there was some indication that successful labor market perfor-
> mance was inversely related to length of stay in the program.
> There are a number of plausible explanations for such a phe-
> nomenon. Perhaps the most reasonable is that youths with
> more severe problems tend to stay in the program longer and
> also to have worse labor market performance after they leave the
> program. Ascribing all of the poor labor market performance to
> the length of stay rather than to some unmeasured personal
> characteristics of the enrollee results in the conclusion that the
> program may be detrimental. (Glennan, 1972, p. 205)

> The evaluators' findings for achievement tests show a predomi-
> nance of negative effects—that is, the pupils enrolled in Follow
> Through models did worse than the control groups on twenty-
> six comparisons. . . . Most evaluators would regard these find-
> ings as evidence of an initial nonequivalence, not fully corrected
> by analysis of covariance, of Follow Through and non-Follow
> Through. (House *et al.*, 1978, p. 141)

While the methodological cautions mentioned in these excerpts are well taken, in the absence of additional information

or analysis it is unclear why a methodological explanation is routinely more plausible than a substantive one, namely, an explanation as to why the program might be detrimental. One reason, perhaps, is the lack of theoretical guidelines for analysis of reverse effects. A more obviously fundamental reason may be that an ameliorative ethic, a faith in interventions as inherently virtuous, the career benefits of being associated with a successful program, and an inordinate sensitivity to failure in a highly competitive policy-planning and implementation system have conspired to preclude attention to regressive outcomes of social programs in general.

A more ingenious attempt than those cited above to lay the blame at the door of methodological self-delusion is the following case. A follow-up study after 40 years was conducted on 80 percent of the males who had participated in a five-year controlled experiment with a personal counseling program in their youth. The study found that those who had been randomly assigned to the therapy group were *more* likely to have committed at least one serious crime, to show signs of alcoholism or serious mental illness, to have died young, and to have or have had high blood pressure or heart trouble. "The results go beyond indicating that therapy was ineffective," stated the researcher at a meeting of the American Association of Psychiatric Services for Children. "They also suggest that treatment based on what appear to be false assumptions can be damaging." In the face of this evidence, a government research psychologist discounted the study by noting that the group that had received therapy was probably more willing to admit personal problems in response to the follow-up questionnaire (*Boston Globe,* January 10, 1978).

These cases of methodological mitigation seem to be typical of the manner in which researchers confront the evidence of unintended consequences. "Evaluation studies are notorious," observes Houston (1972, p. 61), "for appending to negative results the assertion that effects were unquestionably produced, but that no provision was made for their measurement." While Houston was probably referring to side effects, the study of reverse effects is jeopardized even more by the tendency to shift the blame to methodological pitfalls. The counterintuitive nature of regressive outcomes seems to be a clear signal for methodological denial.

Since I have been especially critical of evaluation research for failing to provide guidelines for the measurement of reverse effects, in the last chapter I will offer a conceptual framework for guiding such efforts. But now I would like to turn to another field of social science that one would expect to have some interest in regressive intervention.

THE STUDY OF SOCIAL PROBLEMS

In light of the short shrift that has been accorded regressive outcomes in social theory, organizational innovation, knowledge utilization, and evaluation research, it is perhaps not surprising that one searches in vain in the textbooks on social problems for some sustained or systematic treatment of the topic. By and large, anomie or economic dislocations are seen as sources of crime, but the criminal justice system is not (with the limited exception of "labeling theory"); consumption habits are seen as a source of disease and premature death, but the health care industry is not; class barriers are seen as a source of intergenerational poverty, but the educational and welfare systems are not. The instrumentalities for dealing with social problems are viewed at worst as nugatory—rarely as exacerbative or causative. There are exceptions to this viewpoint scattered throughout the literature on social policy, but they are not seen as part of an underlying pattern of institutional dynamics even by those who stress the reverse effects turned up in their individual researches. Further, social critics outside the universities who launch an assault on the perversities of certain institutions are often dismissed by academicians as disestablishmentarians or chronic debunkers.

A few years ago, two critics (Lee & Lee, 1975, p. 9) of the journal of the Society for the Study of Social Problems, called *Social Problems,* raised these questions:

Where are the contributors who criticize political and sociological pomposities, special interest propagandas, and incompetencies? Why haven't sociologists through *Social Problems* portrayed the politico-economic corruption of our society as an inherent concomitant of domestic and imperialistic plutocracy? Why aren't these articles debating the rewards and ravages of elitism in our profession?

Partly in response to this attack, a content analysis of the journal was undertaken to discern the substantive emphases of the journal during the two decades of its existence. The researchers (Henslin & Roesti, 1976) found ample empirical confirmation of Lee and Lee's charge that the journal was neglectful of macrosocial problems, such as those posed by political institutions. Here are some of their findings:

One can note that while only 2.0 percent of the articles in the journal focused on political problems, three and a half times as many (7 percent) analyzed the many facets of juvenile delinquency; only one percent of the articles in the journal focused on sexism, while none analyzed environmental social problems (including pollution) or resource use and allocation. Additionally, we can note that there were as many articles published on topics dealing with psychiatric sociology as those on aging (including other aspects of the life cycle), health care, and the military and political institutions combined. . . . *Social Problems* . . . has not published articles on organized crime, concentration of wealth, environmental pollution, food pollution, inadequate diets of the poor, deaths by lead poisoning, cancer, assassination, political graft and other corruption, political repression, exploitation of the "have-not" nations, social control activities of the multi-national corporations, price fixing, espionage, the ideological manipulation of the public, chemical warfare, or any directly on capitalism, acquisitiveness, or the pressure on resources of a continually expanding Gross National Product. Similarly, from reading *Social Problems* it would have been almost impossible to know that the United States has recently been engaged in the longest war in its history. (pp. 58–66)

In short, the negative side effects of corporate society and its political and administrative instrumentalities had barely been scratched by a journal that spoke for sociologists preeminently concerned with "social problems." And it is little wonder that the *reverse* effects of government policies had been ignored in view of the fact that political or resource allocation problems of any sort had been scarcely dealt with. But perhaps most telling of all is the omission by the content analysts themselves of a category for *policy-caused social problems*.

CONCLUDING REMARKS

Social scientists have shown a strange reluctance to integrate research, theory, and practice in the study of unanticipated consequences. The importance, scope, and historical pedigree of the concept are stressed by theorists (e.g., Merton, 1936; Henshel, 1976; Schneider, 1978), and certain dimensions, such as predictability, desirability, intentionality, and awareness of outcomes, are reiterated. But there is little effort to apply these dimensions to concrete cases, contemporary or historical. Meanwhile, researchers and astute social observers disclose unanticipated consequences of every hue and shape, including reverse effects; but they fail to set their findings within a conceptual framework, and hence fail fully to understand their dynamics or sources. Moreover, there is the practitioner who believes that hiring an evaluation team will discharge his responsibility for learning about the efficacy of his program so that unanticipated consequences can be safely ignored as irrelevant, but who is often compelled by events to realize that the good that the program did was canceled out by the harm that it did on the side, or that instead of having simply failed to achieve its objectives, it compounded the problem.

To advance theory, to guide research, to improve practice—none of these tasks can benefit from the detection of unanticipated consequences without some assistance from the other domains of effort. While this injunction might seem to entail an unaffordable luxury in a world of staggering complexity and pressing social ills, it nonetheless points to a prerequisite for understanding the potency, ubiquity, and dynamics of unintended outcomes.

But the absence of applied theory is not the only reason for paying so little attention to reverse effects. Men seldom fail to perceive the folly of their ways simply because they lack eyes. The tendency of applied social scientists and practitioners to overlook the broad pattern of regression might also be due to one or a combination of the following biases: the paternalistic bias, whereby benevolent efforts to foster the good life are automatically discounted as a source of the bad life; the elite bias, whereby those in control are viewed as too cleverly prudent to be self-defeating; the rationalistic bias, whereby enlightened thought is believed to be more powerful than all the forces of sentiment, self-interest, and contingency; or the activist bias, whereby doing almost anything is regarded as a better thing than doing nothing.

PART II

Conversion Mechanisms

Patterns of Reverse Effects and Their Sources

INTRODUCTION

In this section, which consists of seven chapters, I will explore two problem areas: (1) the dynamics of regressive intervention: what are the patterns of reversal that take place? and (2) the sources of regressive intervention: what are the social forces that foster the intervention and the collective or individual response to it? Because of the complex provenance of certain interventions and the response to them, and the lack of explicit attention in the literature to explanations of ironic outcomes, my analysis will tend to be speculative. My main purpose with respect to theory, however, is to stimulate thought along certain promising lines of inquiry so that a full-scale theory may eventually be formulated.

Features of interventions that in interaction with their environment produce reverse effects will be called *conversion*

55

mechanisms in recognition of the fact that they convert the intentions of the agents into the opposite outcomes. The seven conversion mechanisms are named *functional disruption, exploitation, goal displacement, provocation, classification, overcommitment,* and *placation*. These mechanisms should not be thought of as exhaustive nor, as I mentioned above, do I have any illusion that the last word has been uttered on the dynamics whereby each mechanism produces reverse effects.

Further, despite the editorial appearance of an inexorable march of theory supplied from time to time with bits of empirical sustenance, my actual manner of proceeding has been highly inductive. That is, my explication of mechanisms has been almost entirely governed by the empirical observations that were found by randomly perusing the literature and journalistic sources (and since many of my conclusions are counterintuitive, I have been generous with direct quotations). The main exceptions to this inductive approach entail the use of certain concepts that were mentioned in my earlier review of social theory. This method suffers the weakness of empirical opportunism; that is, important domains of theory that have been developed *without* specific reference to unanticipated consequences are probably untapped or underdeveloped.

For all these reasons, then, the present effort should be viewed as awareness-raising and heuristic. The main objectives are to demonstrate the ubiquity of the problem, to alert policy makers and program administrators to the occurrence of reverse effects in spite of rational decision-making as currently practiced, to commend the study of ironic outcomes to researchers and theorists in the social sciences, and to suggest that particular mechanisms can be identified to account for the recurrence of these consequences. Later, in a final section of this book, I will apply my analysis to an understanding of future trends in modern society with particular reference to the theory of social evolution and make some concrete suggestions for policy.

CHAPTER 3

Functional Disruption

As I pointed out earlier, Merton's definition of a latent dysfunction entails interference with a requirement of the system as its distinguishing mark. One possible effect of frustrating a system need is to exacerbate the very condition that one has undertaken to alleviate, a possibility that Merton does not develop. This is the issue of concern in the present chapter.

Because it is easier to understand the concept of system requirements with reference to the realm of the natural environment, let me begin by citing some pertinent cases drawn from that realm. Indeed, the study of technological change in underdeveloped countries is rife with illustrative material. Here are some striking instances:

> In Burma, deep ploughing introduced by European agricultural experts broke up the hard pan that held the water in rice-fields. The weeding of rubber plantations reduced the sap. . . . In Turkey, experts trained abroad persuaded some of the younger peasants to remove the stones from their tilled land; when the grain sprouted, the fields of the old men had a better crop, since, in that dry climate, the stones served the function of preserving moisture. (Mead, 1955, pp. 186–187)

58 CHAPTER 3

LINKAGE BETWEEN NATURE AND SOCIETY

The effects of interfering with the functional needs of nature are not limited to the natural environment, of course, but may have repercussions on the social system as well. The abandonment of traditional conservation measures as a result of introducing a cash-crop economy in many areas of the world, with the consequences of soil impoverishment, malnutrition, and death among farmers, is a well known example.

Regressive outcomes for crop production do not stem only from direct interference with the needs of nature, but also from indirect interference via impairment of a need in the social system. Here is an instructive case, also drawn from that cornucopia of unanticipated consequences edited by Margaret Mead (1955, p. 224):

> In Iran a farmer was heard to complain that [DDT] had an adverse effect upon farming; the flies, mosquitoes and bedbugs which had been counted upon to wake the farmers from their afternoon siesta are now gone, and the farmers do not wake up in time to put in sufficient work before sunset.

The lesson here is that social as well as natural systems have requirements, such as being awake and on the job. If the exploitation of nature depends upon the continued fulfillment of such needs, then any intervention in nature (e.g., DDT) that has a deleterious side effect on the human organization for production will be self-defeating. In such manner, nature and society are linked together in the most intimate way.

A more spectacular example of this linkage is the effect of the Aswân High Dam on the productive capacity of Egyptians. As Farb (1978, pp. 454–455) relates:

> Schistosomiasis, a debilitating parasitic disease, had long been endemic in Egypt, attacking a very small proportion of the population. The parasite is carried by snails that inhabit shallow waters, such as those of irrigation canals. Previous to the construction of the Aswân High Dam, the canals dried out each year, thus killing most of the snails and greatly lessening the number of parasites. Now that the canals are filled the year

round with irrigation water from Lake Nasser, the snails have multiplied astronomically. As a result, about half of the entire population of Egypt today suffers from schistosomiasis—and the increase in productivity that had been anticipated as one benefit from the dam has been counterbalanced by the severely debilitating effects of the disease upon human workers. Infected individuals lose up to half of their former strength and vitality, and the weakness persists even after the body no longer harbors the parasite. The consequent reduction in the ability to work suffered by the people currently or previously infected has meant an annual economic loss to Egypt estimated at about $550 million.

Conversely, disruption of a natural system may occur through disruption of a social need, and this may occur even when the express purpose of the intervention is to conserve rather than to exploit nature. For if the intervention causes a social group to seek an alternative means of exploiting the environment in order to fulfill the original need, the ultimate outcome could be environmental harm instead of protection. This ironic pattern can be illustrated by effects of a Florida law that banned the shooting or trapping of alligators. Scriven (1978) has summarized the case as follows:

The legislature in Florida banned the shooting or trapping of alligators in order to save them from extinction. As a result, farmers who owned large areas of swamp land that had proved marginally profitable as long as it was used for the cultivation of alligators proceeded to drain it since their only source of income from it had vanished, and the cost of draining is eventually amortizable against the crops that can be produced in the drained land. So the alligators lost all their habitat and were wiped out completely in the very area where they were supposed to be saved.

In short, the functional requirements of nature and of society stand in so extremely close a relationship that a disruptive intervention in one system might not only rebound negatively on the other, but might ultimately worsen the condition in the system that one hoped to protect or enhance.

The mutual disruptiveness of nature and society reminds us that latent dysfunctions within either system do not stem solely from internal sources, an assumption with respect to society that has pervaded sociological theory despite the efforts of ecologists (e.g., Duncan & Schnore, 1959) to gain recognition of the role of the natural environment. No doubt the contemporary trauma of an "energy crisis" will finally drive the point home. In any event, the interdependency of functional needs between human and nonhuman systems is an inescapable fact in investigations of the context of regressive intervention in the field of technical change.

FUNCTIONAL IMBALANCE

Turning to sources of reverse effects internal to social systems, what I discern to be a common source is the emphasis on a particular requirement at the expense of another, creating what Merton (1961, p. 734) has called a functional imbalance. Such imbalances appear to be of two general sorts, depending on their source. One stems from simple neglect of a secondary need, while the other stems from an opposition between needs that makes it impossible to serve one without jeopardizing the other.

Neglect of Secondary Needs

This type is extremely common in the implementation of social programs. As Zander (1978, p. 66) observes: "Too often a present bias or overemphasis on a specific goal causes planners to ignore or downplay one or another aspect of a proposed or operative program. Absurd unintended consequences then result." Zander gives several illustrations of this effect in programs for the aged. Thus, the implementation of Supplementary Security Income substantially raised the income of many elderly poor; but because payments were now less responsive to increases in the cost of living than under earlier programs, such as Old Age Assistance, many of the recipients found themselves worse off than they would have been had they remained in these other programs. "By the time SSI had been in effect for over a year," Zander (1978, p.64) notes, "a survey of selected public and private agencies indicated that demands by the elderly for hard services—food, shelter, and income maintenance—were increasing, not decreasing." In effect, the recipients' need to adjust to changing economic conditions was overlooked in the drive both to simplify the system and increase benefits.

Another case of ignoring a secondary system need is that of increased Old Age Security Insurance benefits several years ago "which suddenly raised many poor elderly to an OASI income level where they received a few dollars over the eligibility requirements for Medicaid" (Zander, 1978, p. 66). As a result, medical coverage was now denied to the very population that needed it most, while only a few extra dollars were given in compensation. Here the eligibility requirements of Medicaid as well as the needs of the elderly for medical attention were neglected in the pursuit of a higher income level. As Zander points out, such blunders not only increase hardship for older persons but result in unnecessary implementation costs for taxpayers.

This last example puts us on notice that past interventions might well have created needs (e.g., eligibility requirements) that new interventions ignore. Increasingly in an age of ubiquitous interventionism, social reform is a matter of taking into account not only the "natural" needs of social systems but also those "artificial" needs that have been imposed by previous reforms. In effect, one intervention might cancel out the intended effect of another to the distinct detriment of clients.

Antithetical Needs

While such costly mistakes might seem to be preventable by more careful attention to the interlinked outcomes of policy decisions, the second type of functional imbalance is more resistant to anticipatory diagnosis and control, for it entails the simultaneous satisfaction of *opposing* system needs. Merton

(1961, p. 734) has taken note of this social pattern in the following terms:

> A group has diverse functional requirements: to take only one thoroughly investigated example, the requirement of enough social cohesion to keep its members oriented to the group as having value for them and the requirement of working toward the group goals, of getting the job done. It is not unusual, therefore, that the same activities that are functional for one of these requirements prove to be dysfunctional for the other. When this is true to a substantial degree, the group confronts an organizational problem.

Merton here tags one of the key problems in planning for implementation, or of purposive action of any kind for that matter, a problem that has been regrettably ignored: how to weave a course between functional requirements that work at cross-purposes? Rein and White (1977, p. 266) have pointed out that the rational problem-solving image of policy formation does not cope well with such a dilemma. And yet, this type of dilemma lies at the core of organizational action:

> Dilemmas of social policy arise, for example, in the effort to preserve work incentives and to provide adequate income support for those unable to be gainfully employed. Or they arise in manifold ways in efforts to design a program so that it will not reach those for whom it is not intended: administrative screening devices that focus on weeding out ineligibles also reduce the likelihood of reaching eligibles. Dilemmas also arise in education when, on the one hand, one strives for the kind of parity of input or output envisaged in the notion of equality of educational opportunity while, on the other, one tries to provide the disparities envisaged by the notions of pluralism and cultural democracy. (Rein & White, 1977, pp. 266–267)

Or again, as pointed out by Blau and Scott (1962, p. 250):

> The very improvements in some conditions that further the achievement of the organizations' objectives often interfere with other conditions equally important for this purpose. A by now familiar example is that hierarchical differentiation promotes coordination but simultaneously restricts the communication processes that benefit decision-making.

Here are some additional examples of antithetical requirements. Goals must be clearly defined and consensus assured before undertaking a new program; but goals must be diffuse so that leeway in adjustment is afforded, and consensus must be allowed to fluctuate so that alternative perspectives are encouraged. Participatory planning is necessary to give the members a stake in an organization and to insure a supply of fresh ideas; but strong leadership is necessary to enforce standards, cope with crises, and manipulate the environment. Public agencies like schools need to involve the community in planning major new programs in order to avert attack and exploit community resources; but they must close themselves off from the community in order to plan and act judiciously, and to maintain both the reality and sense of professional control.[1] Many functional antinomies of this kind could be cited. Indeed, the problem is so ubiquitous that the philosopher Sidney Hook (1974) asserts that it imbues pragmatism with a "tragic sense of life."

Dilemmas such as those mentioned above set the stage for self-defeating action insofar as there is a tendency toward a puristic commitment to one or the other horn. (Some possible sources of this tendency will be discussed below.) There seem to be two ways in which this tendency invites a regressive outcome.

First, the wholehearted embrace of one of the options can damage the fulfillment of the other to such an extent that the reason for choosing the particular course of action is confounded. For example, the study of planned organizational change has encountered an antithesis between the need for external assistance, on the one hand, and the need for local participation and sense of control over the change process, on the other. Thus, an analysis of a large number of case studies of "organization development" as a change strategy found a negative correlation between the efforts of outside consultants and institutionalization of the project. "Excessive reliance on outside consultants," write the researchers, "seems to reduce ownership, hence institutionalization" (Fullan et al., 1978, pp.

---

[1] For several recent analyses of educational institutions in terms of organizational dilemmas, see Miles, 1978, 1981; Berman and McLaughlin, 1979; and Sieber, 1980.

39, 41). Conversely, Sieber (1978) found that excessive reliance on improvement of internal communication and collective decision-making can undermine the use of expert resources from outside the organization with the result that innovative effort is poorly conceived and carried out.

Laws in behalf of some social good that interfere with the ability of private industry to make a profit can also lead to an effect that worsens the situation. This seems to have occurred with building code enforcement programs in the cities. According to Downs (1973):

> Compelling owners of deteriorated buildings in low-income neighborhoods to bring buildings up to code may cause them to abandon the buildings rather than comply, because it does not pay to rehabilitate them. . . . It is naïve for analysts trying to correct poor housing to suppose that owners will ignore their own economic interests completely, to the extent of causing ownership to result in drastic losses rather than profits. Many would rather give up their ownership first. So about 800 to 900 buildings per year are being abandoned by their owners in New York City alone, and more in other cities.

Second, a belated recognition of failure to satisfy an opposing system need may shift action in a direction that entails renunciation of the intervention altogether, including its basic values. This familiar pattern has sometimes been referred to as a *pendulum* effect. An example is the educational movement of the 1960s that centered on "alternative schools." Contemptuous of hierarchy and rules, these schools tended eventually to experience chaos, or as Deal (1975, p. 489) calls it in a review of the movement, "psychic upheaval, depression, tears, and crisis." A common response to this exclusive emphasis on freedom and equality was reversion to highly traditional structures and learning situations; another was to disband altogether and to spurn future efforts to liberalize education or to embrace any major innovation along those lines.

The utopian fallacy lies precisely in this tendency to overemphasize certain system needs, with the consequence that the system either gives belated recognition to opposing needs or becomes inoperative, the participants reverting with a ven-

geance to older patterns of behavior and thought. As Kenneth
Burke remarked once, "Pessimism is utopianism gone sour."
In a more functionalist vein, one might say that hell has no fury
like a functional requirement scorned, a simple truth that is
often forgotten when we are exposed to the charms of a rival
requirement.

Functional Imbalance and the Dialectic

It would appear that the pendulum effect entails a combination of the historical dialectic and modern functionalism,
two models of social theory that are rarely viewed as compatible. The essential idea of the dialectic is that polarities are
resolved into a new equilibrium by forces that arise from their
opposition. Marx applied this model to the antagonism between the needs of the capitalist system for private appropri-
ation (i.e., the "cycle of investment–production–profit–investment, dominated by private capital," as Giddens, 1979,
p. 142, says) and a socialized mode of production. (For an
explication of this core idea of Marx's theory of capitalistic
contradiction, see Giddens, 1979, pp. 131–164). Out of this
structural antagonism, he believed, would spring a class consciousness among the proletariat that would resolve the antagonism by replacing capitalism with socialism. Thus, change
in the system would be generated internally by contradictory
elements. Now let us look at the pendulum effect in light of
this idea.

If one conceives of the "internal contradictions" of a social
order as entailing antithetical system requirements, then the
ground is laid for an emphasis on one of these requirements at
the expense of the other.[2] Thus, the stress on private appro-
priation, which involves exploitation of workers who are in
close communication with one another, fosters a tendency to

[2] As I pointed out earlier, my criticism of functionalism does not reside in what
   some critics have called a teleological notion of social systems (see Giddens,
   1979) inherent in the idea of system requirements, but in the implication that
   other, historical factors need not also be considered in explaining either the
   maintenance or subsidence of a system.

swing to the other pole, culminating in revolution and dictatorship of the proletariat. But here we must depart from the Marxist dialectic by asserting the role of factors external to the system, factors which might either reinforce or inhibit the tendency to shift toward a polar requirement. Marx's revolution did not come about in capitalist society, but in agrarian societies with traditions of absolutist bureaucratic regimes; and the liberal state inhibited the harmful tendencies of laissez-faire economics from erupting in revolution. Thus, it appears that if external factors are sufficiently powerful, they can either reinforce or inhibit the pendulum. In either case, the system may attain a new "equilibrium". If reinforcement of a swing occurs, then the counterrequirement might be not only violated but effaced (sometimes by state force, as with the elimination of competitive free enterprise in the Soviet Union). If the swing is inhibited by external factors, then new structures might arise to maintain a certain balance over time (e.g., unionism in America as a consequence of the National Labor Relations Act of 1935).

Note that this framework does not depend solely on endogenous forces, as does Marx's version of the historical dialectic, but includes either reinforcement or inhibition of natural shifts of emphasis by exogenous factors. Nor does it depend solely on external disruption of a functional equilibrium, as functionalism implies, since such equilibrium is viewed as a continuous movement between the serving of antithetical system needs. By making slight modifications in each of the two theoretical models, therefore, a fruitful marriage may be proposed.[3] Now let us turn to a consideration of forces that reinforce and even institutionalize swings of the pendulum.

---

[3] For a formulation of several bases for a synthesis of the dialectic and functionalism, one of which is especially pertinent to my analysis, that is, contradiction between "institutional principles," see van den Berghe, 1963. It seems to me, however, that the ubiquity of antithetical functional requisites is the key that has been overlooked.

Sources of Functional Imbalance

At the societal level, the main external factors in democratic societies that reinforce the satisfaction of one need and
thereby create a functional imbalance are pressures from the
electorate and concentrations of power in the hands of highly
organized groups. Here I am not interested in the narrow,
self-defined needs of social groups, which might well give rise
to struggles, but in appeals to basic social or organizational
requirements that are structurally contradictory.

Pressures from the electorate are often couched in
genuine appeals to satisfaction of particular basic requirements of social systems. Thus, appeals to either deterrence or
rehabilitation of deviants, bureaucratic problem solving or
charismatic leadership, continuing growth or zero growth,
centralization or pluralism, and so on through a host of structural antinomies, reflect the shifting demands of the public for
promises of deliverance from some pressing social evil. The
greater the perceived ill, of course, the greater the frustration,
and hence the greater the demand for a strong, immediate,
definitive, and hence simplistic solution. The diverse, one-
sided interventions that are adopted in dealing with profound
social issues may thus be seen as secular expressions of a
millenarian mentality. Instead of a supernatural response, the
commitment of a secular intervention to one horn of a functional dilemma entails an inner-worldly orientation. In both
the religious and secular cases, however, there is resort to a
noncontingent realm of action and belief—that is, a realm
where the attainment of objectives is guaranteed independently of resources or constraints. As political pressure
mounts for resolution of a problem, a noncontingent orientation is more and more likely to be embraced. A clear and
especially pertinent example at the present time is popular
fervor for military ventures against an enemy who has a re-
taliative capacity beyond the reach of any weapons in the
arsenal of democracy. In this instance, security by force of
arms is emphasized to the detriment not only of domestic

welfare, but of alternative forms of security, such as negotiated agreements.

The second source of exclusive emphasis on particular system needs at the societal level is highly organized interest groups. Those who possess the most potent means of pressing their appeals to structural principles of the "good society" are able to foster programs that ignore competing requirements. Whether the issue be war or peace, conservation or more intensive development of energy sources, jobs or price stability, oligopoly or competition, and so forth, the solution will be deeply influenced by concentrations of power. The ultimate source of these concentrations is the degree of differentiation in the system. In simple systems only a few polarizations occur—for example, male and female, old and young, member and nonmember, agriculturalist and herder, or missionary and witch doctor. In modern society, however, they are legion. This situation contains a high potential for reverse consequences of policies, a potential that gains in strength with the mobilization of new resources "which provide one or more contenders with the capacity to press forward old demands more forcefully" (Flanagan, 1973, p. 52). Examples of this process offered by Flanagan are the accumulation of wealth by the bourgeoisie, the organization of the working class, and the igniting of popular enthusiasm by a charismatic figure or a religious institution. Such asymmetries of mobilization are a frequent source of functional imbalance, especially if the demands of the newly empowered had been previously frustrated to a high degree.

PERVERSE DIAGNOSIS

Somewhat different from functional imbalance is a pattern that I shall call *perverse diagnosis*. This occurs when the requirement that is addressed by an intervention is illusory, thereby undermining the system even further. For example, it is well established that punishment was recommended in the

eighteenth century for the treatment of mental illness as a
means of dealing with the irascibility of maniacs. Here are the
words of two eighteenth-century authorities cited by Foucault
(1965, p. 180):

> It is by force that the furies of a maniac are overcome; it is by
> opposing fear to anger that anger may be mastered. If the terror
> of punishment and public shame are associated in the mind
> during attacks of anger, one will not appear without the other;
> the poison and the antidote are inseparable. . . . fear being a
> passion that diminishes the excitation of the brain, it can con-
> sequently calm its excesses, and especially the irascible excitation
> of maniacs.

Such perversity of diagnosis is not restricted to a benighted
past. Thus, persons suffering from depression are not infrequently ordered to "snap out of it" on the assumption that
they are malingering. Far from improving matters, the injunction is harmful because now the individual is made to feel
guilty for being unable to comply with legitimate demands,
which deepens depression.

Perverse diagnoses are perhaps even more common with
regard to social planning. A few years ago in New York City,
additional patrolmen were placed on the streets to reduce the
cost of overtime. But since the major source of police overtime
is court processing of arrests and not patrol duty, the increased
number of policemen only meant more arrests, which in turn
meant more time spent in court. As a consequence, overtime
costs were increased instead of reduced (*The New York Times*,
December 4, 1977). Again, American experts erroneously assumed that the Guatemalan earthquake of 1976 created a need
for emergency food supplies, when in fact the country had just
harvested its largest grain crop in many years. Consequently,
27,000 tons of grain were donated to rural victims of the quake.
This had the effect of knocking the bottom out of the country's
grain market for almost a year, thereby hurting the very population of rural farmers whom the aid was designed to assist
(*The New York Times*, November 6, 1977).

One of the most persistent and tragic instances of perverse diagnosis in the United States is the assumption that crime is caused by the easy availability of addictive drugs, which in turn is attributed to allowing illicit suppliers to operate. In fact, the principle of the price mechanism tells us that the scarcity of a commodity increases its price, and the supplier is then even more eager to satisfy demand. In the case of heroin, this means that the necessity of stealing to acquire the means of purchasing the drug also increases. Thus, a three-year study in Detroit shows that the rate of property crimes goes up when the price of heroin rises (*The New York Times*, May 22, 1977). And, of course, nothing is more likely to reduce supply than a crackdown by police. As Schur and Bedau (1974, p. 20) note:

> Efforts to cut off supply have, in the face of overwhelming demand, utterly failed to deter potential suppliers. On the contrary, criminalization—which by raising the risks of illicit traffic, and to some extent limiting supply, encourages price increases and hence higher illicit profits—actually nurtures and strengthens black market operations.

Or as Brecher *et al.* (1972) have expressed it:

> The profitability of the entire narcotics black market depends on untiring efforts of the law-enforcement agencies to hold the available supply down to the level of effective demand.

If these assessments are correct, then one major cause of crime is the policy of suppression itself. In effect, the taxpayer pays to have himself robbed.[4]

Sources of Perverse Diagnosis

Certain cases of perverse diagnosis share the fallacy of neglecting to consider overriding, proximate causes of prob-

---

[4] Although the topic lies beyond our concern with social intervention, it is worth noting that perverse diagnoses of technological mishaps can pose a major threat to modern life. Thus, the *New York Times* (July 22, 1979) reports of the Three Mile Island nuclear accident: "When the accident occurred, operators shut off the emergency cooling pumps because they thought too much water was going into the cooling system; in fact, there was too little."

lems that are augmented by treating a prior factor that is presumed to be the cause. Thus, while placing more patrolmen on the street might reduce overtime for patrol duty, it overlooks the more important, proximate cause of overtime: more time spent in court. Likewise, while reducing the supply of hard drugs might reduce some crime, it ignores the more critical, proximate cause of crime: the need for money to pay for drugs to which one is addicted, which is augmented by reducing supply. With respect to coping with deviance, this tendency is nurtured by a moralistic orientation that rejects the need to understand system requirements and focuses on willful misconduct.

A related source of perverse diagnosis is discrepant frames of reference between the agent and the target of intervention. This may cause ignorance of the target system's genuine needs and the attribution of certain requirements of the agent's own culture, society, or personality. In the Guatemala case cited above, it was sheer ignorance of the country's recent grain production that caused the trouble. The problem of attribution is acute in public institutions that are staffed by middle-class white professionals who are responsible for diagnosing the needs of lower-class or minority group clients. (For a review of research on this issue in education, see Persell, 1977, pp. 101–134.) The problem is even more serious when the professional and his clients represent distinctly different cultures, as noted by numerous anthropologists. For example:

> When American teachers tried to spur Hopi and Navaho children through introducing competition, or to encourage by singling out for praise, they failed in the first case and caused intense misery in the second, since to stand out is painful and brings insecurity. (Mead, 1955, p. 255)

As Linton (1936) pointed out many years ago:

> Because of its subjective nature, *meaning* is much less susceptible to diffusion than either *form* or *use*. . . . A receiving culture attaches new meanings to the borrowed elements or complexes, and these may have little relation to the meanings which the

> same elements carried in their original setting. (Cited in Rogers &
> Shoemaker, 1971, p. 337)

A slightly different problem arises when the diagnosis of a
target system's need is essentially correct but the intervention
goes astray and addresses itself unwittingly to an audience
that does not share the diagnosed need. This seems to be
commonplace in the field of public information campaigns.
As Merton and Kendall (1944, p. 7) observed with reference to
the "boomerang effect":

> The boomerang which results from contradictory personal ex-
> periences may occur in the health and welfare field precisely
> because their audiences have not been adequately defined. The
> writer often feels that the people who listen to his programs are
> the relatively uneducated who have the greatest need for his
> information. In point of fact, however, it is usually highly edu-
> cated people who listen to educational or "serious" programs.

One possible regressive effect of assuming that the audience is
uneducated is resentment of the messenger for "talking
down," an attitude that might cause a sophisticated listener
not only to discount the message but to abandon the very
practice or belief that is advocated. That is, a sort of blasé effect
might ensue from repeated exposure to a vulgarized version of
a practice or idea that one has already embraced, thereby
prompting the listener to spurn the practice or idea.

Conversely, an educated appeal to an uneducated audience might create suspicion and distrust, as in the following
case:

> A representative of a county medical society broadcast a talk on
> X-rays. He stressed the precautions needed to prevent X-ray
> burns; he indicated that the local government protects the citizen
> by a system of licensing X-ray operators and by inspecting
> equipment; he emphasized the specialized training required to
> attain competence in this field. The speaker was evidently seek-
> ing to prevent his listeners from falling into the hands of quacks
> who have neither competence nor integrity. . . . It is well
> known from related fields of investigation that listeners cannot
> readily assimilate information and attitudes if these are not
> integrated with their backlog of experience. . . . Since the talk

raised issues which it failed to clarify, it led to a *boomerang effect*. . . . the whole emphasis of the speaker led first to impatience, then to disbelief, and finally to distrust. (Merton, 1957, pp. 518–519)

In effect, a correct diagnosis may *become* perverse when the intervention is aimed at the wrong audience. Perhaps the simplest case is that of the surgeon who operates on the wrong patient who, as a consequence of the operation, succumbs on the operating table.

OVERLOAD

Occasionally a diagnosis may be correct, but unwarranted assumptions are made about the target system's capacity to use the prescription correctly. What happens in such cases is that a *new* imperative is imposed upon the target system by the intervention, an imperative whose nonfulfillment may cause more damage than good. Here is an example drawn from a study of "open education" in Boston (Barth, 1972, pp. 137–138):

> Open educators assume that children learn by exploring a variety of materials, by making choices, and by posing and solving their own problems. They also assume that children will welcome opportunities to do these things. Children in the Program did not; the efforts of the young teachers were unsuccessful from the beginning. Following theory and intuition, they encouraged children to make decisions. But many children had limited capacity to attend to a task; the more options made available to them, the more difficult that attending became. A rich environment of manipulative materials only made it less likely that a child could focus on any one.

Unlike functional imbalances and perverse diagnoses, in which system requirements precede the intervention, overload occurs when a key requirement is imposed by the intervention itself and no provision is made for satisfying it. The result can be impairment of the system instead of the intended goal of increased adaptation.

Organizations, as well, may lack the capacity to meet

the latent requirements imposed by an intervention, and, in trying to do so, produce the opposite effect. An instructive case is provided by New York State's strict drug law enacted in 1973. This law prescribed severe and mandatory penalties for drug offenses at all levels. Moreover, plea bargaining was prohibited for persons who had previously been convicted of a felony and were indicted for a subsequent felony. This latter provision *may* have resulted in an increase in the proportion of convicted felony offenders who were sentenced to prison (the trend was in this direction before the law). However, the rise in proportion sentenced "was more than offset by the decreasing likelihood that arrest would lead to an indictment and indictment to conviction" (Joint Committee on New York Drug Law Evaluation, 1978, p. 23). Because of the severer penalties, defendants more often demanded jury trials, and "defense counsel typically posed many challenges and objections in the process of entering a guilty plea" (Joint Committee on New York Drug Law Evaluation, 1978, p. 18). In addition, some judges granted continuances more readily because they felt that rehabilitation was more important than imprisonment under the severe mandatory sentences. Consequently, the law increased court congestion in an already overtaxed system and led to the punishment of a smaller proportion of offenders than before.

The fallacy of presuming that a community possesses the skills or knowledge required for the safe utilization of a new technology can have catastrophic consequences. While few persons would give a loaded gun to a child for self-protection, it appears that certain technologies that are disseminated to developing countries literally threaten their survival. A tragic case is the distribution of baby bottles and infant formulas, an innovation that has contributed to malnutrition and disease. Testimony before a Senate health subcommittee has confirmed the problem:

> Mothers in those countries cannot afford as much formula as
> their babies need, so they dilute it with extra water to make it last
> longer. The water is rarely clean. A nurse testified that in Lima,

Peru, formula powder is sometimes mixed with river water
contaminated with human wastes. Since few people in less-
developed countries have refrigerators, bacteria are likely to
develop in leftover formula even if it was mixed with clean water
to begin with. Another difficulty is that illiterate mothers cannot
follow mixing directions on packages. Overall, said Dr. Derrick B.
Jeliffe, former director of the Caribbean Food and Nutrition Institute in Jamaica, improper bottle feeding is responsible for an
estimated 10 million cases of malnutrition and diarrhea in poor
nations. . . . A survey in Chile showed that the mortality rate
for bottle-fed babies was three times as high as for those who
were breast-fed. . . . (*The New York Times*, May 28, 1978)

On a broader scale, it appears that many economic interventions in Third World countries impose new demands on
the target systems while withholding the very means for meeting these demands. Since the more advanced nations desire to
retain geopolitical dominance over those whom they assist
economically, full economic participation on the world stage
on their own terms is denied these client countries. Also,
lacking the capacity to realize aspirations for political self-
affirmation, low-income peoples cannot be mobilized in behalf
of economic development. Thus they are hampered in their
efforts to develop modern economies at the same time that
they are being pushed to do so.

Goulet (1973) argues that development entails two
categories of change processes:

The first processes concern production, mastery over nature,
rational organization, and technological efficiency; the second
concern structures of power and ideology. Prospects for success
in responding to the first series of challenges are dim unless
nondeveloped societies gain strategic freedom to redefine the
parameters operative in the second set of processes.

Sources of Overload

The source of overload is probably the same as that of
perverse diagnosis, namely, discrepant frames of reference.
The chief difference between the two is that one overlooks the
capacity to cope with *newly imposed* needs and the other over-

looks *preexisting needs*. Thus, discrepant frames of reference that entail ignorance of the target system and projection of one's own capacities are operable with respect to overload as well as perverse diagnosis.

In the case of overload, however, the effect may be amplified as well by the misperceptions of the client. This process can again be exemplified with regard to economic development. When advanced countries behave as if their value priorities and institutions were models of virtue, which they almost invariably do, client countries respond with pride in local traditions and an eagerness to avoid the stigma of backwardness and dependency. Ironically, this response leads the poorer countries to try to rival the advanced countries by *emulating* them. But since only particular cultural elements, instead of the entire societal complex, can be adopted, for example, munitions, construction equipment, consumption habits, or accounting techniques, the capacity to absorb these elements without basic dislocations in economy, polity, and culture is severely strained. Because of its own misperception or lack of information, a developing nation may not be cognizant of the new, ancillary needs that will be generated by adoption of advanced technology, needs which the nation will be sorely taxed to satisfy. This ignorance only encourages the advanced countries, of course, to undertake projects without prior assessment of target system capacities. Thus do underdeveloped countries participate in their own impairment.

THE FUNCTIONAL SHIFT

Before leaving the subject of functional disruption, it is important to recognize a process that tends to perpetuate interventions whose effects are regressive. This process becomes evident when a desirable unintended consequence takes precedence over an original goal of intervention. Such an unintended outcome, or windfall, can divert attention from the regressive effect with regard to the original goal and even justify its continuance. For example, segregating students according to academic or mental ability might be detrimental to learning (the intended, or manifest, function) but contributive to the job satisfaction of teachers who are able to avoid having to tailor their services to individual children (the unintended, or latent, function). Consequently, tracking might be continued. Similarly, the construction of small-town hospitals might be found to be unnecessary and only contribute to inflationary pressures on health cost rather than lessening them, but the program might be perpetuated because it was found to reduce unemployment in the construction trades. Training schools for PINS (youths who are labeled Persons in Need of Supervision) are believed to aggravate tendencies toward deviance (Glasser, 1978, pp. 152–154); but if the $20,000 a year that it costs to keep one PIN in an institution were paid directly to indigent parents for private tutors, psychiatric care, or baby sitters, the employment of public guards, nurses, and specialists and the upkeep of public buildings would be jeopardized. In fact, many of our highly bureaucratized efforts to deal with problems of individual welfare, efforts that are often claimed to be deleterious (e.g., Gaylin et al., 1978; Piven & Cloward, 1971), are probably resistant to change in part because the status and employment functions of the mature bureaucracy have superseded original goals.

But the most sinister illustration of a functional shift in the modern world concerns the production of armaments. Originally undertaken as a defensive measure, it eventually contributed to the proliferation of arms in the world and to the threat of warfare. But it is now extremely difficult to curtail, because it not only provides employment on a vast scale but also affords our main export and is therefore crucial to our international balance of trade. In this case, the shift was expedited by deliberately amplifying the unintended consequence once it had been discovered. As Melman (1974, pp. 107–109) reports:

> When, in 1971—for the first time since 1893—a deficit appeared in
> U.S. trade with other nations, federal officials became alarmed at
> the manifest noncompetitiveness of U.S. industry in the world

marketplace, and the predictions of more to come. . . . the Department of Defense came through with a major plan for enlarging world sales of armaments from the United States, increasing such exports from $925 million in 1970 to $3.8 billion per year in 1973. . . . The enlargement of armaments sales abroad is the largest single effort that the state management devised for restoring a favorable balance of trade to the United States.

Sources of Functional Shifts

Three major sources may be hypothesized: (1) a demotion of the original goal to a position of lesser importance than the unintended outcome, perhaps owing to fundamental changes in the value system or to an assumption that the original problem is being taken care of; (2) shifts in the relative power of groups that are differentially affected by the intervention's outcomes (e.g., the military elite versus consumer groups that would prefer to improve the balance of trade by production of better products rather than armament sales); (3) a belief by the advocates of the original goal that its continued pursuit is worthwhile and can be ensured only if those who are interested mainly in the unintended outcome are appeased, that is, by engagement in an illusory trade-off.

At bottom these explanations depend upon ignorance of the severe harm being done by the intervention with respect to original goals. The reasons for such ignorance are multifarious, as suggested by my earlier reference to biases of various kinds as well as to the lack of an intellectual tradition that fully appreciates the ubiquity of reverse outcomes. Alternatively, of course, there is the possibility of deliberate concealment whereby ignorance is only feigned. In such cases the agent derives some secondary benefit from the intervention and, therefore, has accepted a trade-off that is not illusory but nefarious. Finally, there is the possibility of denial in the psychological sense, that is, a subconscious defense against admission of failure that is perhaps buttressed by peers, companions, and institutional symbols of self-righteousness.

These observations touch on the basic sources of the perpetuation of regressive interventions, a question that I will return to in the final chapter. The functional shift is more in the nature of an *enabling* condition than an underlying source of perpetuation, but it is a condition that arises frequently in a rapidly changing society with many diverse interests and power sources, and with increasing emphasis on bureaucratic and professional means of coping with problems.

CONCLUDING REMARKS

Functional imbalances, perverse diagnoses, overload, and functional shifts account for many cases of regression in a fairly parsimonious and factually satisfactory manner. But there are numerous other cases that seem to elude this functionalist framework or that require additional considerations even if the framework could be applied. (This limitation of functional analysis for my purposes was discussed in the previous chapter.) In general, then, it has seemed advisable to follow the rule that if the imputation of a requirement and its fulfillment or nonfulfillment is primarily a translation of a cause into functional terminology, and if several causes seem to be operating, then the functional model should be held in abeyance and alternative schemata explored. In particular, the translation of a cause into fulfillment of (or interference with) a system need runs the risk of creating a kind of "tunnel vision," inasmuch as the search for additional causal variables and the analysis of their complex interactions are depreciated. This hazard can be illustrated by the doubtful utility of functional analysis in understanding the conversion mechanism to be discussed in the following chapter, namely, *exploitation* which takes a variety of forms as a consequence of its multiple sources.

CHAPTER 4

Exploitation

All interventions entail a concerted mobilization of resources and opportunities. These resources and opportunities may exceed the rewards of pursuing the intervention's goal, may be acquired by hostile parties, or may be taken advantage of by clients in a way that is unintended. These possibilities raise the prospect of exploiting interventions in a manner that subverts or even reverses an intended outcome. I will first consider the question of exploitation by hostile and nonhostile targets of intervention and then turn to exploitation by agents of intervention.

EXPLOITATION BY HOSTILE TARGET POPULATION

Exploitation by parties that are hostile to the purposes of the intervention might be called a *petard effect*. For example:

> Like the government of India that in the early 1960's built a road through Nepal towards Tibet, the GVN [of South Vietnam] had by all its vast efforts at "nation-building" and "rural construction" succeeded only in building an invasion route for the enemy. (Fitzgerald, 1973, p. 209)

The theft of military secrets is, of course, a common and by now thoroughly predictable case of having one's weapons turned against oneself.

This pattern is not restricted to warfare, hot or cold, moreover, but may occur in any hostile relationship. In a case study of school–community conflict, Gold (1977, p. 555) tells of an effort to co-opt parents:

> The idea of using parent volunteers, a strategy for coopting critical parents, boomeranged as parents collected more and more information with which to attack the school.

Similarly, the efforts of a government agency to gain legitimacy by co-opting hostile elements may lead to capture, as in the classical case of the Tennessee Valley Authority. As Salamon and Wamsley (1975, p. 158) have noted, "An agency that began as a force for environmental conservation and social change became, over time, a major threat to the environment, an unquestioning exponent of industrial advance, closely allied with entrenched regional elites." Because of the insecurity of many government agencies, the diffuseness of their ultimate clientele, and the common professional or industrial backgrounds of government personnel and private peers, even agencies that are charged with strictly regulatory functions have tended to become aligned with the very forces that they were presumed to control. As Salamon and Wamsley (1975, p. 159) write of the Food and Drug Administration:

> Lacking active support from the masses of consumers whose interest tends to be diffuse and unfocused, such agencies as the Food and Drug Administration had to reach an accommodation with the handful of producers directly affected by their actions. Since the relevant legislators faced much the same pattern of interest, the result was a cozy triumvirate of legislators, industry, and agency—with the consumer conspicuously absent.

At higher levels of government where political appointments are routinely made, the indebtedness of officials to private benefactors may in similar ways convert the goals of an agency of control into their opposite effects. In the quite recent past, the Justice Department apparently was captured by special interests through the political appointment process. As Anderson (1973, p. 25) observes, "Of the eight top Nixon appointees [to the Justice Department], seven were either campaign functionaries or defeated ex-candidates or both." The outcome was that justice was hoist with its own petard. Anderson (1973, pp. 26–27) catalogues some of the injustices of that agency during the Nixon administration:

> Civil rights laws were not enforced or were enforced selectively. . . . the television stations were threatened with an obscure anti-monopoly action. . . . Prosecutions of militant pacifists, such as the Berrigan group, were launched with ferocious fanfare. . . . Amnesty from prosecution was routinely accorded to lawbreakers who were either politicians or political fat cats. Among them were the twenty-one G.O.P. finance chairmen for the 1968 campaign who patently violated the reporting provisions of the Corrupt Practices Act.

Then, of course, there were the Watergate-related illegalities for which top Justice officials were imprisoned. In sum, as someone has observed, the problem may not be that government agencies of control are unresponsive, but that they are responsive to the very people they are supposed to be controlling. Thus, they too build invasion routes for the enemy.

Occasionally the "resources" that an intervention offers for exploitation by a hostile party are very subtle and unpredictable. Glaser (1975, pp. 94–95), for example, reports that career-oriented or nonamenable criminals who are exposed to "special staff oriented to personal rapport, counseling, and diffuse individual assistance" have *higher* recidivism rates than those who are subjected to conventional prison and parole programs. Similar findings have been reported as a result of psychotherapy on prisoners with lengthy criminal records. Glaser offers the following plausible explanation for this disappointing outcome:

> The counterproductivity of policies with career-oriented criminals that reduced recidivism with conflicted offenders may be explainable by the fact that career criminals have developed favorable conceptions of themselves and prestige with their peers primarily by frustrating authority figures.

In short, the use of "authority figures" to implement the program was exploited in a manner that ran counter to the objective of the intervention. Indeed, occasionally persons who are perceived as hostile are actually *attracted* to the very means that are undertaken to control or punish them. As Marx (1974, p. 23) observes:

> There is the case of those who violate rules and leave obvious clues, because they want to be punished. For some individuals (as false confessions to sensational crimes suggest) the publicity and notoriety that can come from formal prosecution may be positive. . . . Prison, whatever its horrors, also offers a relatively secure and predictable environment with a minimal standard of living, which may be attractive to some highly dependent or incompetent people.

In effect, certain subjects of formal control mechanisms are converted into *clients* by the latent rewards of the intervention.

Finally, we come to the case wherein the exploitation of resources is a matter of *antagonistic cooperation* in which both sides gain advantages. Such cases depend on tacit (and sometimes not so tacit) agreement between nominally hostile parties to take advantage of an intervention that is ostensibly directed against one or even both of them. In a lengthy case study of organized crime and corruption in Seattle, Washington, Chambliss (1978, p. 100) notes: "The laws of the state, county, and city are specifically (and in many cases intentionally) written so as to make it impossible for anyone to operate profitably a tavern, cabaret, hotel or nightclub without violating the law." These laws oblige the operators of such establishments where gambling or prostitution takes place to pay off the crime network, which in turn pays off officials not to enforce the laws. Here the intervention that is exploited for illegal gain by both sides is the law itself. Mutual dependencies between nominally hostile parties may develop around opportunities for exploitation of an intervention (in this case, the threat of overly restrictive laws) that completely subverts the goals of the intervention held by the public.

This pattern is not restricted to situations in which control is directed at only a single party in the relationship. Strategic arms agreements, which aim at control of both sides in a hostile relationship, can be exploited by both parties in a manner that increases rather than decreases the threat of war. As Caplow (1975, p. 109) asserts: "An agreement to limit armaments requires the participants to exchange verified inventories of their existing arsenals, and this augmented flow of information facilitates the strategical planning of each party." Exploitation in this case is similar to a temporary truce that affords both sides the opportunity to assess its relative resources. Imbalances develop once more as a result of one side's exploiting the information better than the other in the effort to gain strategic superiority *within* the limits of the agreement, thereby increasing the threat of aggression. "The terms of modern disarmament treaties provide no defense against this escalating mechanism," writes Caplow (1975, p. 109), "and it is not surprising that escalation begins even before the treaty is ratified and continues unabated until the agreement breaks down and a full-scale arms race is resumed."

Clearly, interventions that promise to conquer the enemy, control deviance, or prevent military conflict are subject to exploitation by the social objects of these actions in ways that turn intended consequences on their head.

EXPLOITATION BY NONHOSTILE TARGET POPULATIONS

The social target of an intervention need not be hostile for exploitation to occur, of course. The fate of the government's efforts of the 1960s to reduce the welfare rolls by giving people the opportunity to become self-sufficient without being penalized by taxation on higher earnings (by means of an "earnings disregard") is instructive:

> Sponsors of the disregard simply overestimated the potential of the welfare population. The emphasis on self-support combined with the earnings disregard did not reduce either the numbers or

the costs of AFDC [Aid for Dependent Children], but had the reverse effect. To disregard a portion of earned income means to accept the principle of aid to the working poor. The number of eligible clients increased as small amounts of client earnings were ignored in computing benefits. At the same time, federal pressure pushed states' needs standards closer to actual minimum living costs. Reporting small earnings did not jeopardize welfare benefits. In short, the disregard brought some of the working poor onto the assistance rolls for the first time, and kept on the rolls some clients who might otherwise have been forced off because of self-help efforts. (Steiner, 1974, p. 62)

A similar pattern can be detected once again in cases in which the poor are attracted to the cities by welfare benefits or employment opportunities that were designed to alleviate the conditions of the inner city but which, as a consequence of this attraction, only aggravate them. Thus, as the *Wall Street Journal* reported in 1968 (cited by Banfield, 1974, p. 242):

A massive industry effort to help avert future riots in Detroit appears to be backfiring as hundreds—possibly thousands—of unemployed persons from out of state come to the city seeking work.

The result: Some out-of-staters have failed to get a job, swelling the unemployment that many believe contributed to last July's riot.

Others have snapped up jobs that might have gone to the city's own so-called hard-core unemployed.

Moreover, it appears that those who do benefit from better jobs as a result of government or private intervention use the opportunity to move out of the ghettos, thereby draining the inner-city shopping centers of customers and creating even more unemployment and urban blight.

A computer simulation by Forrester (1969) of four urban improvement programs—an underemployed job program, a training program, financial aid to local government, and low-cost housing construction—found that all four are likely to be detrimental to urban conditions in the long run because of the attraction of the underemployed to the area, which sets a number of other forces into motion. This is especially the case with low-cost housing construction, according to the assumptions of the model:

> The housing available for the underemployed begins to rise immediately. Because of the increased housing, more underemployed are attracted to the city and the underemployed population rises for the first 10 years. But the low-cost-housing program exerts continuous pressure on the available unfilled land, making the area less favorable for other types of construction. As a consequence worker housing, premium housing, new enterprise, and mature business all gradually decline. As the business units decline in number, the available jobs decrease, thereby bringing economic pressure on all categories of the population and causing them to decrease. . . . The housing program, aimed at ameliorating conditions for the underemployed, has increased unemployment and has reduced upward economic mobility both in absolute numbers and as a percentage of population. (pp. 68–69)[1]

Taking advantage of such opportunities as job programs or housing is not illegitimate, of course. The opportunity is inherent in the design or implementation of the intervention. Nor is it always the case that the "exploiters" are the poor or otherwise disadvantaged. The diversion of resources and superior students to "magnet schools" is an example of middle-class exploitation that worsens the condition that an intervention was designed to alleviate, with the poor and minority groups being the losers. Conceived as a means of encouraging voluntary desegregation and upgrading the education of minority students, these schools were planned to be distinctly different in order to attract students from a wide area. But what has occurred, at least in some cases, is that the schools drew resources away from nonmagnet schools and attracted the children of more knowledgeable parents, that is, educated whites. Consequently, the magnet schools simultaneously weakened the nonmagnet schools and increased

---

[1] It should be borne in mind that these are hypothetical processes based on the simulator's assumptions and limited data. For a critique of Forrester's model, see Hester (1969). Among other things, Hester points out that urban transportation increases the availability of land to a city and that migration is influenced by many factors other than the attractiveness of a specific area to which one migrates.

segregation within the districts. (See Warren, 1978, for a study of several districts.)

To be sure, there are also instances of *illicit* exploitation of resources by clients that make a mockery of the goals of intervention, such as the Chicago welfare client who enriched herself by receiving several welfare checks under assumed names. But such instances are undoubtedly much rarer than the effects of *licit* exploitation. They are also more predictable and therefore easier to control by monitoring.

Further, there is what might be called *semilicit* exploitation in which the gain is neither expressly prohibited nor approved. The dependency needs that are triggered by relationships with a psychotherapist may obstruct the process of developing personal sufficiency, for example. Illich (1976, p. 24) has generalized such "secondary gains" of psychotherapy to the entire field of health care:

> The so-called health professions have an even deeper, culturally health-denying effect insofar as they destroy the potential of people to deal with their human weakness, vulnerability, and uniqueness in a personal and autonomous way.

Such increased dependency or vulnerability may be frowned upon, but it is not subject to punishment or even to stern reprimand, and therefore one is often not even aware of its occurrence. It is a semilicit form of exploitation that may well cancel out the benefits of treatment.

EXPLOITATION BY THE AGENTS OF INTERVENTION

The distinction between illicit, semilicit, and licit exploitation of an intervention in a manner that causes reverse effects applies with equal cogency to *agents* of intervention.

Illicit Exploitation by Agents

The classical type of *illicit* exploitation, of course, is corruption, a topic that was touched on earlier when we discussed the "antagonistic cooperation" between crime network figures and government officials. The problem is an ancient one. A clear case is supplied by the practices of the imperial secret service under the Roman Emperors Diocletian and Constantine, as related by Previté-Orton (1952, p. 16):

> These multitudinous and ubiquitous official spies superintended the imperial postal service, conveyed official commands, and reported real or imaginary delinquencies of all and sundry. They were worse than the abuses they were supposed to prevent; their corruption was notorious, and they added to the ills and oppression of the Empire.

Documentation by a number of investigatory bodies of police corruption in our own time (Neier, 1976, pp. 72–85) demonstrates that Constantine and Diocletian were not the last heads of government to suffer such reversals. A carefully executed study for the President's Commission on Law Enforcement concluded as follows with regard to Boston, Chicago, and Washington, D.C.:

> Counting all felonies and misdemeanors, except assaults on citizens, roughly 1 in 5 officers were observed in criminal violation of the law. . . . Opportunities arise principally in relationship with businesses and businessmen, policing traffic violators and deviants, and controlling evidence from crime. Obtaining money or merchandise illegally is the principal officer violation. (Riess, 1971)

It would appear, then, that the nation's crime rate is substantially increased by the actions of those charged with the responsibility for reducing it. Moreover, one surmises that the visibility of lawbreaking police officers does little to instill a respect for law and order in the bosoms of potential miscreants.

Illicit exploitation in the form of corruption is not limited to the police, of course. Agents of government programs are frequently placed in a position to receive gratuities for nonenforcement of regulations or for other actions that benefit private interests, and this too may have substantial reverse effects. One example will suffice. In the FHA housing scandals of the 1960s, a large number of housing appraisers and other officials were named in grand jury indictments for taking payoffs. Overappraisals of run-down buildings, together with FHA's mortgage interest subsidy, made it possible for speculators to buy cheap and sell dear (at a profit, say, of 1000%). A little cosmetic work was all that was necessary to induce the poor to buy houses that subsequently had to be abandoned by the hundreds of thousands (about one house in every ten was defaulted in Detroit alone). In addition to appraisers,

> supervisors got paid to allow the graft to continue and to ignore complaints from bilked buyers. In the departments that dealt with paper—credit reports, job verifications and the like—the payoffs were from the mortgage companies, to ignore obvious inconsistencies and blatant fraud. . . . The department of property management had almost endless opportunities for graft. . . . In Romney City, the corruption went on up the line, through the department heads and through the deputy directors to the director himself. (Boyer, 1973, p. 83)

The consequences were increased urban blight, loss of credit by defaulters, a serious drain on FHA insurance funds, increased alienation of blacks, and a waste of $80 billion of taxpayers' money.

On a more distant stage, the sapping of resources, public confidence, and private initiative in South Vietnam as a result of widespread corruption induced by the American transfusion of goods and money into an underdeveloped country is another painful example of the regressive effects of corruption on national goals.

Licit Exploitation by Agents

As with the targets of intervention discussed earlier, exploitation by agents of intervention may also be quite *licit*, though the consequences may be nonetheless harmful. This pattern seems to be associated with statuses in society that are highly prestigious and therefore relatively immune to charges of detrimental effects. The health care profession is a prime example. Owing to their prestige, physicians can command an enormous amount of control over their own work, and can even set the level of demand for their services. As Starr (1978, pp. 177–178) observes:

> One of the many anomalies of medical economics is that "demand" normally set by consumers, is in medicine largely determined by the producer, the physician, who decides whether hospitalization, tests, surgery, referrals, and further visits are needed. . . . Rather than being ruled by market forces, American physicians are able to control them.

One of the major consequences is that the more specialists there are available in an area, the more frequently will physicians refer their patients to them. This means that when more physicians are trained, the per capita imbalance between cities and other areas is *increased* rather than reduced. For doctors can continue to concentrate in areas that are already saturated without fostering competition.

A more serious implication of the prestige of therapeutic medicine is the damage done to public health by lack of attention to preventive health care. Not only does therapeutic medicine on the extensive, modern scale undermine a sense of control over one's physical well-being, as suggested by Illich (1976), but its priority over preventive care is a major source of serious illness and its related costs:

> The cost of not following preventive measures can be staggering. For example, the Government spends $1 billion a year to treat the victims of a single occupational disease, black lung, which afflicts coal miners. The disease could have been prevented 30 years ago. The health consequences, all preventable, of cigarette smoking now cost more than $20 billion a year. Circulatory illnesses, about half of which can be prevented by controlling personal risk factors, drain the economy by $30 billion a year. (*The New York Times*, May 30, 1978)

And yet, less than 3% of the nation's expenditures for health is devoted to prevention and less than 1% to health education. The private and public insurance programs have exacerbated the situation by disbursing enormous sums for treatment but virtually nothing for preventive medicine. The high cost of therapeutic medical technology has further abetted the problem. As Dr. John Knowles, the President of the Rockefeller Foundation, points out (*The New York Times*, May 30, 1978), the cost of developing an artificial heart runs twice as much each year as the cost of the most expensive program for preventing heart disease.

While medicine is perhaps the clearest example of the harmful effects of therapeutic professionalism, much the same point can be made with respect to other professions. Many professionals are able to manipulate demand to some extent, to persuade the population of their dependent status by virtue of increasingly complex technical knowledge, to deflect attention from the prevention of problems that require professional assistance once they occur, and to divert funds from alternative, nonprofessional avenues for problem-solving. In effect, the service professions have a stake in the obsolescence of prudent self-care and of communal mechanisms for preventing problems and for coping with them when they do arise. Or, as W. S. Gilbert (1978, p. 633), that lyrical student of institutionalized hypocrisy, once put it:

> The worthy pastor heaved a sigh, and dropped a silent tear—
> And said, "You mustn't judge yourself too heavily, my dear—
> It's wrong to murder babies, little corals for to fleece;
> But sins like these one expiates at half-a-crown apiece.

Licit exploitation seems in general to result from a gradual expansion of prerogatives in response to emergent opportunities, including newly defined human "needs." This process, to which I have referred elsewhere as *role inflation* (Sieber, 1974, p. 572), can be a powerful mechanism of organizational and societal change. One ancient observer who appreciated its ubiquity was Polybius (1966, pp. 214–215). He attributed the rise and fall of different forms of the state, and hence the very course of history, to successive exploitations of the privileges of power. Although some lawlessness and "unscrupulous acquisition of wealth" abetted this cyclical process, by and large the modes of exploitation were legitimate, especially in their early form. It was their degeneration into "arrogance," "insatiable excesses," "reckless conduct," or a "mad desire for glory" that caused the successive leaders to squander their privileges in a manner detrimental to the state, hence, ultimately, with self-defeating consequences. In our own times, the legitimate inflation of the ruler's prerogatives has been evident in the growth of the "imperial Presidency" (Schlesinger, 1973). Suffice it to say that the regressive effects of this trend were epitomized in Watergate.

Of course, technicians and professionals are not subject to public debate, recall, or overthrow in the manner of political leaders; hence, the historical cycle that Polybius attributes to the role inflation of rulers is not likely to occur with these modern statuses. Authority that is based on expertise is buttressed by guild assurances of integrity that are virtually immune to challenge in a highly specialized, service-dependent society. The potential for regressive consequences of this societal intervention is, therefore, bound to be with us for some time.

Asceticism and Wealth: A Case of Licit Exploitation of New Opportunities. It should be emphasized that the resources that lend themselves to licit exploitation need not be an intended or foreseen feature of the intervention, but may emerge in the course of time in the form of perquisites, dividends, notoriety, contributions, and the like. Such resources may even accrue to interventions whose normative codes officially reject them, as in the case of certain ascetic communities. Unless the temptation to exploit these resources is firmly repudiated by such groups, a key value of the agents may be converted into its opposite. In short, the intervention may suffer that regressive effect that Southern (1973, p. 261), in obvious emulation of Weber, calls the "penalty of Puritanism." The penalty was nowhere more evident than in the case of the Cistercians:

> The Cistercian ideal demands complete self-abnegation, poverty, simplicity, retirement, purity, and refinement of the spiritual life. But the historic role of the Order and its reputation among

> uncommitted contemporary observers suggest aggression, arrogance, military (or at least militant) discipline, outstanding managerial qualities, and cupidity. . . . Forbidden to spend on embellishments for their churches and common life, they were often, at least in the twelfth century, faced with the problem of an unexpendable surplus. Almost of necessity they were driven to spend the surplus which they could not devote to present needs and adornments on the improvement and increase of their estates. They did this not from policy, but from the pressure of opportunity. . . . These puritans of the monastic life incurred the penalty of puritanism; they became rich because they renounced the glory of riches, and powerful because they invested wisely.

I noted earlier that Merton (1936, p. 903) cited this historical process as demonstration of the principle that absolute value commitment may cause the agent to overlook the further consequences of his actions, consequences which may negate the original value. I took exception to this explanation on the grounds that it ignored the objective strategy and context of action, and failed to account for the fact that groups with absolute value commitments sometimes do achieve their ends. We may now explore this question with more precision in terms of the agents' exploitation of emergent resources that come to exceed the rewards of pursuing an original goal. First we will look briefly at monastic asceticism, and then we will turn to the role of Protestantism in the spread of mammonism.

In the Cistercians' case, the surplus that was generated was made possible by particular benefactors: landlords with vast tracts of uncultivated land on the frontier of European settlement. The reason that the Cistercians moved into these areas was that other Orders had already filled the religious gap in the settled countryside and towns. Thus, there was a certain amount of pressure to accept the new opportunity that was vouchsafed them. In return for the right to develop this rich territory, the Cistercians offered to give religious comforts to the remote, unsophisticated landlords, to organize their landholdings, and even to provide military defense. In short, an economic and political bargain was struck that redounded to the benefit of lord and monk alike. The ethic of asceticism may have contributed a special zeal to the labors of the monks, but it cannot therefore be accorded the central role in the production of a surplus. As Southern (1973, p. 261) points out:

> The Cistercian Order would never have grown to a great place in medieval society if it had depended on the efforts of small groups of dissidents like those who in the early days had gone out from Molesme to found the abbey of Citeaux or from St. Mary's at York to found the abbey of Fountains. These were the pioneers, but great success depended on great benefactors with the right kind of property. . . . The Cistercians needed much land, but they did not need it where others were already established. They needed it on the edge of the wild, and they found it wherever the frontiers of cultivation were being pushed back.

Moreover, it is unlikely that the ascetic ideal was genuinely embraced by all who flocked to such orders. The demotion of this ideal to the status of lip service was a consequence of the movement's expansion. Thus, as the movement grew in scope, the attractive rewards of exploitation were even more likely to undermine the ascetic ideal of the founders. As Previté-Orton (1952, p. 506) has pointed out:

> The extraordinary growth of monasticism new and old in the century of Church reform undoubtedly brought too many into the cloister, whether as converts or as oblates, who had no true or lasting vocation for the ascetic life; and the enormous landed wealth lavished on them by the laity, either in devotion or in fear of Judgment Day, proved a dangerous ally of laxity and degeneration.

The regressive outcome of monastic asceticism, then, demonstrates not so much that a " 'realization' of values may lead to their renunciation," as Merton (1936, p. 903) puts it, as that a weak value which is confronted with strong economic or political rewards for pursuing an alternative value is subdued and eventually eclipsed. This is especially likely if the outcome poses an embarrassing or inconvenient *contradiction* of the original value and if the actor is free to renounce that value. Monasticism was not able to turn its back completely on its official inspiration, despite its wealth, because of the constraints of Catholic doctrine and its sanctions. But businessmen who accumulated small or great fortunes in the centuries following the Reformation felt no such constraints, and so Protestant asceticism gave way to unvarnished mammonism. The dynamics of this transformation were similar to that of monastic asceticism, however: New opportunities for capitalization and production were supported by a set of religious values that were eventually contradicted by the successful outcomes of economic action.

Just as Catholicism lent itself to exploitation by the church hierarchy, Protestantism lent itself to exploitation by the individual—or more precisely, by the community of the elect. As source of group cohesion in business dealings (and especially in the acquisition of credit), as legitimizer of private property, material success, and unrelenting competition, as engine of self-righteousness in mastery of the world, Protestantism was a powerful spur to capitalism. Calvin's and Luther's insistence on placing service to one's neighbor before service to oneself notwithstanding, the abundant economic opportunities that had opened up in this period of history (and, as we know, the spirit of acquisitiveness long preceded the spirit of Protestantism) were now susceptible to conversion from satanic temptations into godly injunctions. Christopher Hill (1966), following much the same lines as Tawney, has offered one of the most balanced interpretations of the role of Protestantism in the rise of capitalism to be found in that large and controversial literature. Writing of the businessmen of sixteenth- and seventeenth-century Geneva, Amsterdam, or London, Hill observes:

> Such men felt quite genuinely and strongly that their economic practices, though they might conflict with the traditional law of the old church, were not offensive to God. On the contrary: they glorified God. . . . The preachers attempted to spiritualize what men were doing anyway, by telling them to do it for the right reasons. One may suspect that their congregations paid more attention to the general permission than to the careful qualifications with which it was hedged around. "They are very hot for the Gospel," said Thomas Adams of such laymen; "they love the Gospel: who but they? Not because they believe it, but

> because they feel it: the wealth, peace, liberty that ariseth by it."
> . . . It was, if we like, a rationalization; but it flowed naturally
> from protestant theology, whose main significance, for our pres-
> ent purposes, is that in any given society it enabled religion to be
> moulded by those who dominated in that society.

In sum, the legitimative potential of the intervention (Protestantism) in combination with a climate of nascent capitalism,
contributed to the brazen pursuit of wealth.

This interpretation, of course, does not bear on the larger
Weberian thesis that a structure of sentiments that he called
"inner worldly asceticism" is a spur to conscientious, methodi-
cal conduct. (See Nelson, 1973, for a statement that affirms this
central implication of Weber's work.) It does bear on Weber's
tendency to underplay the exploitative potential of Protestantism and of monastic asceticism under particular historical
conditions. It does not mean that sixteenth- and seventeenth-
century businessmen were merely rationalizing their mun-
dane acquisitive (or in the case of scientists, inquisitive) behavior. One need not be a patent hypocrite to find self-
justification in terms of an emergent value system. Indeed,
one may embrace that value system with all one's heart, but its
primary utility in respect to one's vocation, whether it be
business, science, or professionalism, may still be legitimative.
In this sense, Protestantism was rife with exploitative potential
in the context of early capitalism. Consequently, the exploitation of economic opportunity for the achievement of self-
serving ends was viewed as legitimate, and not only in spite of
the doctrine of the church, but with its aid and comfort.

Semilicit Exploitation by Agents

Finally, we come to that peculiar type of exploitation by
agents that lies in the gray area between licit and illicit practices
and which I have called semilicit exploitation. Here we find
practices that are not formally penalized by society, because
they lie within the discretionary authority of certain statuses,
but that also are not wholly condoned, because they violate

certain important values. Their toleration is founded on the rationale that no alternatives are readily available. Because they are judged to be "necessary evils," the true extent of their possible harm is minimized or simply put out of mind. It is not possible, of course, to draw a sharp line between licit and semilicit forms of exploitation. The former may blend imperceptibly into the latter and eventually be condemned as wholly illicit. Indeed, this seems to have been the case in Polybius's theory of the circulation of elites. Some forms of exploitation, however, appear to stabilize at the semilicit phase thanks to basic constraints on tendencies toward wholly illicit behavior.

Questionable forms of status exploitation arise most obviously in cases of unequal power relationships: corporal punishment of school children for minor infractions; undercover police work, including entrapment; abuse of prisoners by guards in settings that are ostensibly rehabilitative; or domination of boards of trustees by executive officers and of grand juries by prosecutors. The interventions that entail these behaviors may lend themselves to reverse effects precisely because of the opportunities for semilicit status exploitation that they afford.

The case of trustees is illustrated by Kerr's (1964) research on school boards: "Under certain conditions the chief contribution of school boards to the continuance of our educational system is their legitimation of the schools' policies, rather than their representation of the community." This reverse effect, which Kerr seems to view as "functional" for school systems, is largely due to the superintendent's ability to use his professional position to control the attention and manipulate the decisions of trustees. Similarly, prosecutors have converted grand juries into weapons of the government. As Senator Tunney (1976) has observed:

> The grand jury was included in the fifth amendment to serve as the citizen's shield against overzealous or politically motivated prosecutions, and as the people's sword against corruption in high places. However, the grand jury has become a rubber stamp for prosecutors and all too often has infringed upon basic

> constitutional rights. . . . Grand jurors are even frequently un-
> aware that prosecutors are their servants, not their masters.

But perhaps the clearest instance of the expansion of status prerogatives with profoundly unsettling implications for the "open society" is the growing practice of undercover police work.

The new wave of undercover work, as Marx (forthcoming) notes, is status-enhancing for the police because it gives them some control over the need for their services, which can then be converted into more favorable arrest records: "Secretly gathering information and facilitating crime under controlled conditions offers a degree of control over the 'demand' for police services hardly possible with traditional re-active practices." Marx clearly reveals the extent to which "plainclothes patrol and related undercover activities, often of a pro-active nature, are coming to be regarded as important police tactics, carried out by cutting edge, carefully chosen elite units."

The proactive feature of undercover work apparently entails a great deal of criminogenic behavior, both intended and unintended, despite its reluctant social acceptance. The undercover seller or buyer of drugs, the *agent provocateur* who infiltrates militant groups, the solicitor of prostitutes and homosexual liaisons or the undercover prostitute herself, the sting operations wherein undercover police set up fencing establishments, the offer of bribes to government officials, the use of decoys to entice purse-snatchers and muggers—all such practices intentionally amplify the opportunity for crime on the grounds that persons who are inclined under normal conditions to commit such crimes will be arrested or deterred. Unfortunately, there is no evidence that such tactics actually reduce crime on an aggregate basis; indeed, there is the distinct possibility that they unintentionally increase it.

A large minority of persons who are stimulated to commit a crime and subsequently arrested are first-time offenders; this fact suggests that they would not normally commit the crime. In the Washington, D.C., fencing operation, for example, about one in three had no prior arrest record. (Career criminals are often able to identify the plainclothesmen in their area and therefore can either wait for more opportune occasions or move elsewhere.) Burglars who are induced to supply illicit goods may do serious harm to victims. As Marx observes, "Part of the increased homicide rate in recent years, particularly among minority youths, has been attributed to vastly augmented amounts of federal 'buy' money." Persons who would ordinarily only use drugs privately have been induced to sell drugs to others by the easy profits demonstrated by the undercover solicitor. Unorganized gamblers and drug dealers have been prompted to organize because they were led to believe that the Mafia had moved into their territory. Undercover agents from different agencies have engaged in gun battles, needlessly endangering not only themselves but innocent bystanders. Citizens who are mistakenly arrested sometimes resist arrest because of the personal appearance of the nonuniformed officer and face death or injury. In all these ways, the exploitation of the discretionary authority of the police to fight crime by "going underground" has been criminogenic or otherwise threatening to the safety of the community. This effect has been amplified, moreover, by the increase in the number of undercover impersonators. "According to one estimate," writes Marx (*The New York Times*, June 29, 1980), "perhaps a quarter of the complaints filed against New York City police officers involve impersonators." This indicates that the petard effect, discussed earlier, can ensue from the enemy's emulation of the aggressor's tactics of status exploitation, thus amplifying the original tendency toward regressive consequences.

The Target Population as Agents

Thus far I have regarded exploiters as either agents or targets of intervention. But these two types may occasionally coalesce. Such is the case with interventions that employ the so-called "power equalization" model of change in which the members of the target population become agents of the intervention through participation in decision making. This is a widely used tactic in organizational change programs.

Organizational theorists, and especially those in the human relations tradition, have frequently claimed that subordinates will tend to resist innovations that are forced upon them. Thus, various means of participatory management, or collective decision making, have been advocated and have become quite popular. But such mechanisms are often more symbolic than real efforts to equalize power. If the decision to innovate is made principally by management, then gestures toward democracy are not sufficient to prevent resistance. Indeed, the subordinates' authority to make decisions about implementation of a mandated project can be *exploited* to sabotage the project. This process seems to have occurred in the Teacher Corps, with the consequence that schools tended to be somewhat *less* innovative than they otherwise would have been. An evaluation of the Teacher Corps by Corwin (1973, p. 265) reports as follows:

> [Teachers'] participation had only a minor effect; and contrary to usual expectations and findings from other studies (Aiken and Hage, 1970), the small effect which does appear is negative ($r = -.26$). The power equalization model presumes that changes are produced from the consent of the parties involved. However, some innovations are forced into a system, which arouses the incumbents' suspicion or opposition. This was often the case in this program. When subordinates fail to agree on the objectives or strategies of these proposed changes, but are relatively professionalized, their participation in the decisions places them in a better position to sabotage the innovation. (Mulder, 1971)

A major resource of the innovation—the power to influence decision making—was apparently employed against other features of the innovation by *agents* who resented being treated as *targets* of reform.

Here it is worth noting that a conversion mechanism that I shall refer to later as a type of provocation (the use of control perceived as illegitimate) is combined with an opportunity to exploit the resources of an innovation (decision-making power) to the distinct detriment of the intervention's ultimate goal.

The interlocking of conversion mechanisms is by no means a rare occurrence, a point to be discussed more fully in the final section of this study.

SOURCES OF EXPLOITATION

It would obviously take us far afield to inquire into the many background features of our society that foster each form of exploitation mentioned here. A few summary observations can be made, however.

First, with regard to the legitimate exploitation of resources by clients (e.g., the expansion of welfare rolls, the migration of unemployed to the city to take advantage of training programs, housing, etc.), it seems evident that the scope and depth of needs is overlooked by policy makers. Thus, persons in need who are located outside of the target population rush to take advantage of new opportunities. If the target population comprises the inner-city poor, then the problem of the city may be aggravated by immigration. A major condition for this effect is the lack of alternatives to exploitation of urban assistance, such as employment opportunities (Harrington, 1977). If the intervention is one that is attractive to the middle class, as in the case of magnet schools, then the superior ability of the middle class to take advantage of the intervention will drain away resources from lower-class areas and exacerbate segregation. Behind these processes are felt needs that program designers have underestimated.

Much the same point could be made about semilicit and illicit exploitation by clients. And in some cases, as with the dependency needs that are gratified by psychotherapy or health care in general, the need is not even recognized as operative. This reminds us that *needs* are seldom biologically dictated. Indeed, in addition to the latent requirements of psychological well-being, social norms that establish levels of aspiration and reward and, hence, a sense of relative deprivation also operate in the formation of felt needs. Accordingly, a high level of affluence in society together with the egalitarian ideal of extending the benefits of affluence (including power) to disadvantaged groups stimulates *demand* of a high order. But since affluence also entails the entrenchment of privileged groups, the resources to meet these demands are strictly limited. Strong pressures to take advantage of what opportunities *do* exist as a result of welfare and similar interventions are therefore generated. Illicit as well as licit exploitation is the inevitable consequence, perhaps especially when agents of the intervention become "policemen" to see that the limited resources are not stolen.

With respect to professional agents or other experts, a paramount enabling condition for exploitation is a high degree of *trust in exogenous expertise*. Such faith becomes vital in a technological society which has a highly refined division of labor and also, therefore, a growing emphasis on functional interdependence as a basis of social order. The halting efforts underway to teach laymen certain aspects of law, medicine, consumer economics, auto mechanics, TV repair, and so on, do not contradict the argument but support it. The need for more endogenous expertise is widely recognized by educators and reformers, but efforts to satisfy the need are virtually impotent. Public apathy, inadequate funding, resistance of professionals and union leaders, and the prohibitive range of skills needed for an individual to become even partially self-sufficient in urban society are some of the reasons.

Another enabling condition of exploitation by agents is that resources that are worth exploiting must be *available*. In the broadest sense, resources include any generalized media of exchange, that is, any media that can be converted into value in a variety of contexts. With the great increase in affluence in modern society, resources belonging to others that can be diverted to one's personal use have increased not only in volume but in accessibility. The channeling of public resources through bureaucratic functionaries and government contractors and the increased dependence on special agents for the handling of assets (banks, investment plans, insurance programs, retirement funds, etc.) mean that liquid assets have become dispersed among second and third parties and therefore increasingly removed from their "owners."

Such opportunities are not restricted to financial or other material gain, however, but extend as well to the enhancement of professional autonomy and security and to the consolidation of political or bureaucratic power. The managerial revolution in the corporate domain; the delegation of power to politicians who are increasingly removed from their constituents (as a consequence of time demands, the fragmentation of interests within constituencies, the complexity of social problems, and so forth); the encapsulation of rights, proscriptions, and sanctions in a complicated body of law that defies comprehension or control by laymen; the increasing complexity of federal and state regulatory and service functions; the rise of police and military establishments in response to mounting threats to domestic and international order; and the growth of professionalism—all of these forces have removed large segments of power and authority from lay society and placed them in the hands of an army of delegates. Thus, power and influence have joined capital assets as free-floating resources available for exploitation.

But even a combination of free-floating resources and opportunities to manipulate trust does not automatically produce *illegal* exploitation by agents. Formal sanctions aside, it is possible that internalized moral norms will prevent a person from engaging in grossly deviant behavior. A failure of internalized norms to prevent deviance can be attributed to one of two sources: (1) inadequate, inappropriate, or ambivalent socialization while growing up (Toby, 1974, pp. 86–90), or (2) forces encountered in later life that neutralize satisfactory socialization. With regard to high-status criminality, for example, corruption, it seems reasonable to assume that the second source of normative breakdown is more influential. This would account for the elaborate rationalizations for their conduct of many white-collar criminals. If moral norms had not been internalized, such rationalizations would be unnecessary.

In a study of embezzlement, Cressey (1953, pp. 136–137) has offered a highly interesting theory in this connection:

> The rationalizations which are used by trust violators are necessary and essential to criminal violation of trust. They are not merely *ex post facto* justifications for conduct which already has been enacted, but are pertinent and real "reasons" which the person has for acting. When the relationship between a personal nonshareable problem and the position of trust is perceived according to the bias induced by the presence of a rationalization which makes trust violation in some way justified, trust violation results.

Cressey's theory that rationalizations are formulated prior to the deviant act implies that certain values in the prevailing culture play a causative role instead of, or in addition to, a merely palliative role. The importance of maintaining one's family in a respectable style of living, for example, is a highly legitimate cultural imperative. Any problem that arises in maintaining this value through honest effort sets the stage for self-serving deviance. It then becomes the role of *widely shared* rationalizations to trigger the decisive step toward illegality. Thus, the widely shared rationalization that "everybody does it and you've got to stay competitive (or keep up)" is an integral part of the culture of American business, politics, and the conduct of foreign affairs. As current history strongly suggests, this particular rationalization played a role in such scandals as corporate bribes to foreign governments, ITT, CIA assassination plots, and Watergate-related dirty tricks. Nor can such a prefabricated type of rationalization be regarded as purely palliative, for it is fully compatible with the cultural emphases on shrewdness, toughmindedness, and utilitarianism.

In addition to the maintenance of a style of living suitable to one's position, nonshareable problems also include financial entanglements of a discreditable nature (gambling, nonmarital sex, drugs, etc.). Problems of this kind are precluded from being shared with colleagues precisely because of the image of integrity and aloofness from vulgar materialism or sensuality that positions of high trust require. In effect, the stereotyped demands placed on certain statuses as a means of legitimizing their trustworthiness can be self-defeating, for such demands cut off the occupants of these statuses from opportunities for sympathy, support, and remediation through legitimate channels. Apparently, the moral consensus that is sometimes claimed to neutralize the Hobbesian war of all against all is capable of neutralizing itself in particular instances (in fact, it might be argued that much of the Hobbesian war takes place clandestinely).

With respect to "antagonistic cooperation" between officials and law breakers, insofar as it entails corruption, it involves the violation of a position of trust and hence can partly be explained in the terms set forth above. But there is also the factor of social pressure from peers, as occurs in police departments where corruption is commonplace and where a single honest policeman can pose a threat to many colleagues. In addition, there is the more interesting factor of *mutual system support,* inasmuch as the performance of the larger system of which the corrupt cop, politician, or legal professional is a part is *enhanced* by nonenforcement of certain laws.

A criminal justice system that spent its time tracking down and punishing all gamblers, drug-users, and sexual deviants would probably have very little time for anything else. The social demand for these services is strong and persistent; therefore, it will be met to a large extent regardless of crackdowns by the police (in the case of heroin, as we have seen, not only will it continue to be met, but crackdowns will occasion more crime). In effect, going easy on so-called victimless crimes is functional for the *other* official pursuits of law and order. New York State's tough drug law of 1973 did not increase arrests in New York City, for example, because:

> It was not the policy of the Police Department to [make mass arrests for drug violations]. The Department had been disap-

pointed with past efforts at mass arrests because they were very expensive and did not appear to hamper the narcotics trade. [Also] the Department believed that the courts would be unable to manage the workload that a mass arrest policy would produce. (On this point, the data collected by the [evaluation] Project support the Department's view.) (National Institute of Law Enforcement and Criminal Justice, 1977, p. 14)

Recognition of the futility and the unaffordable demand on resources for thoroughgoing enforcement of victimless crime laws is probably one of the main reasons for corruption in connection with such crimes. Such recognition greatly relieves the pang of official conscience.

The only major form of exploitation with reverse consequences whose source remains to be discussed is the petard effect, whereby the enemy turns the resources of his antagonist against him. The proximate source is not difficult to comprehend, of course, and can be simply called self-defense. What is more problematic is the source of the original act of *provocation*. Since provocations have reverse effects in addition to the invitation to being hoist with one's own petard, it will be analyzed separately in a later chapter, which will include an examination of its sources.

CONCLUDING REMARKS

In this chapter I have suggested that exploitation of the resources, latent or manifest, of an intervention is a generic pattern of human behavior that accounts for a range of reverse consequences. Nor have I assumed that exploitation is always illegitimate, since licit and semilicit forms can also be found. These latter types might account for the perpetuation of certain regressive practices, a topic that I will deal with later. But more important, they suggest that tendencies to take excessive advantage of an intervention's resources can be treated as a very broad phenomenon, embracing both deviant and conformist behavior.

While certain forms of exploitative behavior might be seen

as functional for the larger system (e.g., nonenforcement of victimless crime laws, which is abetted by corruption), the lion's share seems to be predominantly negative because of the reverse effects that they produce. And while it is sometimes not difficult to detect an interference with system requirements (e.g., the undermining of new enterprise by the attraction of low-cost urban housing programs), in most instances it is not clear what system requirement has been impaired, especially when one can point to several interconnected causes of the effect. For these reasons it seems premature to try to fit the broad pattern of exploitation into a strictly functionalist framework, as I suggested earlier. This does not mean that the ironical effects of interventions that invite exploitation are any the less a matter of prime theoretical concern, of course. If the discussion in this chapter has served to advance this point, then it will have served a useful purpose.

CHAPTER 5

Goal Displacement

Superficially similar to agents' exploitation of an intervention is the well known pattern of goal displacement, whereby an instrumental value becomes a terminal value. Thus, it might be argued that a bureaucratic incumbent derives gratification from adherence to regulations and the exercise of delegated powers and competencies quite apart from goal achievement, suggesting a certain amount of self-serving exploitation of the role. Unlike exploitation, however, the presumed benefits of devoting oneself to the most efficient means are *enjoined*, while exploitation, as that term was used in the preceding chapter, denotes behavior that is largely optional and self-serving. In short, the bureaucrat's compulsive attention to means is a positive requirement.

We find, therefore, that goal displacement may occur even when the agents are committed to an ideology of non-conventional service and satisfaction of a broad range of client needs. The fate of certain Community Action Centers, which were conceived as a key weapon in the War on Poverty of the 1960s, is illustrative. As Hasenfeld (1971) pointed out in his study of four centers: "Our findings indicate that the staff had strong commitment to serve the poor, and a desire to break away from what they termed 'bureaucratized' patterns of services.'' Nevertheless, the following basic characteristics of encounters with clients were found:

> Transactions between staff and clients almost invariably followed a highly routinized pattern, in which the nature of the encounter was rigidly controlled by the demands of the intake forms that staff had to fill out. . . . The encounter itself was, typically, a rather fleeting event. Workers were seldom able to make serious attempts to explore the client's situation beyond the minimum requirements of the intake forms. . . . The decision process of defining the client's problem or "need" was simplified. Workers relied mainly on the client's definition of the situation and tended to classify his problems within a very narrow range of categories: employment and health. Thus the staff did not consider a vast amount of individual variations and idiosyncrasies. Yet the stream of clients who came to the CAC presented a wide gamut of human problems and needs. . . . Decisions about client referrals were made essentially on the basis of age, sex, income, and presenting problems. Utilizing such a small amount of information about the client led to significant errors in the referral decisions. Clients were occasionally referred to agencies for which they were not eligible on the basis of other attributes, or to agencies that could not handle their underlying problems. Concomitantly, clients were often excluded from the services of various other agencies.

Merton (1957, p. 200) has provided an incisive description of goal displacement as it occurs at the level of the individual bureaucrat:

> The process may be briefly recapitulated. (1) An effective bureaucracy demands reliability of responses and strict devotion to regulations. (2) Such devotion to the rules leads to their transformation into absolutes; they are no longer conceived as relative to a set of purposes. (3) This interferes with ready adaptation under special conditions not clearly envisaged by those who drew up the general rules. (4) Thus, the very elements which conduce toward efficiency in general produce inefficiency in specific instances.

This characterization suggests that goal displacement is similar to the *functional shift* discussed earlier, since a dedication to means is said to be a beneficial aspect of all organizational action. But functional shifts refer to unanticipated outcomes of action that take precedence over intended outcomes, while goal displacement refers to the intended benefits of efficiency taking precedence over ends. A closer resemblance may be found to what was earlier called a *functional imbalance* inasmuch as goals and means are not kept in proper alignment. But because goal displacement is a problem endemic to that ubiquitous realm of values that is concerned with rational efficiency and the reverence for technique in technological society, it deserves special attention as a source of reverse effects.

To the extent that an agency is unable to adjust to the personal needs of clients because of organizational imperatives, the agency may be viewed as at least potentially regressive, for clients might be handled in ways that are damaging to them. One clear way in which this occurs is through the undermining of personal development. As Vinter (1974, pp. 48–49) characterizes the typical assessment of the "good" client:

> The model patient or prisoner is one who conforms to the rules and routines; the model clinic client is one who keeps his appointments and learns to reveal himself and to communicate using the language of therapy. Such organizationally valued changes may not merely be irrelevant to community performance requirements, but in extreme form may result in a client's "trained incapacity" to function adequately outside the agency (e.g., "institutionalization" in the mental hospital (Wing, 1962)).

With respect to agencies for the blind, Scott (1967) observes as follows:

> Clients are encouraged to organize their lives around the agency. . . . Gradually a greater and greater portion of the client's contact with the larger community becomes mediated, and often determined by the agency, until the blind person is literally sequestered from the community. At this point, the agency completely negates its original objective, which is to help the blind persons to become independent. . . . By sequestering certain blind persons from the community, agencies for the blind are actually contributing to the very problem which they purport to be solving.

On a macro or historical scale, reverse consequences may also ensue when bureaucracies fail to alter procedures to meet new conditions or public needs. Outmoded regulations and procedures may then contribute to the problem that they were originally intended to alleviate. To take just one of numerous examples, owing to a "mass of archaic regulations on the granting of public transit and taxi franchises, the cities are in effect going out of their way to place obstacles in the paths of those who might offer the public better transportation" (Banfield, 1974, p. 9). More generally stated, the creation of a specialized agency to deal with particular problems in the most efficient manner can preclude its replacement by a superior mechanism at a later time by virtue of the monopolization of resources and legitimacy.

Finally, programs and doctrines that were initially developed to achieve some predetermined goal may generate commitments that divert attention from the goal, thereby opening up the possibility that the effects of such programs or doctrines might run counter to the goal. This is especially likely to occur, it seems, if the goal is inherently incompatible with an emphasis on norms of organizational efficiency and control. This *programmatic* form of goal displacement deserves special attention.

As Selznick (1949, p. 258) observed some years ago:

> Commitment to the tools of action is indispensable; it is of the nature of these tools to be dynamic and self-activating; yet the pursuit of the goals which initiate action demands continuous effort to control the instruments it has generated. This is a general source of tension in all action mediated by human, and especially organizational, tools.

Failure to "control the instruments" in the form of organizational strategies can have consequences that are decidedly counter to goals. A striking example is the practice of spraying a toxic herbicide (paraquat) on the relatively harmless marijuana plant. This practice poses a threat to public health inasmuch as traces of the substance turn up in cigarettes. Indeed, according to Dr. Howard Harris, director of the New

York Police Department's crime laboratory, "tests around the country show that as much as 20% of the marijuana consumed by Americans is tainted with paraquat" (*The New York Times*, April 22, 1978). The consequence of heavy consumption of paraquat is permanent lung damage. Since the preservation of public health was the purpose of the 1970 Controlled Substances Act that banned marijuana, this particular means of implementing the Act is counterproductive. In short, the program is faithfully pursued regardless of its inevitable effect on ultimate goals.

This example brings to mind a much more famous use of herbicides: the defoliation of extensive areas of South Vietnam in the 1960s. Since the ostensible purpose of the American presence in Vietnam was to preserve the life, liberty, and prosperity of the South Vietnamese people, the means that were employed—including bombing, internment, random massacre, and systematic destruction of crops—probably comprised the most spectacular instance of regressive goal displacement in the history of the modern world. As one historian (Fitzgerald, 1973, pp. 459–460) has pointed out:

> The U.S. armed forces in effect drove a steamroller over the densely populated area of the Iron Triangle, flattening the villages with five-hundred-pound bombs, bulldozing the miles of tunnels, and destroying the jungle cover with herbicides. This operation "generated" (in the impersonal military phrase) seven thousand refugees and rendered the area uninhabitable by anyone except the Front troops. . . . In the same year U.S. forces expended tons of herbicides, which ultimately stripped an area the size of Massachusetts of crops and vegetation. The American command claimed that the aim of the "resources control program" was to deny food to the Front troops. The crop destruction, however, affected the civilians almost exclusively. For while the troops, being mobile, could find other sources of supply, the civilians, particularly the women and children, could not.

Returning to our own domestic front, we find several striking instances of reverse effects that arise from situations in which means and goals are inherently incompatible. The emphasis of the criminal justice system on efficiency, for example, seems to contradict the ideals of due process and justice. As Blumberg (1967) has noted:

> The court organization itself . . . possesses a thrust, purpose, and direction of its own. It is grounded in pragmatic values, bureaucratic priorities, and administrative instruments. These exalt maximum production.

The inconsistency between this emphasis and due process is nowhere more obvious than in the practice of plea-bargaining, a bureaucratic expedient that has virtually replaced jury trial. For the practice of coercing a defendant to admit guilt is little more than an organizational "tool of action" in the service of efficiency. As Blumberg (1967) continues:

> A wide variety of coercive devices are employed against an accused client, couched in a depersonalized, instrumental, bureaucratic version of due process of law, and which are in reality a perfunctory obeisance to the ideology of due process. These include some very explicit pressures which are exerted in some measure by all court personnel, including judges, to plead guilty and avoid trial. In many instances the sanction of a potentially harsh sentence is utilized as the visible alternative to pleading guilty, in the case of recalcitrants.

The National Advisory Commission on Criminal Justice Standards and Goals condemned plea-bargaining in 1973 and strongly urged that it be abolished by 1978. If anything, however, it has increased in frequency.

In addition to the ritualism of functionaries and the enshrinement of counterproductive practices or programs, the contradiction between means and ends can be detected in efforts to bureaucratize roles that are based on extraorganizational criteria of performance and success. In such cases, the role may be jeopardized by organizational control, thereby rendering it less effective. This problem, which has been viewed by sociologists in terms of a conflict between professionals and bureaucracy, can be fruitfully recast as a special case of regressive goal displacement. On the basis of his research on locals and cosmopolitans in a university, Gouldner (1957–58, p. 466) has pointed out that despite Weber's suggestion that the expertise of an organization's personnel enhances performance, "there seems to be some tension between an organization's bureaucratic needs for expertise and its social-system needs for loyalty." Indeed, subsequent studies have clearly shown that professionally oriented members of bureaucracies are more likely to assert that organizational procedures interfere with their performance. Thus, in a study of social workers it was found that 50% of those with the highest professional orientation felt that "procedures interfere with helping clients," compared with only 21% of those with lowest professional orientation (Blau and Scott, 1962, p. 73). It was further shown that the professionally oriented workers were far more likely "to deviate from administrative procedures in the interest of professional service to clients." In another study, Corwin (1965) found that the more professionally oriented teachers in public education are more often involved in overt conflict with administrators.

The conflict between bureaucratic and professional standards of performance is enlarged when a type of expertise is introduced whose task is "to test and discard old beliefs" and whose ranking system "is based uniquely on achievement and confirmation by peers" (Bell, 1973, p. 380). Such has been the case with the bureaucratization of science. Bell (1973, p. 405) has summarized the issue:

> For science, bureaucratization imposes a number of severe risks. Within the organization of science, bureaucratization may impede the "recognition system" of work and persons which has been the heart of the community of science through the subordination of individual achievement to the overall goals of a laboratory, or by appropriating the work for the credit of the "bureau" itself. In the over-all organization of science, the creation of a centralized bureaucracy—and centralization is an invariable tendency in these instances—could mean the stifling of inquiry, the demand that scientific work be responsive to stipulated national or social needs and the priority of political goals over scientific work.
>
> Inevitably, thus, tensions will arise between the bureaucra-

tic tendencies of large-scale science and the charismatic dimen-
sion of science, which sees its activities as ends in themselves
that should not be subordinated to other goals.

It seems clear that subordination to other goals is increasingly
the fate of science as it responds to the warm embrace of either
corporate interest or government policy. And although Bell
(1973, p. 406) asserts, "It is likely that the move for the 'dises-
tablishment of science' will spread," one sees little evidence of
effective effort in that direction. Indeed, with the cutbacks in
university teaching positions and government grants for basic
research in certain fields, one has witnessed a flow of scientifi-
cally trained personnel into profit and nonprofit independent
research agencies that survive on government-inspired,
-funded, and -monitored projects or into the government itself. A dilution of the charismatic ethos of science is an inevitable consequence, with the additional implication that traditional scientific value is undermined rather than enhanced by
organizational imperatives.

This regressive effect may have already occurred in the
field of social research on federal programs. A study of con-
tract- and grant-supported evaluations (the former occurring
predominantly in independent agencies and the latter in the
universities) by Bernstein and Freeman (1975) found that
proposals for grants scored considerably higher in quality than
those for contracts. Since grant research is field-initiated,
while contract research is done in response to the government's Request for Proposals, it is clear that the latter is far
more subject to the government's regulatory authority. In
view of the differential quality of these two types of research, it
is not surprising that proposals tended to score higher when
the project directors chose to address themselves to an audience of professionals and colleagues rather than to that of
funding or program personnel. And it is especially noteworthy that the presence of a theoretical framework was strongly
related to the quality of design and procedures. On the whole,
then, one might conclude that the quality of evaluation research has declined over the past generation precisely

because of the rise of an industry that specializes in it, an industry that is highly bureaucratized and dependent upon the dictates of government agencies. Presumably, the satisfaction of organizational imperatives has overridden the objectives of science.

SOURCES OF GOAL DISPLACEMENT

In addition to the inherent emphases of organization on predictability and efficiency, which are buttressed by the promotion and tenure system, *esprit de corps*, and so forth (Merton, 1957, pp. 195–207), a major source of goal displacement is a scarcity of resources. There are two possible ways in which scarcity fosters goal displacement. The first is by abandonment of costly procedures that were designed to ensure the accomplishment of goals. Thus, plea-bargaining entails the elimination of juries and other court expenses that have been traditional safeguards of due process. In essence, less efficient but more effective means are replaced by more efficient but less effective means. As a consequence, the ultimate goal is seriously jeopardized.

The second way in which scarcity fosters goal displacement is by requiring that the organization demonstrate its indispensability to its supporters. A great flurry of activity in predetermined modes is an inevitable consequence, especially when the measurement of ultimate goal achievement is difficult or subject to dispute. Thus, the larger the number of clients, the more paperwork, the more bombing raids, the more arrests, the more herbicide dispensed, and so on, the greater the impression of indispensability. In some human service fields there is a constant drive to recruit clients so that an agency's program can boast a high level of participation. According to Scott (1967), it is the vigorous competition for clients among agencies for the blind that causes these agencies to induct clients into their service mode, resulting in the clients' dependency on the agencies:

> When an agency has the opportunity to provide services to a blind person who is suitable for its program, it is reluctant to let him go. The chances of finding a replacement for the client who leaves are not always good, and with a substantial number of clients on hand, the agency may find it difficult to justify its expenditures to the supporting public.

Vinter (1974, p. 48) suggests that this is most likely to occur when the goals of the agency are ambiguous and therefore not subject to easy assessment:

> Limitations in objective assessment of effectiveness have important consequences for the treatment organization. They induce emphases on intraorganizational behavior, pressures toward goal displacement, and a tendency toward self-justifying doctrine rather than rational planning.

Scarcity of resources and goal ambiguity probably have independent effects on goal displacement, but when combined the consequences are highly predictable.

Other structural sources of a tendency to goal displacement are a weak peer group and high visibility of job performance to superiors both of which conditions increase the member's vulnerability to control by dint of status-anxiety. Then, too, there is sheer "pride of craft," which may inhere in a superior knowledge of rules and regulations. In such cases, the bureaucrat is similar to Colonel Nicholson, the British officer of engineering in *The Bridge over the River Kwai*, who risked life and limb to defend the instrumentality that he had so proudly constructed for his captors.

Not all goal displacement is regressive. Only when dedication to the tools rather than to the ends of action generates rewards that conflict with ultimate goals is a reverse outcome likely to occur. Once it does, however, it is highly resistant to correction, for, unlike many forms of exploitation discussed earlier, goal displacement is virtually self-legitimizing.

This is especially true because of the modern emphasis on "technique," or the notion that there is one best way to achieve any designated objective and that all else, including the careful examination of ends, is subordinate to the discovery and realization of that particular way. According to Ellul (1964), all of our institutional endeavors have been technicized, and "when technique enters into every area of life, including the human, it ceases to be external to man and becomes his very substance. . . . Our civilization is first and foremost a civilization of means; in the reality of modern life, the means, it would seem, are more important than the ends. Any other assessment of the situation is mere idealism" (pp. 6, 19). Clearly, a cultural emphasis of this sort is highly favorable to goal displacement with regressive consequences. The ultimate tragedy is that the likelihood of such consequences remains less impressive than the noble ingenuity that produces them.

CHAPTER 6

Provocation

One of the most obvious sources of reverse consequences is the provocational nature of many interventions. While this pattern is most familiar with regard to actions intended to punish or deter behavior defined as hostile or deviant, it applies in a broader sense to the arousal, incitement, or stirring up of any attitude, desire, or passion, either individually or collectively, that leads to a reversal of intended outcomes. While there are probably as many types of provocation as there are latent affective drives, four types are especially common: the provocations of illegitimate control, implicit threat, truncated therapy, and enticement.

ILLEGITIMATE CONTROL

Few principles of human interaction are as firmly rooted in common experience as the idea that any threat or display of force that is viewed as illegitimate tends to engender counterforce, and in many instances to amplify the proscribed or threatened behavior. The prospect of counterforce is so universal as to have bred one of the world's most familiar moralisms—that he who lives by the sword shall die by the sword or, as Aeschylus (1973, p. 124) expressed it:

> You smote and were smitten
> You killed and were slain
> By the spear you killed
> By the spear you died
> Wretched in acting
> Wretched in suffering.

Indeed, the principle has even entered into our criminal justice code as grounds for mitigation of murder under the rubric "provocation" (Loewy, 1975, pp. 31–34).

The reverse effects of force perceived as illegitimate are most obvious in the instance of aggressive war. In fact, the formidability of one of the world's leading powers, the Soviet Union, owes a good deal to the provocations to which that country has been exposed for many generations. As Schuman (1962, p. 21) points out: "the major territorial aggrandizements of Russia in Europe (I speak now not of Asia) have been more often a result of unsuccessful military aggression against Russia by Western Powers than a result of successful military aggression by Russia against Western Powers." Schuman cites the Swedish, Lithuanian, Polish, and Turkish seizures of formerly Russian territories six hundred years ago, the Polish occupation of Moscow three hundred years ago, the Napoleonic invasion, the Allied invasion of 1918–1919, and the Nazi invasion, all of which attacks culminated in the expansion rather than the subjugation of Russia.

While the military commander is aware that his actions will very likely arouse counterforce, other managers of men's destinies have been curiously insensible of this rule, with the not infrequent result that the behavior that is attacked springs back with a renewed vitality that can shape history. Thus, early Christianity received its single greatest impetus from martyrdom. "The blood of martyrs is the seed of the Church," pronounced Tertullian in a phrase that has reverberated through the centuries. This has been affirmed by modern historians:

> Persecution, so far from driving the church underground, had the opposite effect. When one governor in Asia Minor in the second century began persecuting the Christians, the entire Christian population of the region paraded before his house as a manifesto of their faith and as a protest against the injustice. (Chadwick, 1967, p. 55)

Even Machiavelli, who has been upbraided for overreliance on force as a political technique, was aware of its counterproductive possibilities. Thus, he cautioned the prince who had gained power by treachery to inflict injuries quickly and then to moderate his cruelties as soon as possible in a bid for legitimacy:

> On seizing a state, the usurper should make haste to inflict what injuries he must, at a stroke, that he may not have to renew them daily, but be enabled by their discontinuance to reassure men's minds, and afterward win them over by benefits. Whosoever, either through timidity or from following bad counsels, adopts a contrary course, must keep the sword drawn, and can put no trust in his subjects, who suffering from continued and constantly renewed severities, will never yield him their confidence. (Machiavelli, 1954, p. 77)

But Machiavelli's advice would seem to have been infrequently taken, for history offers numerous examples of a curiously myopic attitude toward dissent reflected precisely in "continued and constantly renewed severities." Nor is it by any means the case that the lesson has been absorbed by contemporary authorities. As Attorney General Ramsey Clark in 1968 plaintively warned those who yearned to deal with the urban rioters of the 1960s with unrelenting force:

> There are few acts more likely to cause guerrilla warfare in our cities and division and hatred among our people than to encourage police to shoot looters or other persons caught committing property crimes. How many dead twelve-year-old boys will it take for us to learn this simple lesson? Far from being effective, shooting looters divides, angers, embitters, drives to violence. It creates the very problems its advocates claim to avoid. (cited in Harris, 1969)

Similarly, in objecting to the withdrawal of aid from students who participated in campus disturbances in the 1960s, it was necessary for the U.S. Commission on Violence (cited in Harris, 1969, p. 179) to point out:

> If aid is withdrawn from even a few students in a manner that the campus views as unjust, the result may be to radicalize a much larger number by convincing them that existing governmental institutions are as inhumane as the revolutionaries claim.

The problem of what might be called "misplaced deterrence" has been increasingly recognized by students of criminal justice and corrections. The inability of prison sentences to deter crime has been a main source of this recognition. As one expert on corrections (Schrag, 1974, p. 733) observes:

> Long sentences, with or without treatment, do not have a better record than short ones. Indeed, if type of offense, prior convictions, and related variables are held constant, the prospects for repeated offenses increase with the length of the sentence (Lamson & Crowther, 1968). And the greater the number of times an offender is incarcerated, the greater the risk he will be incarcerated again.

This appears to be the case especially with youthful offenders, as noted by Glasser (1978, pp. 153–154) on the basis of an authoritative study in Philadelphia of several thousand boys: "The more punitive the treatment (institutionalization, fine, or probation) a youngster receives, the more likely he is to commit more serious crimes with greater rapidity than those who are less constrained by the judicial and correctional systems." In general, it appears that deterrence by force is a futile method of dealing with crimes of passion and other unpremeditated crime and is counterproductive as well in dealing with youthful offenders, many career criminals, and offenders who are motivated by ideology or visions of status enhancement. Perhaps the main positive impact is on individuals who are highly sensitive to derogatory labeling by the criminal justice system, such as white collar or "avocational" criminals (Geis, 1974, pp. 277–279). This latter observation suggests that a side effect of imprisonment may be more effective as a deterrent than coercion itself, at least with certain types of lawbreakers.

It is unnecessary to cite the many historical cases in which social control efforts that were perceived as illegitimate have led to revolt, revolution, or successful protest. And, of course, revolt is not confined to the "masses" but may characterize the "classes" as well, as exemplified by that famous harbinger of revolution called the Boston Tea Party. A more recent example that might also have far-reaching consequences for American society is California's Proposition 13. According to Kuttner (1980), the groundwork for this tax revolt, which entailed a reduction of property taxes by more than half, was laid in the late 1960s when property assessments were suddenly brought up-to-date after several years of scandal and laxity. Thus, many homeowners were confronted with tax bills that were three times higher than before. In effect, a measure that was intended to increase taxes eventually led to their reduction by stirring the middle class to revolt.

A thorough comprehension of the reasons why illegitimate control efforts (or rather, efforts *perceived* as illegitimate) generate counterforce would require a social-psychological treatise of some length. No doubt such processes as alienation from authority, confirmation of negative beliefs, reaction against humiliation, rationalization of guilt, and the like, play a role in individual cases. Here I will confine my remarks to collective reaction.

There appear to be three basic ways in which control defined as illegitimate produces collective defiance and deviance on an increased scale. First, a threat to persons of like status induces a closing of ranks, a coming together of the persecuted that generates interpersonal ties, increases value consensus, and promises a buffer in the face of potential or intermittent defeat. Consequently, the group becomes an end-in-itself, an end that elicits constant reaffirmation of its dissident goals and of the norms that govern its inner life.

A second source pertains to subcultures that engage in certain illicit behaviors primarily to symbolize their rejection of dominant group values. If their behavior is further proscribed and assaulted by forceful means, its symbolic value is simply enhanced, and this enhancement in turn increases the likelihood that the behavior will recur. This suggests that a more reliable means of eliminating such behavior is to ignore it, if at all possible. This alternative approach is supported, for example, by experiences with decriminalization of marijuana in the state of Oregon, the first state to have taken this step. According to surveys conducted by the Drug Abuse Council (1975), the use of marijuana did not increase in the years following decriminalization. On the contrary, those who had smoked the drug before the law was liberalized reported a decrease in use: 40% the first year and 35% the second year said they smoked less often than before, while only 5% reported that they smoked more often. Since marijuana consumption was a key symbol of the youthful counterculture of the 1960s, its decrease in Oregon may well have occurred because its symbolic value had been undercut by liberalization.

A third source pertains to threats to material welfare, such as exorbitant taxes. Here revolt seems most likely if those affected are subjected to an arbitrary system of collection, feel underrepresented in policy making in general, have rising expectations of civil participation, and are subject to other forms of official abuse. These conditions apparently characterized the French peasantry prior to the agrarian revolt of 1789 (Tocqueville, 1955; Lefebvre, 1967).

Sources of the Resort to Forcible Control Despite the Probability of Reverse Effects

While it may be admitted that the display or threat of force operates as a deterrent in many cases, the frequency with which it produces the opposite results means that it is often resorted to inappropriately. This unsuitable use of force is most obvious in cases where more effective, alternative means for dealing with deviance or hostility (including ignoring it) are available. This raises the question of why force is so often embraced in spite of its all too common amplification effects.

One reason for the inappropriate use of force is that its influence on the enemy's collective will to resist is underesti-

mated. Thus, the strength of possible retaliation is miscalcu-
lated, and the prospect of a destructive boomerang is not seen
as lying within the realm of possibility. A powerful nation, for
example, may assume that an equally powerful nation will
present a substantial threat if provoked, while a weaker nation
can be attacked with relative impunity in spite of anticipated
counterforce. In effect, the physical means of counterforce are
calculated, but the *social* means may be ignored or discounted.
This tendency can be detected in the contrast between the
American attitude toward the Soviet Union, on the one hand,
and toward North Vietnam, on the other, in our recent history.
Shortly after the confrontation with the Soviet Union over
Cuban missiles, President Kennedy held a press conference in
which, according to Wicker (1975, p. 333), he expressed the
view that:

> powerful nations ought to be wary of inflicting major defeats on
> each other. Had the Soviets actually gotten an operational mis-
> sile base into Cuba, which would have been a substantial Ameri-
> can setback, Kennedy felt he would have had to react strongly.
> But that had not happened, and Kennedy thought he had made
> the ultimate Soviet defeat in Cuba not so harsh or extreme as to
> force Krushchev into some strong retaliation.

It is instructive to contrast this cautious attitude with Kennedy's stance toward North Vietnam, a country viewed as
militarily weak that eventually retaliated with overwhelming
force, largely because of its superior social organization for war
and its will to resist:

> [Over two years] he doubled the number of troops Taylor re-
> quested, posting sixteen thousand American soldiers as advisers
> to the ARVN. At the same time he increased military aid to the
> Saigon government, reinforced the Vietnamese units with
> squadrons of American helicopters and airplanes, and under-
> took a CIA-sponsored program of clandestine sabotage opera-
> tions in Laos and North and South Vietnam, all directed against
> the DRVN. (Fitzgerald, 1973, p. 164)

The will to resist that was reinforced by these measures was
overlooked by those who continued to prosecute the war in
Vietnam.

A second reason for the use of force despite a strong potential for reverse consequences is that the agents of force are motivated by the symbolic value of their action. In brief, their standing among peers and followers depends upon stalwart refusal to be intimidated by the presumed enemy. This attitude is especially common among specialists in violence and perhaps also in cultures that stress violence as a mode of social control. Thus, a resort to force may be no less a symbol of subcultural reaffirmation than the resort to marijuana, rioting, or martyrdom. Resistance or defiance only enhances the symbolic value of force by confirming the wisdom of its application in the first place, thereby short-circuiting the rational feedback process. In this way, force may become an end-in-itself dictated by the imperious needs of group belonging.

As an example, let us consider briefly the well documented case of the use of maximum force to quell the Attica revolt, an action the tragic paradox of which shocked the nation. Recall that 10 of the 50 hostages were killed and 3 others wounded by the bullets fired by the attackers. The assumption that freeing the hostages unharmed was the primary goal of ending the revolt was widely shared by the public and the inmates themselves. According to a poll of the survivors, 47 % of the inmates did not expect guns to be used at all in the assault (Wicker, 1975). As one of the inmate leaders later recalled with respect to the hostages: "We felt that their lives meant something to the administration. How can you come in and kill the man you sat down with last week and drank a beer with or bowled with. . . . [We thought] you couldn't come in like that, shooting fish in a barrel." But as Wicker (1975, p. 312), one of the official observers at Attica, pointed out:

> This calculation left completely out of the picture all the pressures from *outside the prison* that were converging on Oswald and Rockefeller, pushing them to "reopen the institution" at whatever cost and without further dealings with "murderers and thieves."

Not the least of these pressures was a flood of telephone calls and telegrams from wardens all over the country urging the use of force. The absence of prompt action, correction officials at all levels claimed, would be interpreted by prisoners throughout the country as a sign of weakness within the profession of violence.

A third source of violence and one that has a high potential for escalation, is an illusion on the part of violence specialists that they are under attack. Apparently a facile resort to force tends to be taken for granted by those whose training and occupational life are devoted to its swift employment. Hence, there is a tendency for threatening or harassing actions to be interpreted as harbingers of violence against authorities, and a consequent tendency to overreact.

This phenomenon was strikingly revealed by the Kerner Commission's investigation of the police reaction to urban riots in the 1960s. As a consequence of the belief that sniping by ghetto blacks was rampant, the police and National Guardsmen themselves engaged in rampant firing. "What is certain is that the amount of sniping attributed to rioters—by law enforcement officials as well as the press—was highly exaggerated," stated the Kerner report (1968, p. 335). "According to the best information available to the Commission, most reported sniping incidents were demonstrated to be gunfire by either police or National Guardsmen." In an episode in Newark, fireworks thrown out of a building caused two columns of National Guardsmen and state troopers to direct mass fire at the entire housing project. Of the 23 persons killed in the riot, one was a detective, one was a fireman, and 21 were Negroes, 6 of whom were women and 2 of whom were children. A thoroughly ironic consequence of the violence in Newark was that 400 armed police occupied the black area of Jersey City several days before any disorder broke out.

Still another source of counterproductive force needs to be mentioned: the inability of the perpetrators to concede that the motivation for dissent or hostility is highly legitimate in the minds of their opponents. White prison guards with a local, small-town background often discern little basis for the protests of black inmates against "political imprisonment," for example, or even for their demand for civil rights while imprisoned. With respect to police escalation of riots, Clinard and Quinney (1978, p. 144) have observed:

> Criminal violence by the police in these confrontations [i.e.,
> Chicago] occurs in large part because of the views the police
> share regarding protesters. That is, "organized protest tends to
> be viewed as the conspiratorial product of authoritarian
> agitators—usually 'Communists'—who mislead otherwise contented people." (Skolnick, 1969)

Indeed, when real communists are the objects of attention, the American statesman is sometimes unable to discern anything but treachery in his opponent's demand for concessions. In such circumstances, a threat of force becomes not only a means of self-protection, but a pious instrument of moral retribution. Moreover, one's avowal of the righteousness of force probably increases the provocational effect tenfold, for it directly assaults that moral consensus which serves as the enemy's basis for existence. Once again, therefore, we detect the role of discrepant frames of reference in the promotion of reverse consequences.

The failure of authorities accurately to perceive or diagnose the values of the target system (and here the military parentage of the phrase is grimly to the point) might also be due to gradual changes in attitudes toward authority apart from specific acts of official violence. In other words, popular conceptions of the legitimate boundaries of force may shift over time without corresponding shifts by government. Widespread de-legitimation of authority, as has occurred in the past decade or so, is a seed bed of provocation, especially if the perspectives of government agents lag behind the climate of public opinion.

IMPLICIT THREAT

While force explicitly confronts an individual or group with a threat to physical or social well-being, many interventions pose threats that are not fully intended or not intended at all. Such threats remain implicit. This seems to be a major source of the boomerang effect of propaganda as described by Merton (1957, pp. 517–524). Here is an example:

> A preliminary analysis of the X-ray program . . . found two major themes. The first dealt with the value of X-rays. The second revolved around the dangers of incompetently administered X-ray. The final message was that an X-ray examination is desirable, but that the patient should be certain that he is in the hands of a qualified technician.
>
> We suspected that this twin message would be understood by only a fraction of the audience. There were nine times as many references to the dangerous aspects of X-rays as there were to its value.
>
> This is the way listeners reacted:
>
>> Sick people would get frightened after listening to the talk and not even go to the doctor. All that voltage and all that. It isn't even necessary. . . . I think the talk left people not wanting X-rays. It sounded so dangerous. (Merton and Kendall, 1944, pp. 4–5)

Reactions of this kind are more likely to occur when latent fears are associated with the topic. As Merton and Kendall (1944, p. 6) note: "If the latent fears of losing one's job, contracting tuberculosis, and so on, are stirred up by the talk or dramatization, the response may well be a defensive discounting of the whole program."

The anxiety-provoking effect of an implicit threat might reinforce behavior in much the same manner as explicit force, namely, by prompting persons to seek out others who are engaged in the same undesirable behavior in order to allay their fears. Thus, social interaction would tend to reinforce the behavior that is being attacked. As Schacter (1959, p. 24) has put it: "Misery doesn't love just any company, it loves only miserable company." Havelock (1969, ch. 4–12) has made an interesting deduction from this tendency:

> These results raise some problem for the public health educator. If he attempts to reduce cigarette smoking through an increase in threat, anxiety and the like, he may actually be pushing the

listener into the arms of friends who smoke. For, under conditions of high anxiety or ambiguity, individuals will seek out
others similar to themselves (i.e., those who smoke) in order to
make an "accurate" comparison or evaluation of their actions.

Propaganda and educational campaigns are by no means
the only vehicles of implicit threat. Another often mentioned
source is the outsider or stranger who strives to reform the
target system. But here a distinction must be made between
the geographical outsider and the social outsider; for it is the
latter who tends to incite suspicion and group resistance, even
if he is a formal member of the group, that is, a geographical
insider. Thus, public school teachers are often more receptive
to teachers in other school systems who demonstrate new
practices than they are to university specialists who visit the
schools or to co-workers with deviant backgrounds. The latter
pose an implicit status threat because of their prestige, ideological differences, or dissonant statuses. For example, an evaluation of the Teacher Corps by Corwin (1974) found that the
amount of dissonance between the change agents (i.e., interns
within the schools) and the members of the host organizations
was *negatively* correlated with the successful introduction of
new technologies in the schools. This finding was contrary to
one intention of the program, which was to create strong ties
between institutions of higher education (whence the interns
came) and the public schools as a means of exposing the
schools to the cosmopolitan stimuli of the university. As Corwin (1974, pp. 711, 717) points out:

> Independent field observations and interviews also confirmed
> that interns were often a source of friction and tension in the local
> schools, and that schools tended to react defensively when even
> a few of these critical, liberal, change-oriented newcomers were
> introduced. . . . The characteristics of interns contributed to
> the explanation of both (a) the number of conflict incidents
> reported among members of the program, and (b) the proportion
> of teachers reporting that the program had created problems for
> them. The differences in the liberalism of the interns and
> teachers, and the proportion of liberal arts majors were both
> correlated with each variable. The defensiveness of schools in
> the face of this conflict is also revealed in (c) parallel effects which

the presence of liberal newcomers appear to have had in promoting organizational inflexibility; five characteristics of the interns explain more than half the variance (R^2 = .55).

In contrast, it appears that the liberalism of the university faculty that provided the preservice training for the interns was *positively* correlated with success. This seems to have been explained by the higher quality of such faculty, which factor was associated with liberalism. In effect, then, the geographical outsider's status difference was shielded from the school personnel, which made it possible for their quality to influence the schools without posing a status threat. This veil of distance was not afforded to the interns, who were perceived as *social* outsiders despite their geographical proximity and who therefore had a dampening effect on the schools' tendencies to innovate.

Status threats appear to be implicit in many, if not most, organizational efforts at innovation for two reasons. First, changes in technology or established ways of doing things disrupt hierarchical relationships and customary modes of interdependency. "Innovation threatens also the hierarchy of power and prestige on which the corporation's system of control is built," writes Schon (1967, p. 58), "for its political structure is tied to an established technology." Second, the seeking of advice is an admission of failure to cope autonomously. As Zaltman, Duncan, and Holbek (1973, p. 87) point out:

> Another barrier to the flow of new knowledge to the organization is a status discrepancy between the potential recipient and potential donors (Rice, 1963). The higher the status of the potential donor organization relative to the recipient organization, the less likely information will flow between them (Czepiel, 1972). The rationale behind this is that seeking information is an admission of inferiority.

These observations suggest that the higher the degree of hierarchical differentiation in an organization (or any collectivity, for that matter), the greater the resistance to change. As Burns and Stalker (1961) note: "Fear of depreciating one's status within the organization can cause considerable resistance; when such fears are widespread within firms the organization can be immobilized with regard to change."

While such generalizations will come as no surprise to organizational theorists and wise administrators, there is an implication for regressive outcomes of change efforts that seems to be overlooked. To the extent that repeated assaults on status relationships by well-meaning innovative efforts harden the resistance of members to renewed efforts, a history of implicit status threats is regressive. Indeed, there is the possibility that neutralization of even a single status threat entails a reinforcement of traditional behavior as a form of defensive reaction. The practice that is attacked might not only remain impervious to change, but might also increase in intensity.

The resistance of many white parents in the cities to initial desegregation may also be viewed as a regressive response to an implicit status threat, although here the reference is to a social class status rather than to hierarchical relationships in an organization. What are sometimes claimed to be the explicit threats of desegregation—inferior education or marauding blacks—might be minor compared with the implicit threat of downward status mobility symbolized by daily association with blacks on a *de jure* basis of equality. Since children are often viewed as the vehicles of their parents' class aspirations, the threat of status demotion is felt even more keenly when one's children are involved. This reaction might be strongest among recently arrived members of the urban middle class who have moved out of mixed racial areas into "purer" neighborhoods. (For a case study in a northern city that supports this interpretation, see Rogers and Swanson, 1965). The consequence, of course, is that many schools become more segregated as parents move to the suburbs or set up private schools in the city, at least in the first year or so.

Anxiety can be unintentionally induced at even deeper layers of the personality than those ordinarily reached by status or class threats. Such anxiety might not only jam out all other signals of the intervention, so to speak, but cause reactions that are contrary to those intended, or reactions that are even totally incapacitating to the subject. Presumably, the more central the threatened need, the greater the anxiety aroused. Thus, because of the affective salience of parents to young children, the threatened loss of love posed by severe parental punishment may not only stimulate *fear* regarding the consequences of the proscribed behavior, but may induce a state of *anxiety* that undermines self-control and drives the child to compulsive reenactment as a means of tension release. This process might account for the following conclusion of child psychologists:

> The unhappy effects of punishment have run like a dismal thread through our findings. Mothers who punished toilet accidents severely ended up with bed-wetting children. Mothers who punished dependency to get rid of it had more dependent children than mothers who did not punish. Mothers who punished aggressive behavior severely had more aggressive children than mothers who punished lightly. (Sears *et al.*, 1957, p. 484)

Apparently, anxiety has taken precedence over fear. Goldstein (1940) has distinguished between the responses generated by these two states as follows:

> In the state of fear we have an object before us that we can meet, that we can attempt to remove, or from which we can flee. We are conscious of ourselves as well as of the object; we can deliberate as to how we shall behave toward it, and we can look at the cause of the fear, which actually lies before us. Anxiety, on the other hand, gets at us from the back, so to speak. The only thing we can do is to attempt to flee from it, but without knowing what direction to take, because we experience it as coming from no particular place.

In short, an explicit threat (force) can be canceled out by a greater, implicit threat (anxiety), producing a result diametrically opposed to one's intentions.

TRUNCATED THERAPY

There is still another way in which intense emotional forces are provoked: by means of psychotherapy. A generation or so ago therapy would not have compelled our attention as a major source of adverse effects, in spite of the circulation of disparaging anecdotes. At least the therapist remained available to deal with untoward consequences, and indeed to put certain side effects (such as transference) to work in guiding the patient toward self-enlightenment and the resolution of conflict. But with the advent and widespread growth of therapeutic programs such as encounter groups, sensitivity training, group therapy, and special programs in a variety of institutional settings, psychological treatment has been packaged into sessions that last only a short time, are oriented to getting quick results, have few standards or guidelines for their conduct, and are often led by persons with limited training or experience. This mass marketing of psychological aid has produced the hazardous phenomenon of truncated therapy.

While impressions of the percentage of participants who are definitely harmed by encounter group sessions vary widely, what seems to be one of the most systematic and intensive investigations found that overall (for a variety of techniques) the casualty rate was 9.6% for the experimental groups and none for the control group. With certain techniques, the rate was even higher (Lieberman, Yalom, & Miles, 1971). Since this study also found that group leaders were unlikely to know when a casualty had occurred, studies that depend on the estimates of adverse consequences by leaders are probably quite unreliable.

After surveying the results of a number of studies of sensitivity training, Back (1972, p. 193) reported:

> Immediately after the training, 18 studies showed definite improvement, while 14 studies gave no positive results. Where there were control groups, the evidence is similar: 19 studies showed positive results and 14 showed negative measures or

mixed results. . . . When follow-up is considered, of course, the number of relevant studies became smaller; of those without control groups, 12 studies showed substantial or incipient improvement during the follow-up, and 7 showed either reverses or continued nonimprovement.

Here we run into the common problem of separating regressive and null effects, since investigators and reviewers often lump them together under the label "negative" results. It seems clear, however, that reverse effects predominated in at least a minority of the studies. As Back aptly notes:

> The general tendency of publication procedures as well as natural inclination of the researcher would be to stress positive results and to neglect no-difference findings. The mixed evidence, therefore, probably reflects an even bleaker reality.

That it is the short-term nature of much sensitivity training that is responsible for detrimental results is strongly indicated in a study by Wyant (1974) of laboratory training in elementary schools. In examining the effects of different amounts of training, he found that short amounts (between 6 and 22 hours) yielded regressive effects on three tests of communication during emotion, procedures in meetings, and effectiveness in meetings. That is, schools with a little training had lower scores than schools with no training at all. Interestingly enough, the results were especially regressive on communication during emotion. Greater amounts of training tended to raise scores on the three tests. In a review of the study, Runkel and Bell (1976, pp. 131–132) concluded as follows:

> Apparently, small amounts of training serve to bring problems to the surface and to make staff members more cognizant of the problems that exist in the schools; but small amounts of training are not sufficient to enable a staff to deal with the problems constructively. . . . In practical terms, this result means that the isolated two-day workshops that are only too common in laboratory training for organization development will probably have moderately destructive results.

The reverse effect of truncation is not limited to popularly packaged programs for individuals or small groups, however, but may occur as well in more traditional psychotherapeutic interventions that are subject to organizational constraints. A comprehensive review of techniques for dealing with serious juvenile offenders (Mann, 1976) studied the impact of therapy and concluded as follows:

> A number of youths who had no history of violence apparently rebelled violently against required therapy, perhaps because it is felt to be personally intrusive; perhaps because achieving self-understanding tends to be painful; perhaps because psychotherapy makes strong demands for interpersonal relationships and commitments. Marohn (1974) comments: "Offering a psychotherapeutic relationship often constitutes a trauma by stimulating a maternal transference characterized by fears and wishes for closeness, mothering and merger, which seemed to throw the patient into shock and trauma."

Whatever the precise dynamics of the regressive effect of short-term individual or group therapy, it appears that the arousal of intense emotional forces without extensive follow-up is a major factor.

ENTICEMENT—THE FORBIDDEN FRUIT EFFECT

One of the more genial perversities of man is his tendency to desire an object all the more when it has been expressly forbidden. Thanks to the moralistic Watch and Ward Society of Boston, as Schur (Schur & Bedau, 1974, p. 90) reminds us, "the verdict, 'Banned in Boston,' was once the guarantee of large audiences for a spicy play and of big sales for a racy book." Indeed, mankind as we know it was launched thanks to the temptation of Eve. Since that happy occasion, we have witnessed the enticement effect with a growing appreciation of its potency and perseverance and with an ill-concealed sense of the absurdity of those who sponsor it. As Spinoza wrote in the heyday of puritanism:

> All laws which can be broken without any injury to another, are counted but a laughing-stock, and are so far from bridling the desires and lusts of men, that on the contrary they stimulate them. For "we are ever eager for forbidden fruit, and desire what is denied." Nor do idle men ever lack ability to elude the laws which are instituted about things, which cannot absolutely be forbidden. (cited in Grinspoon, 1977, p. 361)

While numerous examples of the enticement effect could be cited, ranging from a child's raid on the pantry to the widespread appeal of marijuana, I will give only one case. According to Jerome Skolnick in an article on crime and justice (distributed by United Press International, September, 1977):

> By passing a law we may even make the prohibited conduct more popular. President Hoover's Wickersham Commission, which studied the effects of Prohibition on the nation during the 1920s, concluded that a new institution—the speakeasy—made drinking fashionable for wide segments of the professional and middle classes who had previously not experienced the sinful delight of recreational boozing.

Women and adolescents in particular apparently increased consumption as a result of Prohibition. Moreover, since the quality of the beverages declined, greater health risks were involved, and "public drinking halls declined from being merely disreputable and became a criminal institution controlled by the underworld" (Caplow, 1975, p. 124).

The dynamics of enticement appear to consist in the following sequence: An act that is gratifying is singled out and publicized by condemnation. This not only arouses and focuses curiosity, but puts everyone on notice that somewhere people have been indulging in the act to their hearts' content. This provides confirmation of the pleasures of the act and raises the prospect of acting out rebellious or deviant tendencies in the company of others in a relatively safe way. For some, the threat of discovery might add a certain degree of apprehension that increases the need for the tension-release properties of the act, hence making it all the more enjoyable.

For others, the act might be symbolically gratifying as well, especially if it is a subcultural vehicle for expressing rejection of dominant values. An important condition for these dynamics to work themselves out, however, is the ultimate inability of authority to suppress the act by force. This is especially likely to occur if "the minority is numerous and dispersed through the population in such a way that it cannot be attacked as a body." (Caplow, 1975, p. 122). For all these reasons, actions that are banned as immoral are often pursued with renewed gusto.

CONCLUDING REMARKS

The unintended arousal of debilitative anxiety, resistance to change, status threats, tendencies toward deviance, and emotional forces that are unresolved by therapy is probably rooted in most of the same factors that prompt the use of illegitimate force—in particular, overconfidence in one's capacity to control or shape others, the symbolic significance of the provocative act to the actor and his peers, and discrepant frames of reference. In addition, a commitment to puritanical values that seem to be violated by a minority, perhaps representing a status threat to nativistic elements, as Gusfield (1963) suggests in the case of Prohibition, is no doubt operative in the banning of certain deviant behaviors.

It seems likely that several types of provocation discussed here will be amplified in the years ahead owing to a few major trends. One is the proliferation of special interest groups, which entails social conflict and resort to governmental sanctions (e.g., the proabortion versus the antiabortion forces and the fight over a Constitutional amendment). Another prominent trend, which thus far seems to have escaped solution, is the international arms race. Furthermore, if American society continues on its present conservative course, one might expect repressive efforts to increase on the domestic front. Finally, there is the continuing pressure for organizational change in many fields as a consequence of the transition to a post-industrial society based on the application of new technical knowledge. Those who view such trends with dismay might take heart in the counterproductive tendencies of provocation. Unfortunately, there are collateral evils of rampant conflict and induced social change, regardless of the final outcomes.

CHAPTER 7

Classification

Classification as an interventional technique is rooted in three of the most basic trends in modern society: differentiation, professionalization, and bureaucratization. In particular, the growth of professional "people-processing" agencies has been phenomenal. As Hasenfeld (Hasenfeld & English, 1974, p. 1) observes:

> This trend reflects, on the one hand, the shift of socialization and social control functions from primary groups such as the family to the state, and on the other hand it reflects the development of complex people-processing and people-changing techniques that can no longer be implemented in small social units. . . . Examples of such organizations are the public schools, hospitals, welfare agencies, employment placement offices, and police departments.

In fact, it does not seem unwarranted to assert that the self-images as well as the objective constraints and opportunities of the great proportion of the population over six years of age stem from the categorizations of such agencies. The reverse effects of three types of classificatory modes will be discussed: the derogatory mode, the deferential mode, and the exemptive mode.

DEROGATORY CLASSIFICATION

All schools classify students according to grades, test scores, and teachers' impressions, and many allocate them to special programs, levels, or "tracks" according to these measures. As a consequence, undesirable patterns of behavior that are supposed to be altered are often reinforced, especially if treatment is either slipshod or merely custodial. This process is now widely believed to have occurred with mentally retarded children:

> What happens is that children labeled as mentally retarded are placed in special classes which theoretically provide them with special attention. More often, these classes tend to fulfill the expectancies of the label—children are moved along very slowly, are not challenged, etc. . . . because of inadequate knowledge and the lack of expertise of many special class teachers, the children are not taught with specialized techniques but instead are often treated with a lack of concern for their intellectual growth and a type of special care which prevents them from escaping from this type of class. (Havelock, 1969)

Even more common is the practice of allocating normal students to different programs according to academic ability or IQ. As I noted earlier, a recent review of numerous studies of tracking found "substantial losses by the average and low groups" (Persell, 1977, p. 92). An earlier review of the literature characterized the practice as follows:

> It has the following three attributes which, in all probability, were unintended in the conception and subsequent development of the ability grouping scheme: (1) it segregates children along class and caste lines; (2) it stigmatizes and discourages children who are assigned to low groups; and (3) it definitely lessens the attainment of children who are members of low groups. (Almony, 1970)

A system of derogatory classification may induce both subjective responses (self-imagery and expectations held by others) and official reinforcement in a vicious circle. The *subjective* aspect has been notably covered by Goffman (1961, pp. 355–356):

> In response to his stigmatization and to the sensed deprivation that occurs when he enters the hospital, the inmate frequently develops some alienation from civil society, sometimes expressed by an unwillingness to leave the hospital. This alienation can develop regardless of the type of disorder for which the patient was committed, constituting a side effect of hospitalization that frequently has more significance for the patient and his personal circle than do his original difficulties.

Glaser (1975, p. 83) points out that stigmatization may not only shape the expectations of others, but may have a transvaluation effect on lawbreakers:

> The . . . criminalizing effect of labeling . . . occurs when being labeled delinquent or criminal generates a stake in nonconformity with the law or decreases the stake in conformity. . . . People acquire specific ideas of what a delinquent or criminal is like, and as soon as they hear that someone has committed a crime they assume that he or she has all the traits they associate with such offenders. . . . Criminal labels generate a state in nonconformity with the criminal law when they become a source of pride, perhaps the basis of a reputation to live up to.

The *objective* aspect of derogatory labeling can be equally counterproductive. Perhaps the clearest example, and one that persists on an enormous scale despite criticism, is the influence of laws and regulations that preclude employment of persons convicted of crimes or even of those arrested without a conviction. Thus, a person with a criminal record is commonly barred by law from being a barber, a cabaret operator or entertainer, a bartender, a real estate salesman, a boat captain, a lawyer, a physician, a teacher, a fireman, and so forth. As Neier (1976) comments:

> Millions of people are denied jobs and licenses because of criminal records. Arrest records not followed by convictions are often equally damaging. . . . They are denied the stabilizing influence of steady homes and jobs and are forced into crime. The records virtually guarantee a repeat performance. . . . The handicaps of criminal records imposed on millions of people are, I believe, among the major causes of crime in the United States. (pp. 202–209)

In addition to official exclusion, the mere fact of having a record often gives employers pause. According to a carefully controlled study of the effects of a criminal court record on the employment opportunities of unskilled workers, a person accused of a crime, regardless of conviction, is subject to substantial discrimination:

> Of the twenty-five employers shown the "no record" folder, nine gave positive responses. . . . Of the twenty-five approached with the "convict" folder, only one expressed interest in the applicant. . . . Another important finding of this study concerns the small number of positive responses elicited by the "accused but acquitted" applicant. Of the twenty-five employers approached with this folder, three offered jobs. Thus, the individual accused but acquitted of assault has almost as much trouble finding even an unskilled job as the one who was not only accused of the same offense, but also convicted. (Schwartz & Skolnick, 1975)

Even prior to being labeled an arrestee or convict, many are viewed as criminals by the legal code for actions that do little more than offend the community's sense of propriety (and often that of only a minority). Thus, almost half of the arrests in America are for "victimless crimes," or crimes in which the participants voluntarily participate. The use or distribution of illicit drugs, public drunkenness, prostitution, gambling, and pornography are the most common of these crimes today. Many, if not most, of those who engage in these acts are otherwise law-abiding citizens. However, since the term *criminal* is associated in the public's mind with acts that are deliberately harmful to one's fellow men, perpetrators of victimless crimes are assimilated to a category of heinousness that is not only subjectively stigmatizing, but objectively reinforcing of participation in an underworld community. In short, the very act of labeling might create "criminals" and genuine crime. (What has come to be known as *labeling theory* has generated a large literature. The reader who is unfamiliar with this domain of social thought would profit from the reviews by Taylor, Walton, and Young, 1973; and Henshel, 1976.)

In addition to the reinforcement effect of the constraints that are imposed by authorities, the group into which one is cast also reinforces one's behavior. Thus, the very tendencies that are decried may be encouraged by one's peers. And since few individuals are able to hold themselves aloof from the pressures and rewards of group membership, even coercive assignment to a negative reference group might set the stage for socialization away from the very goal of segregation. Thus, first-time offenders who have committed minor crimes are exposed to the lore and possible fruits of a criminal career while incarcerated. In a case study of a man who was sentenced to six months for selling a few ounces of marijuana to a police informer, the subject stated in an interview toward the end of his prison term:

> I know I didn't hurt anybody, so there's no reason for me to feel that I'm suddenly a better man for having spent all those months in jail. In fact, the temptation is much greater for me now to go into a life of crime—if dealing in a harmless drug is a life of crime. Because I've met people who are involved in the drug trade, I know a lot more about the drug trade from sharing a cell with them, and about crime generally from the other criminal elements in there that I've met. It's a way of life that I certainly don't think is right. Because I feel wronged by the court in having been given a six month sentence, and when I think of the money I've lost from my legitimate business, the temptation now is for me to get back my due. (Sieber, 1977, p. 148)

As the preceding testimony suggests, a sense of illegitimacy toward the use of government force, together with economic losses incurred by imprisonment, heightens one's susceptibility to the lessons of professional criminals during incarceration. Indeed, a survey of a hundred judges in New York City yielded a consensus that the stricter penalties for drug violations enacted by Governor Rockefeller made matters worse by recruiting youngsters into the drug traffic through incarceration (*The New York Times*, Jan. 2, 1977). (Furthermore, as I pointed out earlier, several studies of recidivism have revealed that longer sentences are associated with greater likelihood of rearrest, other factors being equal.)

With regard to client-serving organizations, it is sometimes claimed that one means of overcoming the negative impact of formal segregation is to give the client some freedom in choosing his own niche. This was the hope of the early supporters of educational vouchers, which aimed to give parents a range of options in the expectation that this would foster healthy competition among schools. What emerged, however, was a tendency for parents to select schools according to the child-rearing values of their particular social class (Bridge, Blackman, & Lopez-Morillas, 1976). As the researchers found:

> Different kinds of schools attracted different kinds of children, and parents' choices reflected their instrumental child rearing values. Working class families tended to emphasize obedience and respect for external authority, and their children were over-represented in highly structured, traditional classrooms. In contrast, middle class families tended to emphasize independence, imaginativeness, and intellectual performance, and their children were overrepresented in less structured open classrooms.

This self-selection process had the effect of reinforcing segregation according to academic ability and strengthening the barriers to social mobility. As one of the researchers concluded: "To the extent that schools are supposed to foster social mobility, increasing family choice in schooling would appear, on the surface, to be counterproductive" (Bridge, 1977). In sum, the attempt to abolish segregative practices by shifting control from the organization to the client may enhance a tendency toward self-classification that is ultimately more segregative.

DEFERENTIAL CLASSIFICATION

Many of the processes discussed thus far are familiar to sociologists and social psychologists. What seems to have been overlooked, however, is the possibility that not only can a demeaning categorization of individuals be deleterious, but a deferential one can be equally harmful. Thus, the awarding of educational degrees to unqualified persons, to persons who must enter underpaid positions in order to utilize their skills, or to persons entering occupations that are saturated might well have reverse effects. This classificatory process can be called *overentitlement*. Since it operates through raising expectations to unrealistic heights, however, I will defer discussion of this process until the following chapter on overcommitment in general. It is noteworthy that stigmatization has monopolized our attention, despite the fact that over-entitlement can be detected in every classificatory system that is devoted to the training or processing of people. Our commitment to equality of opportunity, or even to equality of result, should not blind us to the possibility that faulty classification may push the disabled and promote the inept beyond their capacities, or prepare the able for a system that cannot reward or even tolerate them. These issues and evidence of negative consequences will be discussed later.

EXEMPTIVE CLASSIFICATION

Finally, we come to a third way in which classification might produce regressive consequences—through what might be called exemptive reinforcement. Individuals are often given official exemption from particular obligations: the poor, certain categories of the unemployed, the physically or mentally unfit, and several normal statuses that are relieved of such burdens as jury duty, taxation, labor, and conscription (e.g., children, females, students, and teachers).

Inherent in this practice are two dangers: that an individual will fraudulently claim an exempt status and that one who is initially qualified will perpetuate his exempt status by behaving in such a way as to ensure continued certification. In either case, unless the grounds for exemption are irremediable (e.g., blindness, and even here there is leeway in self-sufficiency), the goal of providing support and services until a person is able to meet normal social obligations may be undermined. The exemptee, in effect, may conclude that an ultimately remediable condition is not worth the trouble of remediation, thereby deliberately forgoing fuller participation in society or self-actualization. The existence of an array of pejorative labels for such individuals—draft-dodger, welfare deadbeat, psychosomatic, rip-off artist, pious fraud—is indicative not only of moral disapproval of such pseudolegitimate deviance, but of the possible magnitude of the problem in a humanistically oriented but nonetheless bureaucratic society.

This reminds us of a pattern that was earlier called semilicit exploitation by clients, wherein the resources of an intervention are exploited for "secondary gains." Such gains, I noted, might well be regressive if one goal of the intervention is to develop greater personal sufficiency. The point I wish to stress now is that such exploitation is facilitated by classificatory systems that apply definitive labels of inadequacy. Self-images and notions of particular rights and obligations are reinforced by such systems. And while this process may be enhanced by goal displacement in a client-serving agency (e.g., undermining the self-sufficient behavior of the blind by inducting them fully into the agency as a means of gaining further support for the agency), it occurs even in the absence of goal displacement by virtue of the simple process of official categorization. Cloward and Piven (1975, p. 23), who are far from joining those who claim that welfare destroys moral fiber, have noted the self-fulfilling effects of bureaucratic procedures that are based on a view of the poor as inherently marginal human beings:

> Bureaucratic procedures are also punitive, reflecting the premise that the poor are unworthy and the constant fear that the client will lapse into sloth and chicanery. Such procedures in fact make people into what they are already said to be, for when their rights are ignored, men do indeed live by their wits, evading what is capricious and arbitrary or lapsing into apathy.

Cloward and Piven here point to a key mechanism of exemptive reinforcement. Although exempting agencies are regarded as offering free (or very cheap) services, they do exact a price—compliance with agency expectations. A core feature of such compliance is confirmation of one's dependency, both objectively and subjectively. In the extreme case, the client is expected to express gratitude for the privilege of being allowed to repudiate his or her autonomy.

This process is by no means restricted to welfare clients. One of the most striking instances of exemptive reinforcement can be found today in the opposition of many American women to the proposed Equal Rights Amendment that, in their view, will remove their exemptions from certain formal and informal obligations. This threat to exemption is being fought despite the threats to civil liberties and self-ac-tualization entailed in the continued discrimination against women.

SOURCES OF CLASSIFICATION

I have already noted that a major source of classificatory systems is the growth of people-processing agencies, which in turn stems mainly from the shift of functions from the family and community to specialized agencies. Another and broader source is the need to identify strangers in a world that is characterized by great mobility (both geographical and social), high population density in many places, and the rapid turn-over of clients or members of formal organizations. Thus, social recognition (including knowledge of how one is ex-pected to behave) is facilitated by widely shared labels refer-ring to community of origin, educational level, occupation, skills, personality type, and even consumption habits. (Ironi-cally, the recurrent application of such labels may restrict the sense of freedom that is promised by the anonymity of urban society.) Thus, it is not necessary that every new encounter entail a lengthy process of mutual interpretation, as certain symbolic interactionists suggest. For example, Dreitzel (1970, pp. xi–xii) claims:

> Out of a mutual process of defining and redefining the relevant "meaningful" elements of situations, something like a social

structure, however unstable, gradually emerges. The precarious nature of such social structures lies in the fact that they are subject to constant revision in accordance with the changing interpretations of the involved actors.

The resort to prefabricated classes precludes this process to a significant degree. The negotiation has already been worked out, and one needs only to adopt the pattern of interaction that has been ordained as appropriate between persons thus labeled. In any event, it is clear that definitive schemes of classification, together with the regressive tendencies noted here, are a paramount product of social differentiation and the decline of community.

CONCLUDING REMARKS

Because of its close relationship to goal displacement and clients' exploitation of available resources, classification might not be readily viewed as a distinctive mechanism of conversion. But its rootedness in the broad social process of differentiation means that it has an impetus independent of these other mechanisms. Even if goals are not subordinated to means, and even if clients do not exploit an intervention's resources (e.g., the mentally retarded who are shunted into "special" classes and there neglected), classification can have reverse consequences. However, the relationship to these other common processes is a reminder that conversion mechanisms often work hand in hand to produce adverse effects and that such codetermination might make it especially difficult to overcome the production of such effects.

This difficulty in overcoming the problems of classification is perhaps especially severe in the case of deferential treatment as a result of the strong emphasis on credentialism in a society that allocates highest prestige to professional–technical personnel. This issue will be elaborated in the following chapter.

CHAPTER 8

Overcommitment

Overcommitment as a consequence of intervention may manifest itself in several ways: *objectively*, whereby (1) resources are exhausted in the successful accomplishment of ends while expectations remain relatively stable, or (2) resources are inadequate at the outset to meet expectations; and *subjectively*, whereby expectations are elevated beyond the capacity of the intervention to meet them, regardless of a rise in resources. In the objective case, the problem is due essentially to insufficient resources; in the subjective case, it is due to rising expectations regardless of resources.

Overcommitment may be viewed as a type of functional disruption, a conversion mechanism discussed much earlier, inasmuch as the requirement of a balance between resources and demand is violated. It merits special attention, however, because of its broad impact, its many contributing causes, and its longstanding interest as a source of societal tension. Indeed, a number of leading social analysts have attributed our present malaise to the outdistancing of resources by demand (see, for example, Gans, 1974; Ginzberg & Solow, 1974; Nisbet, 1975). The distinction between objective and subjective types of overcommitment is not explicitly drawn, however, and the

way in which each comes about as a result of particular interventions is therefore neglected. Let us look at some examples
of each type.

OBJECTIVE OVERCOMMITMENT

The classic case of exhausting one's resources in the successful pursuit of ends is, of course, the Pyrrhic victory. On a
broader scale, and in a more complex manner, the fate of the
Roman general has been shared by the leaders of the world's
empires. For it appears to be in the very nature of empire to
overextend itself and hence to suffer disintegration, subjugation, or both. In the drive to monopolize trade by military
means, an expansive power requires an ever larger bureaucracy to rule its subjects, repress revolts, regulate commerce,
collect taxes, and maintain the royal household. This bureaucracy not only absorbs too much of the profit, but fosters political intrigues that often lead to civil war and dismemberment of
the empire, especially upon the death of the ruler. In particular, the powers of military leader, supreme judge, and tax
collector may be concentrated in local officials, allowing them
to become independent or prompting continuous struggle
with the central power (e.g., the ancient Near East). Even
apart from such struggles, conflict with peoples on the empire's borders may exhaust its resources, thus rendering it
vulnerable to yet another contender for universal power (e.g.,
the emergence of Macedonia over both Persia and Greece). In
short, in Hintze's (1973, p. 163) view, the essential weakness of
empires is extension "beyond the limits set by the cohesion of
the population, the natural unity of the territory, and the
possibility for effective administration." Empires, then, may
be said to suffer from the Pyrrhic effect insofar as resources
(including power over local governors) are exhausted precisely as a consequence of winning too many battles.

In our own times, of course, the major issue of objective
overcommitment concerns the world's dwindling supply of

vital resources. Confronted with a possibly finite limit to some of these resources and a world population that will double within the next forty years, the reverse consequences of objective overcommitment are becoming painfully obvious. On a smaller scale, the problem has recurred at many times and places. Harris (1977) argues that intensification of production, the "recurrent response to threats against living standards," is inevitably counterproductive because it leads to a depletion of resources and a decrease in productivity, which in turn lead to lower standards of living. In response, society must either reduce its population or "invent new and more efficient means of production." The former solution never having been acceptable, the latter is embraced and the cycle starts all over again.

In the case of many domestic social programs, the failure to provide the wherewithal to meet a given level of demand is seldom a matter of finite resources; this fact brings us to the second type of objective overcommitment: the lack of resources even to achieve initial victories. Often a legislature will authorize a new program or agency without allocating available resources (including power to operate the agency) that are necessary to breathe life into the intervention. In such cases, a new, defective layer of organization is imposed on an already complex, overburdened system. When the task of the new agency is precisely to coordinate existing services, then a deficit of resources may sabotage whatever services were already being provided. Alford (1974, pp. 145–146) has noted this problem in the health field, although it could be generalized to many areas:

> Historically legislators have responded to pressures for reform by establishing a series of agencies—none of which has sufficient power to do its job. Few of these are abolished, and subsequent legislation incorporates the previous agencies into the list of those to be "coordinated," thereby further complicating the system. . . . the new stratum [for coordinating and integrating the component units] cannot carry out this function because it is a staff operation with little power and usually the instrument of one particular leadership faction within the organization. Thus,

their recommendations frequently fail to carry enough weight to
be implemented. . . . the net effect of the activities of the corporate rationalizers is to complicate and elaborate the bureaucratic
structure.

Much the same process seems to occur with regard to
mechanisms set up by advocates of equal access to health care
in the community. In the absence of sufficient power to carry
out their grandiose mandate, further complications are created
for the intervention system.

Because these bodies are not given enough power, there is little
incentive to set up procedures and create a composition which
will lead to effective decision-making processes. Just the opposite incentives exist: to make them large and unwieldy—as "representative" as possible—so that all points of view will be heard
but none implemented, save those interest groups who already
hold power. . . . One consequence of this particular scenario is
that even the professionals who started the project with a sincere
desire to "get the community involved" will become cynical
about the competence and skills of community groups and leaders. (Alford, 1974, p. 149)

In sum, the greater structural complexity and unintended
legitimation of existing power groups fostered by such
mechanisms have the additional adverse effect of alienating
those who were initially the most committed to community
participation. In such cases, an intervention never even has
the chance to experience a Pyrrhic victory but falters at the
outset in such a way as to undermine existing arrangements or
to alienate those who were meant to be involved.

The withholding of resources to operate an agency or
program is not restricted to allocations of power, of course, but
also includes allocations of money. The underfinancing of
certain reforms of the 1960s, despite the political fanfare and
apparent orgy of congressional spending, is well known. As
Ginzberg and Solow (1974, p. 10) observe:

The Great Society programs in the four fields of education,
health, housing, and welfare were each funded by about $3
billion in new outlays, once the Social Security tax payments for
Medicare are deducted. To keep the size of these programs in

perspective, it helps to remember that the budget of the Department of Defense during this same period increased from $46 to $77 billion, or by an amount greater than the total combined expenditures for these new human resources programs.

And as Levitan and Taggart (1976, p. 290) point out: "The most pervasive shortcoming of the Great Society was its underestimation of the scale of domestic problems and the distance to be covered in providing even minimally for the welfare of all citizens."

As I noted earlier, several prominent defenders of the social programs of the 1960s have attributed their failures and negative outcomes to underfinancing (see, for example, Harrington, 1977).

SUBJECTIVE OVERCOMMITMENT

The second type of overcommitment is due to rising expectations rather than to inadequate resources to satisfy the existing level of expectations. Indeed, it often stems from an actual increase in resources, which opens up horizons of expectation that are wholly new. At the time that a new resource is made available, demand might be almost entirely latent, but later on it might grow in magnitude to a point where it exceeds the very resources that stimulated it. The demand for rapid transportation over considerable distances increased enormously with the invention and development of the automobile and airplane, for example. The same process may occur with the provision of social services, but, unlike technological development, such services are not subject to market pressures and therefore do not automatically expand in response to rising demand. The consequence may be an erosion of client satisfaction that produces effects that are contrary to intended goals. Alford (1974, p. 150) affords evidence of this outcome with regard to community health agencies:

Because of the inadequacy of other health facilities in poor areas, the very success of a neighborhood health center is likely to be its downfall. If it attempts to "deal comprehensively with patients' problems," the center becomes the "repository of all the unmet needs of our patients. . . ." Thus, even though the staff may have begun work there in the full flush of idealism, ready to serve the community's needs with great energy and devotion, their very commitment will cause patients to flood in demanding care. The resulting overload of work will reduce the quality of care, the enthusiasm of the staff, and the sense of gratitude of patients. . . . the net effect may be cynicism on the part of the previously idealistic staff and a new sense of hopelessness in the population, which has been led to expect real improvement.

The lack of resources to keep up with the demand that has been engendered by an intervention, with the possibility that original goals are confounded, can be discerned in many domains of effort. The use of public parks is a familiar example. Unless strict limits can be imposed on the number of persons who may use such facilities, the result may completely negate the goal of providing open space, natural beauty, and the serenity of woods and fields, especially for hard-pressed urban dwellers. Here is a description from the *New York Times* of Yosemite National Park on a Labor Day weekend (cited by Bell, 1973, p. 273):

The constant roar in the background was not a waterfall but traffic. Transistor radios blared forth the latest rock tunes. Parking was at a premium. Dozens of children clambered over the rocks at the base of Yosemite Falls. Campsites, pounded into dust by incessant use, were more crowded than a ghetto. Even in remote areas, campers were seldom out of sight of each other. The whole experience was something like visiting Disneyland on a Sunday.

In similar fashion, the expansion of highway facilities may engender a demand in excess of the new space that has been provided, leading to even more congestion than before. As Greer (1961, p. 609) reports: "The Hollywood Freeway in Los Angeles carried, within one year, almost twice the number of vehicles it was expected to carry in the remote future." This failure of prediction is a dramatic example of the utter futility of social forecasting that ignores this mechanism of reverse consequences.

The elevation of ends beyond the capacity to fulfill them has long been recognized as a potent force in countries undergoing technological development. Goulet (1973, p. 38–51) points out that a self-concept of underdevelopment in the Third World is produced by a new consciousness of earthly opportunities, a consciousness that soon overtakes capacity and thereby fosters new dependencies on uncontrollable external forces. Subjection to a neocolonial form of exploitation buttressed by the internal structure of dominance is often the consequence. A further outcome, of course, is often rebellion and a paroxysmic refusal to be "domesticated."

Programs that require individuals to meet certain standards of admission or achievement have the problem of coping with the frustration of those who are unable to meet such standards. With respect to manpower training programs, Cain and Hollister (1972, p. 129) report:

> Programs which engender high hopes among some applicants or entrants may lead to a further alienation and hostility for some who are rejected or otherwise refused admission or for those who enter and fail. Admission policies are, in fact, just one example of administrative discretionary behavior that can have considerable separate influence on the positive or negative effects of programs—a point brought out in debates about the relative merits of self-help programs, transfer payment programs, and welfare and relief programs.

Such failure can render the individual even less well adjusted than before the program's advent. The psychological dynamics of this reverse effect have been described in the context of technical change efforts in underdeveloped societies:

> If the dissipation of the tension is not successful, the individual remains in a state of maladjustment or frustration. A common consequence of such a state of frustration is that the individual returns to the old responses that he had begun to abandon. But these old responses are likely to seem less satisfactory than they once were, and so he may remain maladjusted. The illiterate who attempts to learn to read and fails is a very much less satisfied person than the peasant by whom learning to read was

never considered a possible or even a suitable activity. (Mead, 1955, p. 272)

In addition to *failure to meet* standards, frustration of expectations may also flow from discovering that one is not appropriately rewarded for having *successfully met* standards. This pattern was referred to in the previous chapter on classification as *overentitlement*. It will be recalled that my use of the term is not restricted to persons who are undeserving of a particular classification but includes as well instances in which society fails to render rewards consonant with the classification, or is even completely unable to absorb or to avail itself of whatever skills or other attributes are certified. For example, a person may be educationally overentitled relative to his actual skills, relative to the rewards that he receives for plying his skills, or relative to the availability of jobs or career-lines that could utilize his skills. Entitlement refers to formal certification rather than to moral deserts.

To pursue the educational example, labor economists have noted the frequent mismatch between training and occupational position, referring to persons who are unable to be absorbed into the labor force in a manner consonant with their training as "underutilized." This term refers to the third meaning of overentitlement mentioned above, that is, the unavailability of positions. Since it fails to take note of the possibility that the first meaning may also account for mismatching, that is, that a person may be unqualified for a job despite certification, it prejudges the issue to some extent. In any event, overentitlement in the first or third meaning is apparently enormous. An analysis of Bureau of the Census data for 1971 indicates that 51 % of the labor force with at least four years of college were in jobs that required skills below their level of training (Berg, 1976, p. 286). And Berg has summarized a forecast of the Bureau of Labor Statistics as follows:

> In the period 1972–85, 15.25 million people will enter the labor force with college degrees. Growth in occupations currently filled with college graduates, along with attrition, will generate a demand for only 11.5 million of these graduates. Three million of

the residual 3.75 million will fill openings that will have been educationally upgraded. That is, graduates will be given jobs previously held by workers with less education. In the meantime, for 1972–80, of the 8.8 million jobs that BLS forecasts will be allocated to college graduates, 20 percent will be jobs that have been upgraded.

In an earlier work, Berg (1971, pp. 128–129) reported the findings of a survey of job satisfaction that sought to measure the reactions of people to underutilization, and the impact seemed clear:

> The explanation of the fact that men with more education are more dissatisfied with low-skilled jobs than are those with less education appears to lie in expectations: Better-educated men expect to do better. . . . When these aspirations are not satisfied, when their desire to be promoted seems likely to be disappointed, all of these workers are more dissatisfied with their jobs, but those with relatively more education and less skill are especially disaffected; the proportion who are dissatisfied increases by 25 percent.

Moreover, it appears that the important compensatory effect of income on job dissatisfaction will gradually decline (Freeman, 1975).

This state of affairs can have stupendous political significance if the frustrations of those who suffer "status inconsistency" evolve into a right-wing protest movement that threatens democratic society, as occurred at an earlier time in our history (Hofstadter, 1955). Or it could promote a left-wing movement of alienated workers from minority groups who are encouraged to pursue their education as a result of affirmative action programs and open enrollment. To reiterate an earlier point: While sociologists have focused on the maladjustive effects of stigmatization, an equally detrimental outcome of classification systems might lie in the domain of over-entitlement.

Thus far I have stressed the adverse consequences of subjective overcommitment for persons who are processed or served, but it is important to note that agents of intervention may suffer similar consequences. According to Lampman

(1974, p. 80), for instance: "Some found that the troubles and risks of taking part in the 'politics of the poor' outweighed the gains, and they became even more cynical than they were before about participation." Much the same reaction seems to have occurred among the interns in the Teacher Corps (Corwin, 1973, p. 189):

> The more aware they became of the way the program was actually being used—to provide assistance to the schools instead of to promote innovation—the more convinced they were that the change they wanted would not be realized through the Teacher Corps. Having lost faith in the one program designed to bring about change, they lost hope for the profession as a whole. Consequently, the interns who initially had been more liberal and more committed to teaching tended to lose interest in teaching during the program. . . . The clearer the problems became to them, the more powerless they probably felt. They gave up their incentive to lead change in the system, and many began to "mark time."

Considering the numerous experimental programs in education, health services, the justice system, and so forth, that have yielded negligible results at best, it would not be surprising if a sense of "lost hope for the profession as a whole" was a frequent outcome of reform efforts. An observation by Rossi (1972, pp. 19–20) on the likely impact of social programs in an advanced society suggests that this situation may be endemic to many contemporary interventions. As Rossi points out, improvement becomes less and less likely as problems that were more accessible to treatment are alleviated. "The more social services already supplied," he concludes, "the more difficult it is to add to benefits by supplying additional services." This suggests that while we are left with the hard-core problems of society, we might tend to judge our success in dealing with them in terms of past breakthroughs on soft-core problems. The reverse outcomes of subjective overcommitment, then, might be more likely to occur the closer we approach the toughest problems of our society after dealing with relatively easy ones. Perhaps much of our current cynicism can be traced to this source. The overarching danger, of course, is that such cynicism will become self-fulfilling.

SOURCES OF OVERCOMMITMENT

The exhaustion of resources in the course of achieving ends (the Pyrrhic effect) probably stems from one or more of the following factors: (1) a longer required duration of time to gain ends than originally anticipated; (2) an underestimation of the scope and depth of needs to be serviced (or enemies to be subdued); (3) an assumption on the part of resource-providers that, since an intervention has proved its capability in operating at a given level of resource, it therefore needs no additional support; (4) attrition of leaders and other key actors in the course of achieving a succession of hard won victories; (5) escalation of conflict (or social control efforts) as a result of renewed resistance to the intervention, requiring more resources than originally planned; and (6) increased delegation of authority to take charge of conquered territory (or successful service projects), which invites self-serving status exploitation and balkanization. For all these reasons, and there are probably others, short-run gains may cause long-run defeat.

The second type of objective overcommitment—lack of adequate resources at the outset—probably occurs most often when the symbolism of an intervention takes precedence over its instrumental value. Thus, just as a legislature will pass bills without making any provision for funding, it will make the even more impressive gesture of providing funds to launch the program (but not necessarily to run it)—all for the sake of symbolizing its interest in meeting the demands of some sector of its constituency. The latter practice is probably more harmful than the former, since existing services could be jeopardized by a new and faulty program that strives to coordinate them. Further, unfulfillable expectations not only are kept alive but are raised, although in the meantime the politician may have gained his short-run goal of reelection or neutralization of critics. This tranquilizing function of legislative decision making has been analyzed by Edelman (1977) and will be discussed in the following chapter as part of a broader pattern of placation that serves as a distinctive source of regressive consequences.

So far as the sources of subjective overcommitment are concerned, the first and most obvious is the triggering effect of relative deprivation, which can occur simply by virtue of one's becoming aware of people elsewhere, usually of like status in some respect, who are enjoying greener fields. With the rise of the idea of citizenship in civil society, the lowest rung may legitimately compare itself with the highest rung in terms of certain benefits, such as legal rights, medical care, food, and any other necessities defined as essential. If these benefits are felt to have been deliberately withheld by privileged groups, then the years of accumulated relative deprivation may produce a special *urgency* of deliverance when some new intervention promises to alleviate inequities. But even under conditions in which grievances have not accumulated, it soon appears that a new kind of relative deprivation emerges: deprivation with regard to an individual's or group's *imagined future attainments* as fostered by the intervention's promise. Thus, the expectation that at some future date one will become secure, equal, saved, wealthy, and so forth, establishes a new standard against which to measure one's current situation. This means that even if one is better off in absolute terms as a result of the first fruits of action, a failure to deliver fully on promises as subjectively scheduled may incur rejection of the intervention *in toto* and even of the basic values that it represents. Thus, a certain degree of urgency may be unintentionally fostered by the intervention itself, requiring more resources than were originally allocated.

The reverse effects of failure to meet subjective deadlines can be observed in the response to the civil rights programs of the 1960s. As Ginzberg and Solow (1974, pp. 11–12) point out:

> The more surprising development was the attack both from
> many in the liberal camp who had been in the forefront of the

reform movement and from some of the beneficiary groups themselves. The riots in Watts, Harlem, Detroit, and other urban centers had been a warning to the Johnson Administration and to the American people that many blacks had lost faith in the country's intention to deliver on its long-delayed promises. At a minimum, they were tired of waiting. Constant harassment of blacks who sought to register to vote, the use of excessive force against black suspects, and the violation of their rights in the courts only convinced the activists that talk about civil rights and equality was hypocritical.

An overcommitment on the part of the *agents* of intervention may stem from the same sources as overcommitment by clients insofar as the former identify with the latter; indeed, sometimes their backgrounds are virtually identical. But there is also another force acting on agents. Many reform movements require a high level of personal commitment and sacrifice on the part of their leaders and most active followers. Thus, to encourage people to undertake such enterprises it is important to elicit a degree of fervid commitment that is almost bound to exceed the prospects of success. Indeed, a willingness to make sacrifices can best be induced by underestimating the obstacles in the way of success. Consequently, such obstacles are only tardily recognized in the course of implementation. If the rewards do not justify the expenditure of extreme effort within a certain period of time, the agents may grow cynical. They may turn against the goals of the intervention as hopeless and even reject the values that the goals symbolize, as evidenced by the case of political activists in behalf of the poor and the Teachers Corps interns cited earlier. In effect, the agent may develop that sense of "misplaced consideration of others" that even the saintly Albert Schweitzer (1953, p. 24) refers to in a personal anecdote as the source of a lifelong regret.

The source of educational overentitlement is again somewhat different from the raised expectations of underprivileged groups, although it too is prompted by notions of the right to participation in the mainstream of civil society. As Dreeben (1971, pp. 99–100) points out:

The expansion of schooling can be interpreted as part of the general development of citizenship in nation states, particularly in its "social" aspects, as T. H. Marshall defined them. To attend school becomes a right, a sign that one has gained full participatory membership in a nation. Accordingly, we should construe school attendance, and increasingly attendance at institutions of higher learning, in the same way we understand universal suffrage (and the recent movement to lower the voting age to 18), and the right to a fair trial (and the recent movement to allow juvenile offenders to retain legal counsel), where both these contemporary movements represent attempts to extend the boundaries of citizenship.

But there is another factor that is unique to overentitlement: the demand for persons with degrees *independent* of the particular skills that are required for the position. Thus, Collins (1974, p. 440) has found that employers require high school degrees of manual workers "as an indication of character (perseverance, self-discipline, drive, etc.) rather than knowledge." In short, employers view education as a guarantee that the worker will be disciplined and compliant. This demand, together with the symbolic meaning of education to students, creates an overproduction of individuals in particular areas of skill. Since this gives a distinct advantage in the labor market to employers, it reinforces their demand for educational certification of a still higher order, which in turn may well frustrate the symbolic meaning of education to workers, who must now settle for an occupational form of second-class citizenship.

CONCLUDING REMARKS

It is possible that we are witnessing a scaling down of expectations domestically as a result of resource shortages, inflation, and unemployment, as critics sometimes claim. But the traditional symbols of achievement in American society—education, home ownership, middle-class jobs, etc.—will not soon be repudiated. Also, austerity often evokes new types of intervention by centralized authority to alleviate conditions (or at least to placate critics), and these might serve to revitalize hope. New leaders, too, will probably emerge with fresh promises of redemption. Furthermore, it is quite conceivable that, in order to deflect public protest from domestic leadership and to exploit chauvinistic responses to social stress, foreign targets will be sought. Thus, overcommitment may shift from the domestic stage to the international military stage. In sum, it is unlikely that overcommitment of either a subjective or an objective sort will be abated in the foreseeable future.

CHAPTER 9

Placation

It does not require a Machiavellian perspicacity to realize that many interventions are chiefly a means of placating certain parties whose support is considered necessary or whose attacks require neutralization. But it does require a certain sociological perspective to realize that the partners to such agreements are often well intentioned and deceive themselves as much as they do others. Indeed, the placation effect is probably an inherent feature of every intervention that is launched with the express purpose of alleviating a problem. For even in the absence of guarantees that the intervention will be successful, the plain fact of taking deliberate action tends to reassure the public, the agents, and the objects of the intervention (if any) that help is on the way. The facts of the case, however, might be quite the contrary.

Placation gives rise to reverse consequences in two basic ways: by means of a *lulling* effect that permits the situation to deteriorate and by means of an *exasperation* effect that causes the target of an evasive ploy eventually to rebel and to present all of his accumulated grievances at once. This latter effect reminds us that placation is especially common in situations wherein sharp differences need to be reconciled. Before noting examples of conflict situations that have called forth interventions that are essentially placatory, it is important to underscore one point: The lulling effect that allows a situation to deteriorate is also quite common and can have catastrophic effects.

THE LULLING EFFECT

One of the most famous examples of a destructive lulling effect in the twentieth century is the French Maginot Line, that nominal solution to the threat of German invasion that helped the Germans to overrun the country in 1940. The term *Maginot Line mentality* has been spawned by the event, a state of mind that consists in ignoring one's defenses on the assumption that absolute confidence can be placed in a particular provision. This state of mind can be generalized to any inordinate reliance on safeguards, a reliance that permits a good deal of laxity in the way in which the safeguards are maintained.

The lulling effect is often a facilitator of the conversion mechanisms analyzed earlier inasmuch as attention is diverted from the reverse consequences of an intervention by welcome reassurances of its effectuality. Thus, it is possible that our foremost contemporary equivalent of the Maginot Line is our faith in technology to preserve us from the dire effects of depletion of vital natural resources. As Meadows *et al.* (1972, p. 159) observe:

> Technology can relieve the symptoms of a problem without affecting the underlying causes. Faith in technology as the ultimate solution to all problems can thus divert our attention from the most fundamental problem—the problem of growth in a finite system—and prevent us from taking effective action to solve it.

Placation can also facilitate the regressive exploitation of an intervention's resources, including the use of the intervention against its instigators, that is, the petard effect. Thus, because of their presumptive responsibility for enforcing standards to protect the public, the federal regulatory agencies are often claimed to be a major source of reverse consequences due to exploitation by the regulated. As Edelman (1977, p. 38) puts it:

> Some of the most widely publicized administrative activities [of regulatory agencies] can most confidently be expected to convey a sense of well-being to the onlooker because they suggest vigorous activity while in fact signifying inactivity or protection of the "regulated."
> One form this phenomenon takes is noisy attacks on trivia. The Federal Trade Commission, for example, has long been noted for its hit-and-miss attacks on many relatively small firms involved in deceptive advertising or unfair trade practices while it continues to overlook much of the really significant activity it is ostensibly established to regulate: monopoly, interlocking directorates, and so on.
> Another form it takes is prolonged, repeated, well publicized attention to a significant problem which is never solved.

Not only do the groups that are thus deceived retreat from the field with a sense of relief and quiescence, but they now lend support to the very system that seduced them. "Groups which present claims upon resources may be rendered quiescent by their success in securing nontangible values," writes Edelman (1977, p. 40) with reference to the symbolic reassurance gained by such groups. "Far from representing an obstacle to organized producers and sellers, they become defenders of the very system of law which permits the organized to pursue their interests effectively." The public has become a stout defender of our antitrust laws and of our progressive tax laws, for example, in spite of their possible reverse consequences. With regard to tax laws, Edelman (1977, p. 28) notes:

> While the fervent rhetoric from both sides turns upon the symbol of a progressive tax and bolsters the assumption that the system is highly progressive, the bite of the law into people's resources depends on quite other provisions and activities that are little publicized and that often seriously qualify its progressive character. Special tax treatments arise from such devices as family partnerships, gifts inter vivos, income-splitting, multiple trusts, percentage depletion, and deferred compensation. . . . By and large, the recipients of larger incomes can most easily benefit from exemptions, avoidance, and evasions.

The government is not the only source of a lulling effect with regressive potential in modern society, however, as indicated by our earlier comments on the opportunities of highly esteemed status groups, such as professionals, to engage in self-serving exploitation. Thus, the false sense of security that is provided by advances in therapeutic care deflects attention from inadequacies of preventive medicine. And increasing dependence on the professions in general may undermine efforts to develop personal sufficiency and to explore alternative methods of solving problems by reliance on neighbors, family, work associates, and friends—methods which in many cases may be superior to those of professionals. A thorough review of research on the competence of psychiatrists to judge people, for example, reached this conclusion:

> It is astounding that judges and correctional officials continue to view psychiatrists as experts on human behavior when there is considerable experimental evidence and other research which shows laymen superior to psychiatrists . . . in the judgment of people's motives, abilities, personality traits, and action tendencies. (Hakeen, 1958, cited by Henshel, 1976, p. 145)

Because of the prestige of professionals, professionalism may be invoked to lend legitimacy to decisions that are directly detrimental to clients. The professionalization of welfare work, for example, reduced rather than expanded the number of poor persons who were accepted as clients as psychosocial criteria were substituted for moral criteria in determining who "deserved" poor relief (Piven & Cloward, 1971, pp. 176–177). Or again, the professionalization of the federal bureaucracy reduced rather than increased the responsiveness of certain agencies to broad public interests as the interests of *colleagues* came to the fore. As Salamon and Wamsley (1975, pp. 169–170) comment:

> Far from equipping agencies to resist the pressures from "relevant others," professionalism has frequently made them more responsive to such pressures. Presumably objective, scientific, professional work routines and evaluation standards effectively shield agencies from outside scrutiny by the nonprofes-

sional public, but simultaneously make them much more understanding of the "problems" of "relevant others" with whom
they share the professional mystique and collegial empathy.

Here we witness a formidable combination of placatory
sources: a federal agency devoted to serving the public and the
participation of professionals. When still another source of
reassurance is added to this combination, namely, complex
techniques for determination of needs and feasibilities, we
encounter a powerful triumvirate of legitimation indeed.

An illustration of how such techniques can lull the public
and their representatives into a false sense of security resides
in the application of esoteric formulas, such as those found in
cost–benefit analysis, operations research, simulation, and so
forth, all of which are highly quantitative fields. Speaking of
such techniques, Marshall (1970, p. 257) notes that "recommendations based upon them tend to be authoritative in the
sense that they become surrounded by the aura of science."
However, as Marshall, among others, points out, many of the
estimates that serve as the empirical bases for the application
of these techniques are rather soft, and the analytical models
for handling the data are open to dispute. Consequently,
Marshall asserts, "This leaves great discretion to the technicians, and the danger is that consciously or unconsciously they
will manipulate the analysis to come to preferred conclusions." He illustrates this problem by reference to a decisive
discrepancy between the cost–benefit ratios calculated by the
Corps of Engineers, on the one hand, and a Presidential
Commission, on the other, in determining the need for water
development programs in the Missouri Basin:

> The benefit–cost ratio calculated by the Corps was 1.9 to 1; but the
> Commission could find only enough benefits to justify a ratio of
> 0.8 to 1. If the Commission's findings were correct, the project
> should not have been constructed. Discrepancies of this mag-
> nitude are typical of the literature in question. One can only
> conclude that benefit–cost analysis, aside from eliminating the
> most hopelessly ineconomic projects, has been used principally
> as a means of clothing politically desirable projects with the fig
> leaf of economic respectability. (Marshall, 1970, p. 259)

Several of the examples of regressive placation that I have cited fall within the domain of paternalism, that is, ostensible protection of the subject in a manner that undermines his capacity for adaptive behavior. What is often overlooked is that paternalism may be applied to the strong as well as to the weak. In the former case, it is a matter of *over*protection, while in the latter, it is *under*protection that may cause reverse consequences.

The inducement of diseconomies by protecting powerful business interests from their own miscalculations is a common form of overprotection. In a discussion of the "perverse incentives" of government economic policies, Schultze (1973) gives several examples of programs that seek to protect vested interests from economic losses that are self-inflicted and which consequently exacerbate the problem. With respect to protection of businesses in flood plains:

> The present policy, which concerns itself almost solely with public projects, not only fails to consider the establishment of incentives for economic private investment in flood plain lands, it sets up a series of monetary and political incentives which induce distinctly uneconomic investment decisions.

With respect to maritime subsidies:

> Our current maritime subsidies, which directly and indirectly cost some $500 million per year, seem to have been designed to insure the minimum possible efficiency in our merchant marine. . . . The basic operating subsidy that we now pay essentially makes up the difference between American and foreign operating costs. Any productivity gains result in lower subsidies—inefficiency leads to higher subsidies. . . . Even accepting the need for a subsidy program, we have designed one which is guaranteed to produce decreasing relative efficiency in the American merchant marine compared to its foreign competitors.

In the case of the weak, paternalism does harm by *under*protection. In a few words, the espousal of benevolent ends lulls the public into believing that the weak are being humanely treated. This is not to say that the deception is always intended. Paternalism directed toward the weak is often seized upon as a well-meaning solution to a normative dilemma. Confronted with a situation in which a customary response is regarded as illegitimate (e.g., imprisonment of juveniles with adults or rejection of demands by the poor for economic relief), authorities sometimes adopt an evasive alternative that lulls the public and even themselves into a sense of benevolence. The ultimate consequences may be nonetheless detrimental for having been produced with a clear conscience. This problem appears to be endemic to our social institutions of caring. As Glasser (1978, pp. 106–108) notes:

> A common phrase—*social services*—arose to describe these institutions and they came to be widely perceived, especially by political liberals, as entirely humanitarian and benevolent. . . . we adopted the fiction that the interests of clients were identical with the interests of social service agencies, a fiction we have not completely shed. . . . Vast discretionary power thus came to be vested in an army of civil servants, appointed by examination and organized into huge service bureaucracies, which began quietly and silently to trespass upon the private lives and rights of millions of citizens. . . . Because such professionals were presumed to be acting in "the best interests" of their "clients," no one thought to question the excesses of their power.

Glasser gives examples of such excess with respect to students, the sick in mental hospitals, the young in foster care institutions, the poor in public housing, adolescents in training schools, and so on. In all such cases (which seem to involve semilicit status exploitation), it is hard to escape the conclusion that the goal of caring has been turned on its head. A study of juvenile justice interventions by the Rand Corporation (Mann, 1976) has this to say:

> The philosophical orientation which presumes that everything will be done in the child's best interest has in fact resulted in denying young people their due process "rights" and subjecting them to social control programs in the name of "treatment." . . . This is true of police discretion, prosecutorial discretion, the discretion of correctional officers and staff, parole board decisionmaking, and—in some cases—even judicial discretion, which is the most visible and scrutinized of all.

The ostensibly therapeutic treatment of prisoners is a grim example of the way in which a nominally humane solution is converted into a more refined weapon of repression and punishment. Mitford (1974) has reported the observations of several medical authorities:

> Dr. Bernard L. Diamond, professor of criminology and of law and clinical professor of psychiatry at the University of California, told me, "In 'good' prisons, like those in California, physical degradation is replaced by psychological degradation. I call these 'pastel' prisons; they look good, shiny, sanitary. But inmates will tell you thousands of ways in which they are psychologically degraded. (p. 108)

> Dr. Powelson [a former psychiatrist at San Quentin] writes, "that psychiatry in the prison consists primarily in therapeutic practices which can have punitive or disciplinary implications: electric shock, insulin shock, fever treatment, hydrotherapy, Amytal and Pentothal interviews, spinals and cisternals and so on—that is, everything except psychotherapy." . . . Shock treatment was "pretty clearly" used as punishment: "It would take the form of telling the prisoner 'unless your behavior changes you're going to get more of this.' " (p. 111)

A psychoanalyst has attacked the paternalistic hypocrisy of prison therapy in the following terms:

> The rehabilitative model, despite its emphasis on understanding and concern, has been more punitive than a frankly punitive model would probably have been. . . . Under the rehabilitative model it is possible for society to abuse prisoners, without disabusing its conscience. (Gaylin, 1977)

A final and obvious type of the lulling effect that permits exploitation of an intervention needs only to be mentioned, namely, agreements between hostile parties that involve treachery from the outset. The major example in our own times, of course, is the Munich pact. Paradoxically, the transparency of this catastrophic solution led to a similar one elsewhere in another misguided effort at self-defense: the Soviet Union's nonaggression pact with Hitler in response to what appeared to be England's and France's lack of determination to resist Germany. The near consequences of both agreements was the eclipse of the west.

THE EXASPERATION EFFECT

An accumulation of grievances by the parties to a placatory intervention, which then erupts in a burst of ungovernable exasperation when the elements of the compromise become unbalanced, is a further outcome of this sort of intervention. Thus, the various compromises that preceded the American Civil War allowed the dissension between North and South to grow apace at a subterranean level. With reference to the Compromise of 1850, Nevins and Commager (1967, p. 201) note:

> For three short years the compromise seemed to settle nearly all differences. A majority in both Whig and Democratic parties cordially supported it. Yet under the surface the tension remained and grew. The new Fugitive Slave Law [of the Compromise] deeply offended many Northerners. They refused to take any part in catching slaves; instead, they helped fugitives to escape. The "underground railroad" from slavery to freedom became more efficient and unabashed. . . . Harriet Beecher Stowe was inspired by the Fugitive Slave Law to write *Uncle Tom's Cabin*. . . . The rising generation of voters in the North was deeply stirred by it.

Four years later the "popular sovereignty" doctrine of the 1850 Compromise, whereby new states could decide about the status of slavery within their borders, was applied to the territories of Kansas and Nebraska in the Kansas–Nebraska Act. This contradicted a second vital feature of the 1850 Compromise, the provision that slavery would be barred from the Kansas–Nebraska territory. The maneuver enraged the antislavery forces, caused the tragedy of "bleeding" Kansas, led to the founding of the Republican party, and pushed the nation irrevocably toward civil war.

The maintenance of a compromise, even over the short run, usually depends on particular structural props: a certain balance of power, a common enemy or economic threat, a certain distribution of resources between contending parties, a nominal head of state or charismatic personality, general societal stability that has defused the conflict, and so forth.

When a major prop of this kind is removed or substantially weakened, the compromise may degenerate into a renewal of conflict that is more intense in proportion to the buildup of grievances and the past suspension of techniques of day-to-day conflict resolution. As Duverger (1972, p. 226) has remarked, "The contrast between conflict and compromise is not absolute. Compromise is not the end of the struggle, but only a truce, an armistice."

The response of colonial peoples to the dawn of nationalism is illustrative. Geertz (1971, p. 367) illustrates this process with the example of Indonesia, where peoples with "opposed styles of life and world outlooks managed to coexist" until the rise of nationalism, at which point "a kind of 'cultural balance of power' became an ideological war of a peculiarly implacable sort." Nationalism had this effect by "raising settled cultural forms out of their particular context, expanding them into general allegiances, and politicizing them." Thus, nationalism produced far less unity than existed before its advent by virtue of eliminating the structural props that kept the earlier half-solution intact.

To return to my earlier example of the dangerous weakness of formal compromise: Not even the Civil War settled the differences between North and South over the basic issue of civil liberties for blacks, of course, and placatory measures continued to be adopted. Thus, the Supreme Court rendered a number of decisions that sought to "square the separate-but-equal doctrine of the Plessy decision with basic constitutional principles of equality and fairness," as Barth observes (1975, p. 44). Indeed, the separate-but-equal doctrine was itself a compromise that permitted the discriminatory effects of segregation to pile up year after year. As Justice Harlan presciently observed in his dissenting opinion in Plessy:

> The present decision, it may well be apprehended, will not only stimulate aggressions, more or less brutal and irritating, upon the admitted rights of colored citizens, but will encourage the belief that it is possible, by means of state enactments, to defeat the beneficent purposes which the people of the United States

had in view when they adopted the recent amendments of the
Constitution. (*Plessy v. Ferguson,* 1896)

The boomerang of compromising policies may be witnessed on an even larger scale today. Huntington (1975, p. 78)
attributes the alienation from government prevalent today in
the West to the failures of compromise within a highly
polarized political context·

> Polarization over issues generated distrust about government,
> as those who had strong positions on issues became dissatisfied
> with the ambivalent, compromising policies of government.
> Political leaders, in effect, alienated more and more people by
> attempting to please them through the time-honored traditional
> politics of compromise.

On occasion the chief beneficiary of a compromise may be
unaware that a compromise has been struck. This blindspot
may encourage self-confident action in a direction that violates
the implicit agreement, thereby amplifying the natural tendencies toward exasperation. Reedy (1970, p. 70) supplies an
example of this sort of political ignorance in the case of the
landslide election of Lyndon B. Johnson in 1964:

> As Democratic leaders jubilantly surveyed their sweeping vic-
> tory, it appeared as an unalloyed triumph. There was no cloud
> on the horizon (even as big as a man's hand) to indicate that
> trouble was ahead. The trouble, of course, was created by the
> euphoria which resulted from victory. President Johnson and
> most of his close advisers interpreted the election result as a
> mandate from the people not only to carry on the policies of the
> Johnson administration but any other policies that might come to
> mind. There were very few voices raised at the time to warn the
> president that a sizable share of his victory had come from
> people who were literally frightened into the Democratic camp
> by the grotesque and preposterous campaign tactics of the op-
> position. The Democratic administration assumed that it was in
> step with the American people and proceeded accordingly with-
> out a backward look or any probing below the surface.

When the war in Asia was subsequently expanded in a way
that would have pleased the defeated candidate, Johnson's
original power base was rent asunder in a manner so resound-

ing that it forced him to withdraw from the 1968 campaign and split the liberal consensus.

One need not look to history for examples of destructive compromise, explicit or implicit, however, since they abound in every sphere of daily life. In his case study of school–community conflict, Gold (1977) tells how the school board had promised to include at least one self-contained classroom in a new "open" structured school in order to gain passage of a bond issue. When it appeared that the promise was not being honored, the community rose up in arms. The Board's second effort at placation was a survey to determine the wishes of all parents. Gold (1977, pp. 343–346) reports the almost inevitable outcome as follows:

> The Board's decision to require the community survey seemed crucial: it sharpened school–community conflict in many respects, though it was designed to reduce it. . . . The survey permitted the Board of Education (and the educators) to bypass the original issue of whether or not the plans for the school honored the original design.

Placatory solutions are not confined to relationships between secondary groups; they occur as well within primary or closely knit groups. In fact, as Coser (1956, p. 151) suggests, the closer the group, the greater the adverse effects of suppressing conflict:

> If conflict breaks out in a [closely knit] group that has consistently tried to prevent expression of hostile feeling, it will be particularly intense for two reasons: First, because the conflict does not merely aim at resolving the immediate issue which led to its outbreak; all accumulated grievances which were denied expression previously are apt to emerge at this occasion. Second, because the total personality involvement of the group members makes for mobilization of all sentiments in the conduct of the struggle. Hence, the closer the group, the more intense the conflict.

Not only the more intense, but the more deadly as well—since brothers, as Simmel (1950, p. 168) remarks, possess "the most deadly weapons precisely against this specific adversary."

SOURCES OF PLACATION

There are two basic dimensions to the question of the sources of placation: the conditions that foster quiescence on the part of the public or contending groups and the reasons why intervening agents resort to measures that are essentially placatory.

Edelman (1977, pp. 30–35) adduces five social psychological conditions "under which groups are prone to respond strongly to symbolic appeals and to distort or ignore reality in a fashion that can be politically significant." These are: situations that are unclear or provocative emotionally; low tolerance of ambiguity, causing stereotyping and over-simplification; the need to alleviate anxiety; lack of demands, even when socially supportable, for increased economic resources or political participation; and widespread social reinforcement of the foregoing responses. In short, stereotyping, oversimplification, and striving for reassurance are the only means of adjustment by "groups not in a position to analyse a complex situation rationally."

One consequence of oversimplification is the tendency to cope with the *symptoms* of problems rather than with their underlying causes, a tendency that is immediately conducive to reassurance that the problem is being dealt with. Thus, virtually all the resources of the field of law enforcement are devoted to relieving the most obvious signs of deviance (e.g., street crime); expenditures for preventive health care are minuscule; and many government programs are designed to give temporary economic relief to vested interests while diseconomies are allowed to increase.

With regard to compromises between hostile parties, symptoms may be stressed because they entail less intense feeling than underlying sources of conflict that might pose greater immediate threat to the relationship if explicitly addressed. The greater likelihood of a long-run resolution by treatment of underlying causes of conflict is therefore nullified. In addition to postponing a serious issue and allowing hostility to build up, the treatment-of-symptoms approach runs the added risk that certain features of the intervention will continue to compound the problem. In short, the preoccupation with symptoms might divert attention from the operation of such conversion mechanisms as exploitation, goal displacement, or provocation. A strictly punitive approach toward law breakers, for example, diverts attention from the reverse effects of provocation by virtue of focusing on the superficial level of symptoms.

The conditions mentioned above refer only to the public's lack of rationality, or of political and sociological sophistication. What also needs consideration is the active role of symbolic reassurance deliberately played by authority. One reason that we delegate individuals to deal with complex, emotion-laden issues in our behalf is precisely the realization that these issues are too complex and serious for us to deal with ourselves. To this extent, we *are* behaving rationally. When the authorities to whom we have delegated decision making launch a new law, regulation, or program with much fanfare, we are reassured to the extent that we trusted them at the outset and that they now appear willing to do something. And yet, authorities are influenced by *organized groups* rather than by the public at large, and such groups may advocate actions that would arouse public opposition if they were widely known. Consequently, authorities must reassure the public at large in order to shield the role of organized groups in the actual allocation of resources. In short, agents of intervention may play an active part in deliberately fostering the stereotyping and acquiescence of the unorganized and minimally informed.

Indeed, threatening situations that have a complex aspect may be amplified or even contrived by authorities so that they may benefit from the symbolic reassurances that they will then be able to dispense. This is, of course, the time-honored tactic of the snake oil salesman who arouses anxiety about the numerous ills that flesh is heir to as a means of marketing his all-purpose placebo. Some possible examples of anxiety-provoking situations that are made more complex than necessary are the arms race, tax law, and regulatory policies. Moreover, that all three of these examples entail reverse consequences for the trusting public, as I have already mentioned, might well be a factor contributing to the prolonged mystification in which officials have shrouded them. Here, then, we are put on notice that interventions that are regressive for the many may be perpetuated by the few for their own benefit. (Such interventions are *partially* regressive, as I pointed out in my first chapter.)

The placation effect is not limited to political leadership and government administration, as I noted earlier, but extends as well to professionalism and its technical trappings. The potential for regression that is nourished by the placatory effect of professionalism is traceable to several sources: an excessive and growing reliance on exogenous expertise, which in turn is stimulated by increasing technological complexity; the "defensive expenditure" in education that is necessary to compete in the job market (Thurow, 1972); and the monopoly of the "definition of professional excellence in the hands of a small self-selected minority" (Yarmolinsky, 1978, p. 160). Moreover, the emphasis on visible treatment instead of obscure prevention that characterizes medicine and law—treatment that becomes all the more urgent in proportion to the neglect of prevention—enhances public dependency in these fields.

One area in which professionalism has been particularly regressive is in the operation of social service agencies, as we have seen, an outcome that is attributable in large part to the reassurance of benevolent care. The hypocritical contrast between the espoused goal of caring and the practice of violating rights, undermining personal sufficiency, and fostering recidivism (in the case of training schools) may be traceable to a cultural stress on helping the unfortunate, on the one hand, and on pursuing one's private interests through self-reliant means, on the other. Thus, the reassurance that good is being done is gratefully taken at face value, while the actual impact of day-to-day practices is not scrutinized because of the emphasis on self-reliance and the resultant distaste (if not distrust) aroused by the image of the mentally or socially handicapped.

This process operates most clearly, perhaps, in the field of welfare. According to Piven and Cloward (1971), poor relief programs are instituted by the government under the threat of political revolt, and the public (including many of the poor themselves) are thereby reassured that benevolent ends are being served. These programs are then cut back to a level that satisfies local demand for cheap labor without regenerating protest, which by now has been siphoned off. Even though many welfare recipients are thrown off the rolls and others are locked into the marginal labor force because benefits are suppressed below local wage rates, the lulling effect of the earlier program prevents the poor from mobilizing support for another revolt. Even the idea of canvassing the poor to insure that they are receiving the benefits for which they are eligible is regarded as preposterous. In effect, a cultural stress on self-reliance precludes serious attention to the possible malevolence of a symbolically benevolent program.

CONCLUDING REMARKS

Perhaps the greatest significance of placation for the generation of reverse effects is its diversion of attention from the operation of the conversion mechanisms discussed earlier. While I have stressed the manner in which symbolic reassurance may permit exploitation to take place, it also permits functional disruption, goal displacement, provocation, overcommitment, and the adverse effects of classification to proceed with minimal interference from the public or other supporters of the intervention's goals. Once a supporter has been comfortably reassured, any attack on the intervention is experienced as an attack on one's peace of mind. And a broad attack on a whole range of cherished interventions is experienced as an attack on one's sense of fundamental rightness, of an ultimately benign universe, of Weberian "meaning."

This suggests that the idea of progress is itself a placatory device that serves to shield from view those persistent tendencies in history that yield reverse consequences of purposive action. Little wonder that the idea is always resuscitated after periods of profound doubt and that it flourishes when men are in the early phase of pursuing new forms of mastery over the world. For great enterprises require strong denial of the possibility of self-defeat and other negative consequences.

In the following chapter I will return to the idea of progress as it has been reconstituted by one school of sociological theory and subject it to critical scrutiny in light of my analysis of regressive interventions. But first it will be useful to review the ground we have covered and to summarize my main conclusions.

PART III

Summary and Implications for Theory and Policy

CHAPTER 10

Summary

We have seen that the regressive outcomes of intervention are not only quite common but flow from an array of social and psychological mechanisms. Some of the ways in which these consequences are produced are quite familiar and have even gained a niche in commonsense social theory, for example, the forbidden fruit effect and the provocation of illegitimate force. Others are less well appreciated and require considerable attention by social scientists, for example, the functional shift, overload, the lulling effect, and perverse diagnosis. Still other sources are implicit in certain well known sociological concepts that need only to be elaborated in terms of reverse consequences, for example, goal displacement and exploitation.

My procedure of focusing on only a single source of reverse effects at a time, however, has diverted attention from a critical point: conversion mechanisms may occur in concert. In fact, one may depend upon another for a reverse effect to be triggered. A stress on the system's need to recruit and motivate personnel engaged in reform efforts by exalting goals to the neglect of the need for reinforcement at a later date through incremental success (a functional imbalance) may produce subjective overcommitment, the final outcome being frustration and rebellion. Goal displacement may be responsible for the symbolic use of force (a form of provocation if the force is viewed as illegitimate). Placatory interventions may facilitate provocation or exploitation. And so on.

Further, several conversion mechanisms may be brought into play by a single intervention. An apt example of interlocking mechanisms that lead to the same outcome is supplied by a study of the impact of revenue sharing in El Paso, Texas. As Hudson (1980, p. 900) reports:

> One of the aims of Nixon's "New Federalism" reforms was to promote political decentralization in the federal system. An examination of the impact of revenue-sharing and block grant programs in El Paso, Texas, reveals that the New Federalism seems to have had the opposite effect in that city. El Paso is now more dependent, politically and economically, on federal grants than it was prior to the New Federalism and local autonomy is significantly reduced.

Several mechanisms seem to have been responsible for this outcome. In the first place, El Paso did not stand in need of more autonomy from federal grant programs because of its low past participation in categorical programs. Thus, "El Paso did not fit the model of a city constrained by stringent federal guidelines." This suggests a case of *perverse diagnosis* in which the wrong patient is being operated on. In the second place, a *paternalistic* effect is evident in the increased dependency on federal funds that was created, thereby undermining the self-sufficiency of El Paso by providing opportunities for clients' (including local politicians) exploitation of resources. As Hudson notes: "Traditionally the city has not taken responsibility for improvements such as street paving, curbing, street lighting, and drainage, in El Paso's poor neighborhoods, especially the Southside Mexican–American barrio." With the advent of large-scale federal funding, this responsibility could be completely shirked. Third, the infusion of federal funds raised citizens' expectations substantially: "Aldermen tend to perceive increased demands resulting from federal funds as citizens now come to expect such improvements in their neighborhoods. . . ." While no evidence is given that demands exceeded the newly available resources, they clearly contributed to greater rather than less reliance on federal support. Thus, the threat of *overcommitment* was staved off by decreasing autonomy. Fourth, some *goal displacement* may have been involved in the new federal emphasis on procedural compliance:

> For example, the Police Department found its traditional practice of informally reassigning officers to different divisions as work loads varied to be in potential violation of equal employment opportunity guidelines. Mindful of possible criticism from CETA auditors, the Police Chief decided to institute formal (and time consuming) procedures for temporary transfers. (Hudson, 1980, p. 904)

Fifth, the dual emphasis of revenue sharing on service improvement and more local autonomy entails a contradiction of functional requirements, which leads to an *imbalance* that, in the present instance, interfered with autonomy. Hudson argues that the reverse outcome for local independence can probably be generalized "throughout the federal system," in spite of certain unique conditions in El Paso. In sum, revenue sharing may amplify rather than reverse the twentieth-century trend toward governmental centralization.

The interlocking of conversion mechanisms is even more likely to take place in interventions that represent institutional complexes. For example, I have suggested that the criminal justice system fosters crime and injustice in several respects: by police corruption at the bottom and political influence at the top, by labeling certain mildly offensive behaviors as crime, by coercion of defendants to plead guilty, by "covert facilitation" of crime as a means of improving arrest records, by resort to force for symbolic reasons, by compromising due process because of an emphasis on efficiency, by suppressing the supply of addictive drugs, by provoking counterforce when actions are perceived as illegitimate, by promoting socialization into criminal roles by imprisonment and "therapeutic" abuse, and by denying normal occupations to persons with arrest or conviction records. Thus, exploitation, classification (stigmatization and segregative reinforcement), perverse diagnoses, and goal displacement are all prominent features of this single institutional complex. Moreover, the lulling effect of the criminal justice system as a nominal solution to the problem of social disorder may permit these mechanisms to continue operating with impunity. (For an eloquent statement of the argument that the primary function of law is to "comfort" society rather than to "guide" it, see Arnold, 1962, p. 34ff.) In short, through its reassuring promise of order and justice for all, a legal system may be able to produce disorder and injustice on a substantial scale.

As I mentioned in my first chapter, my survey of regressive outcomes suggests a reexamination of certain contemporary ideas about the evolutionary directions and adaptive capacities of modern society. If those fundamental processes that purportedly enhance the adaptive capacities of a society invite interventions that are regressive, then devolutionary forces might counter the enhancement of adaptation. Further, I have promised to offer some observations on the policy implications of my study. Before addressing these issues, we might recapitulate the patterns of regression that have been discussed, with particular attention to the sources of these patterns and the conditions that enable them to have as marked an impact as they do. We shall then be in a better position to assess theory and policy in light of my extended analysis.

The first conversion mechanism was called *functional disruption* because it clearly entailed interference with system requirements. Four types were delineated. A functional *imbalance* involves emphasis on one imperative at the expense of another, a tendency that is especially likely to occur when antithetical needs demand fulfillment. The external sources of functional imbalance were said to be political pressure for decisive and publicly comprehensible action to deal with a deeply felt problem and sufficient concentrations of power to dictate solutions. *Perverse diagnosis* was attributed to the tendency to neglect overriding, proximate causes of problems that are augmented by treatment of the presumed cause. In attempts to deal with deviance, this tendency is encouraged by moralistic interpretations of social reality instead of a more objective "systems" approach. Another source of perverse diagnosis was said to be discrepant frames of reference, involving simple ignorance of the target system's structure or culture and fallacious projection of the needs of one's own social system or personality. *Overload,* or the failure to consider the target system's capacity to fulfill a new need imposed by the intervention, was attributed once again to discrepant frames of reference. Finally, a *functional shift* was said to occur when the unanticipated satisfaction of a system need takes precedence over an original goal that continues to be subverted. The sources of functional shifts were said to be concentrations of power that favor the windfall goal, a shift in the value system that demotes the original goal, or an assumption that the original goal is being served.

The second conversion mechanism was called *exploitation,* and here we distinguished between agents and the target system as exploiters, between hostile and nonhostile target systems, and, with regard to nonhostile target systems and agents, between licit, semilicit, and illicit types of exploitation. The major sources of exploitation by hostile target systems are the desire for self-defense and factors that prompt provocation (see below). With respect to nonhostile target populations, sources of exploitation were said to be the unrecognized scope and depth of needs, heightened levels of aspiration thanks to generalized affluence together with the tendency of the privileged to hoard their resources, and accessibility of generalized media of exchange (involving both the volume of resources and their free-floating nature in a highly differentiated society). Exploitation by agents of intervention was attributed to: excessive reliance on exogenous expertise in a society with a growing division of labor and increasing professionalism; the availability of free-floating resources once again, including

power in particular; the neutralization of moral norms, chiefly as
a consequence of *a priori* rationalizations and their cultural en-
dorsement; and "antagonistic cooperation" between officials
and law breakers. A special type of exploitation that flows from
the power-equalization model of innovation was also discussed, that is, the exploitation of opportunities to participate
in decision making to sabotage an imposed intervention.

I then discussed the familiar concept of *goal displacement* in
terms of reverse effects. Several sources were emphasized: a
ritualistic tendency induced by organizational imperatives;
scarcity of resources, which causes a shift to the use of more
efficient but less effective means and a stress on process indi-
cators of indispensability (e.g., more arrests, more herbicide
dispensed); goal ambiguity, which makes assessment of outcomes difficult; and a cultural emphasis on technique.

The fourth conversion mechanism was called *provocation*.
Illegitimate control results in reverse outcomes because of: a
tendency for groups under attack to coalesce into defensive
entities whose survival becomes an end-in-itself; the fueling of
symbolic deviance; and certain conditions that foster revolt
against deprivation. The resort to such force was explained by:
underestimation of the enemy's will to resist; the symbolic
value of force among specialists in violence, especially in cultures with a historical pattern of violence; illusory threats (or
the projection of violent intentions onto the potential target
system); and discrepant frames of reference that interfere with
comprehension of the opponent's standards of legitimacy.
The provocations of *implicit* threat were traced to: the hierarchical and functional prestige system within organizations
that are subjected to reform efforts; in-group versus out-group
antagonisms; and discrepant frames of reference that occasion
the projection of one's own attributes onto the target system.
At a deeper level of personality, the cancellation of fear by
anxiety may produce compulsive reenactment of the proscribed behavior as a means of tension-release. *Truncated
therapy* was attributed to the mass distribution of psychological
therapy (or other self-actualization interventions) that pre-

cludes follow-up on subjects to deal with the powerful emotional forces that have been released by the initial stages of the
therapy. Finally, *enticement* was seen to operate in a regressive
fashion by publicizing the opportunity for deviance, arousing
latent desires, and creating a climate of possible detection that
raises anxiety and leads to increased indulgence for tension
release. Puritanical values, a symbolic effort to chasten disesteemed groups that pose a new status threat, and a tendency
to attack symptoms rather than causes of deviant behavior are
some of the reasons for resorting to measures that lead only to
an enticement effect.

The fifth conversion mechanism, *classification*, was
viewed as producing reverse effects by means of stigmatization, segregation, overentitlement, and exemption. The roots
of these processes were said to be the paramount trends of
social differentiation, professionalization, and bureaucratization. Also, the need to identify strangers because of increasing
social mobility and high population density, places a premium
on labels that facilitate interaction.

Overcommitment was discussed next and was described as
being either *objective* or *subjective*. The former type entails the
exhaustion or withholding of resources necessary to ac-
complish a task that has already been set, while the latter
entails a rise in expectations that exceeds the capacity to fulfill
them. Objective overcommitment wherein resources are
exhausted was said to stem from an underestimation of the
time required to achieve goals, an underestimation of needs to
be serviced or enemies to be subdued, an assumption by
resource providers that the intervention's operation indicates
that its resources are adequate, attrition of key actors or leaders, escalation of conflict, or exploitation by persons delegated
to take charge of successful subprojects or conquered territory.
Objective overcommitment due to insufficient resources at the
outset was attributed to the placatory function of launching
programs for political benefit with little regard for operational
requirements. Subjective overcommitment was seen to occur
when a sense of relative deprivation is aroused by the inter-

vention's promises of future gain and thus creates an urgency that was unanticipated. With respect to agents of intervention, subjective overcommitment may flow as well from the need to arouse a high level of commitment that minimizes obstacles. In the case of overentitlement, the symbolic value of education in the pursuit of full participation in civil society and the demands of employers for guarantees of discipline and compliance converge to produce underutilization of skills in the occupational structure.

Finally, the seventh mechanism, *placation*, was discussed in terms of a lulling effect and an exasperation effect. One source of placation was said to be the need for groups that are unable to analyze a complex situation to adjust and to be reassured by symbolic action. Another source is the practice of shielding the influence of organized groups from public scrutiny, which involves deception by authorities. Even more deceptive is the practice of contriving or amplifying problems so that authorities can offer solutions that will enhance their support. Expertise and professionalism are further sources of placation which can be attributed to a high level of functional interdependency in a highly differentiated system and which thereby invite exploitation. (Placation, it was noted, is often a requirement for the operation of the other conversion mechanisms discussed here.) In addition, the increasing pluralism of group interests was seen as a major source of evasive compromise with possibly regressive outcomes when external props, including a particular distribution of power at a particular time and place, are removed or modified.

Now let us turn our attention to the implications of my analysis for the development of social theory and social policy.

CHAPTER 11

Implications for Social Theory

In this chapter I will suggest a few lines of theoretical inquiry that might be fruitfully pursued with reference to patterns of regressive intervention. First, I will examine the Parsonian theory of social evolution in light of my analysis, and then I will turn to some other domains of theoretical interest that might be illuminated by the study of regressive intervention.

PARSONS'S THEORY OF EVOLUTION

As I mentioned in an earlier chapter, Parsons (1966) proposes a small number of fundamental historical processes that, in his estimation, combine to produce "greater generalized adaptive capacity." These processes are: differentiation, adaptive upgrading, integration, value generalization, and inclusion. Differentiation within a society refers to the allocation of functional tasks to new, distinct structures. Thus, the separation of economy and polity or of household and occupation and the increasing division of labor within occupations or organizations are all instances of lateral differentiation. In addition, differentiation can be vertical, as in the case of social stratification. *Adaptive upgrading* refers to the increased "adaptive capacity" or productivity of each newly differentiated substructure and entails freeing the participants from ascriptive limitations on their mobilization. *Integration* is the process whereby these new substructures are articulated or coordinated. *Value generalization* draws attention to the emergence of values that can be shared by the substructures, or "moral consensus," over those that are specific to certain subgroups. Finally, *inclusion* means the absorption of groups that were previously excluded from participation and influence in society and which have "developed legitimate capacities" to contribute to the functioning of the system.

In Parsons's view, these processes are related to one another by what might be called the contingent fulfillment of functional imperatives, which can be summarized fairly easily. In order for differentiation to lead to a "more evolved system," it must be accompanied by adaptive upgrading of the new substructures (becoming freed from ascriptive limitations). But in order for this to occur, there must be inclusion of groups that were formerly excluded (i.e., "more generalized resources that are independent of their ascriptive sources"). Further, problems of integrating the new substructures must be solved. This latter process is contingent on two other developments: value generalization, whereby the new substructures develop some degree of consensus, and, once again, inclusion. The theory is graphically summarized in Figure 1.

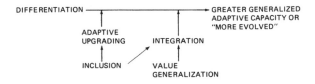

Figure 1

Let us accept the five basic processes as recognizable and significant trends in the emergence of modern society, at least for the sake of the argument that I wish to propose. What seems far more questionable is the net contribution to adaptive capacity that these trends are claimed to make. There are four basic reasons for disputing this claim.

First, each of the five processes releases forces that produce regressive intervention. Second, several of these resultant forces conflict with one another (e.g., increased political pluralism as a result of inclusion versus new concentrations of power as a result of adaptive upgrading). Thus, two kinds of problems will arise: reverse outcomes of interventions and conflict between emergent forces. Third, both of these problems will lead to greater emphasis on social control measures (assessment, regulation, adjudication, force). And fourth, this expansion of control and its attendant organizational forms will produce further regressive consequences. In the final analysis, any "increased adaptive capacity" will be countered by increased incapacity to adapt. If this conclusion is approximately correct, then the study of evolutionary tendencies needs to be complemented by the study of devolutionary tendencies. In effect, it is the net outcome of these two competing forces that must ultimately be investigated at different historical periods.

Let us begin with a consideration of *differentiation*. As I have noted at several points, a seemingly inevitable outcome of differentiation is discrepant frames of reference, which contribute to reverse outcomes in a number of ways. In particular, they are partly responsible for perverse diagnosis, overload of a system, and the application of illegitimate force. Moreover, differentiation affords many opportunities for exploitation as mutual visibility is reduced and blanket legitimation is allotted to functionally interdependent relationships. In the domain of bureaucracy, differentiation also fosters goal displacement and, when reform is attempted, resistance to implicit threats to hierarchical relationships and interdependencies. Thus, even when new substructures are *adaptively upgraded*, especially in the form of professional or scientific bureaucracies, there is a high risk of reverse consequences. Further, the very act of achieving breakthroughs in productivity may divert attention from the problem of finite resources within an expanding system, thereby fostering objective overcommitment.

There are other adverse consequences of adaptive upgrading that need attention. Since adaptive upgrading entails greater productivity, free-floating resources will probably be augmented, a development that invites further exploitation. Moreover, exploitation will be enhanced by the lulling effect of adaptive upgrading, which might in turn undermine preventive care and development of personal sufficiency. Meritocratic concentrations of power, another result of upgrading, will probably also create functional imbalances. And within the context of increasing emphasis on certification, there will no doubt be an expansion of overentitlement with the possibility of widespread status discrepancy. Thus, even if *inclusion* provides a new supply of nonascriptive resources for adaptive upgrading, the processing of recruits to the newly differentiated statuses runs serious risk of raising expectations to unrealistic levels. Conversely, those who are shunted aside along the way may suffer, not only from unmet hopes, but from stigmatization. (This negative consummation, of course, was the theme of Young's *The Rise of the Meritocracy*, 1959.)

It might be said in mitigation that *integrative* processes will serve to bridge discrepant frames of reference, counteract exploitation in spite of the low visibility and blanket legitimation of functional interdependencies, and reduce concentrations of power. Indeed, although Parsons admits that integration is the central problem, he claims that we are moving in the direction of greater "associationism" rather than in that of bureaucracy. First, there is the process of inclusion, or greater participation of social categories with productive capacity, which he believes will contribute to integration. But inclusion also suggests political pluralism, and, as we have seen, pluralism involves placatory compromises that often exacerbate conflict. Inclusion also produces subjective overcommitment on the part of groups that are encouraged to expect full participation in civil society. As Bell (1973, p. 469) points out:

> There is probably more participation today than ever before in political life, at all levels of government, and that very increase in participation leads to the multiplication of groups that "check" each other, and thus to the sense of impasse. Thus increased participation paradoxically leads, more often than not, to increased frustration.

Since more time and effort will be required to arrive at programmatic decisions, which will often entail fragile compromises, frustration and recrimination will be enhanced.

A supplemental source of integration is therefore required, and Parsons calls this *value generalization*. Thus, one might suppose that the increased sharing of basic values would prevent particularistic squabbling as well as illicit exploitation. However, as I have suggested, the internalization of moral norms may not be sufficient to overcome a combination of greater access to free-floating resources and the increased legitimation of functional interdependencies that accompany the advance of professionalism and technologism. As for overcoming pluralistic clashes of interest, Parsons points to a "highly developed legal system" as the modern functional equivalent of religion and ethnic uniformity. Admittedly, the "attenuation of local autonomy," the universalistic criteria of "citizenship" buttressed by a Constitutional framework, and the historical emphasis on "equality before the law" are all formal, idealistic aspects of our legal system (Parsons, 1971, p. 94). But as Mayhew (1971) has pointed out, despite the formal enunciation of such norms, our legal system has been unable to impose them on society by virtue of its poor articulation with other systems:

> A differentiated legal system may lack sufficient articulation with the other differentiated systems of society and so lack the capacity to exercise successful social control. There is considerable evidence that this is true in America today. (p. 188)
>
> The capacity of the legal system to change the society through

> alterations in the order of legal norms is limited. In a sense the
> legal system is too isolated. . . . It is not just that citizens resist
> legal changes; rather, the structural conditions of effective legal
> control do not exist. Hence, when new legal standards are enun-
> ciated, the values of the system are reaffirmed and its promises
> made more visible and specific, but tangible changes are not
> forthcoming. When the legal attack upon the problem fails, the
> next round of demands challenges the legal system itself. (p. 199)

In short, the American legal system is limited to being only a
formal source of integrative values, a state of affairs that both
reflects particularistic demands and allows their reinforcement through the lulling effect of a system that is only nominally universalistic. Of course, as I have already suggested, the
legal system may even be self-defeating, inasmuch as it often
produces the very tendencies it is partly designed to alleviate
(by means of provocation, classification, status exploitation,
and goal displacement).

The response to all of these problems of exploitation,
conflict, unfulfilled group aspirations, and the patent gap between universalistic norms and organizational practice will
very likely be the imposition of regulatory mechanisms, or, to
put it bluntly, increased state control. This may be especially
true in a postindustrial society. As Bell (1973, p. 475) asserts:

> Where the relation among men (rather than between man and
> nature, or man and things) becomes the primary mode of
> interaction—the clash of individual interests, each following its
> own whim, leads necessarily to a greater need for collective
> regulation and a greater degree of coercion (with a reduction in
> personal freedom) in order to have effective communal action.

Yet, there is the distinct possibility that the consequences of
such control will be increased exploitation of bureaucratic resources, goal displacement, and provocation—that is, less *actual* control. Further, together with greater demand for participation in controlling the state apparatus (inclusion), there
may well be subjective and objective overcommitment as previously disfranchised groups compete for a larger share of
political power. New concentrations of power will no doubt
emerge from time to time as the professional–technical sector

and the polity join forces on particular issues, thereby creating functional imbalances and refueling the demand for participation on the part of less powerful or less highly trained groups.

It surely would not do to claim that society is "totally corrupt," as Parsons accuses those of doing who are highly critical of modern institutions (1971, p. 242); nor do I believe that my analysis merely reflects a sensitivity "to the gaps between expectation and performance" (1971, p. 142n), which seems to be his diagnosis of those who suffer from "ideological pessimism," to use his term. What it does reflect is sensitivity to the frequent confounding of purposive action, often as a consequence of the very processes that Parsons views as enhancing the adaptive capacity of the system. This suggests that forces of retrogression are inherent in the forces of progress, a suggestion the flat denial of which can only be branded as ideological naïveté. While modern society may not contain the seeds of its own destruction, it may well contain the seeds of its own neuterization.

OTHER THEORETICAL ISSUES

The implications of studying regressive intervention go far beyond the reexamination of evolutionary theory. There are at least three major strands of social theory that could benefit from such study.

First, investigation of reverse effects might shed light on the structure of social systems through the detection of hitherto obscure sources of system maintenance. The null effects and side effects of a program invite more attention to deficiencies in the program than to unanticipated constraints in the situation itself. Accordingly, better design, more thoughtful salesmanship, or special assistance with implementation is often recommended when such effects become visible. But a reverse effect requires a vigorous search for obscure features of the situation (provided of course, that the whole matter is not swept under the carpet). To put it somewhat differently, regressive interventions may illumine the social structure with special vividness because they compel recognition of the *least* anticipated consequences and subsequently draw attention to the *least* expected aspects and their interdependencies in a given social system.

Functional requirements, for example, may be detected by tracing a reverse effect to interference with some system need that had been overlooked. Numerous examples of this process were given in our discussion of the conversion mechanism of functional disruption. Indeed, the only means of demonstrating the importance of fulfilling a particular system need is to *interfere* with such fulfillment and observe the consequences. For various reasons, including ethical ones, this is manifestly difficult to do. Reverse effects of intervention, however, provide natural experiments of this sort in many instances. Thus, a strategic test of functional theory is offered by the study of regressive outcomes of purposive action. Or again, system vulnerabilities may be detected by tracing the source of exploitation to certain free-floating resources together with certain rationalizations for deviance that were hitherto undetected. (Whether such causes may be translated into functionalist terminology depends upon the complexity and multiplicity of factors involved, the level of theory for which one strives, and one's willingness to accept certain functionalist assumptions about system boundaries and internal relationships.)

A second theme of interest to social science that might be fruitfully addressed by the study of regressive effects is the problem of the limits of rationality. Such limits may be detected: (1) in the failure to consider key features of a target system that might subvert objectives (failure of anticipatory diagnosis); (2) in the refusal of actors to recognize the chronically regressive consequences of their actions (failure of reflexivity); (3) in the reluctance or inability to redesign interventions that are believed to be at least potentially regressive (design retreat); and (4) in the disinclination of policy makers to attack those larger features of the situation that appear to have confounded their plans (policy retreat).

Investigation of the grounds for these apparent defaults of rationality might point, for example, to unintended positive outcomes that take precedence over original goals. Thus, as we noted earlier, educational tracking might be found to make the teacher's job easier, although its effects on learning are subversive. (The reason that this latter effect was not anticipated at the outset involves a failure of *anticipatory diagnosis*.) This effect on original goals may not be recognized (failure of *reflexivity*). If the innovation is unmodified in spite of indications of counterproductivity (*design retreat*), then one might hypothesize that the requirement of job satisfaction was discovered to be of greater value than that of service to clients. To protect this preferred outcome, school administrators and policy makers might argue that alternative means for alleviating the burdens of "heterogeneous" instruction are not available (*policy retreat*).

This example, incidentally, reminds us that simple ineptitude is by no means the sole factor in the production of null or regressive effects, as claimed by some critics of the neoconservative assault on all reform projects. Replacing inept administrators with more skillful ones will not expunge the windfalls of social action that take precedence over original goals or eradicate the antithetical functional requirements of a system. Indeed, the more sophisticated the administrator, the more attentive he might be to enhancing such windfall effects as mentioned above. If he is not *specifically* attuned to the importance of anticipatory diagnosis, reflexivity, redesign, and so on, with respect to a *range* of potential regressive effects, then he (as well as many of his expert advisers) will fail to cope with the regressive nature of the intervention. I shall return to this point subsequently.

The foregoing illustration of limits on rationality suggests a third major theme of interest to social theorists that might benefit from the study of regressive intervention: the legitimation of power. If it is the case that deleterious programs are occasionally perpetuated, then the question arises: what makes it possible to *sustain* actions that have reverse consequences? For it should be emphasized that regressive effects do not necessarily recoil on the responsible agent or agency. While they do sometimes lead to the discrediting of a policy maker or the dismantling of a program, such penalties do not automatically follow. The perpetrator may be unknown to the public, or forgiven because his surprise is shared by everyone (despite the fact of his presumably superior expertise), or even transformed into a hero because of his heroic efforts against overwhelming odds (e.g., the Custer myth). Again, the evidence of detrimental impact might be concealed, or disbelieved, or obscured by controversy (including methodological debate), or mitigated by pleading that any alternative would be even more detrimental. The latter argument is often advanced to justify imprisonment, despite the widespread belief among criminologists that prisons are criminogenic. Finally, evidence of possible reversals may simply stimulate the agents of intervention to redouble their efforts, thereby shifting attention from basic defects in the strategy within a given context to the lack of resources, personnel, dedication, and so forth, that are required to make the strategy work. Nor is it inconceivable that the acquisition of such resources (including more authority and power) might entail a functional shift of emphasis from the original goal to the sheer amassing of resources, that is, that evidence of a reverse effect might be *exploited* to increase the power of an agency to the neglect of any basic modification in the strategy of its intervention. The enforcement of antinarcotics and antimarijuana laws is a prime candidate for this type of self-perpetuating self-defeat. (Here, of course, the intervention is only regressive in terms of *original* goals which are no doubt still held by the public and their elected representatives but not necessarily by the intervention's agents. Such interventions would be viewed here as partially regressive, as I pointed out in Chapter 1.) All of these means of legitimation are assisted, of course, by the lulling effect of governmental expertise and espousal of good intentions.

The multiplicity of ways in which regressive interventions may be perpetuated suggests that such interventions may be *more* successfully maintained than those which are moderately effective in achieving their goals. For in nurturing the latter, the agents are not prompted to undertake campaigns of heroic self-justification nor to weave rationalizations that, in due course, become impregnable doctrine. As is well known, recurrent threats to a group engender powerful measures of self-defense and even counterattack. If the group has governmental legitimacy and is nominally concerned with a social problem that arouses deep anxiety (crime, national security, cancer, etc.), then not only are its actions highly immune to assault by those who claim that the group is actually harmful, but the resources it commands can be employed to neutralize its critics. In short, the provocation effect may ensure that the strength of a regressive intervention is increased by virtue of the attack upon it. Thus, we are confronted with a profound dilemma that can be resolved only by making progress toward recognizing and coping with reverse effects *especially before they are allowed to occur*. These desiderata bring us to the final concern of this book: implications for policy.

CHAPTER 12

Implications for Policy

Few intellectual tasks are as challenging as the effort to anticipate the hitherto unanticipated, and perhaps none is so fool-
hardy. For it is quite possible that our efforts in this direction
are doomed to be as hit-and-miss as the prognostications of a
fortune-teller. Reverse consequences of purposive action will
continue to plague us no matter what we do because of the
powerful social forces that lie behind them, as our discussion
in the preceding chapter must make clear. This does not mean,
of course, that certain precautions should not be taken; but it is
important to bear in mind that our precautions, *being themselves interventions*, are also subject to self-defeat. Thus, whatever recommendations one might offer for policy must be
regarded as hypotheses that require investigation and debug-
ging in their own right.

One has reason to hope, however, that reverse effects of
many government projects can be substantially tamed. Draw-
ing on a wide array of interventions that culminated in such
effects, we have seen that there are certain types that are
frequently and catastrophically overlooked. If we ruminate on
the more manageable sources of these doleful occurrences, it
may be possible to derive a set of policy guidelines that will be
worthy at least of experimentation. Such guidelines can be

applied to two phases: before an intervention is put into effect and while it is underway. Thus, I will offer precautions that might be taken *before* launching a program or project and certain guidelines for monitoring unanticipated consequences *in the course* of implementation. This latter issue brings us back to the need stressed in Chapter 2 for evaluation guidelines in the observation of unanticipated consequences.

With regard to precautions, my recommendations are organized according to each of the seven conversion mechanisms discussed earlier. In each case, I will enunciate a few principles that ought to be borne in mind in formulating procedures for avoiding the pernicious effects of each mechanism and then offer a few specific recommendations for illustrative purposes.

FUNCTIONAL DISRUPTION

Avoidance of functional disruption depends primarily on identification of system requirements, including new requirements imposed by the intervention, and of the likely impact of the intervention on their fulfillment. The assumed dependencies of the target system on its physical and social environment should also be thoroughly investigated. This general task requires objective self-assessment as well, in order to avoid a projective bias in observing the target system. Finally, the multiplicity of goals, of target populations, and of agents or instigators is a factor that is especially important to bear in mind in developing strategies for avoiding functional disruption.

Illustrative Recommendations

Functional Imbalance

1. Analyze functional requirements of target system, including those imposed by previous interventions, and identify those that are antithetical or secondary to primary requirements.

2. Design strategy to serve antithetical requirements either on alternate occasions or simultaneously by distinct mechanisms.
3. Analyze pressures on policy or programs that might produce an imbalance, and strive to alleviate such pressures or balance with other pressures.

Perverse Diagnosis

1. Model the sequence of factors contributing to a problem, and note whether the chosen point of intervention will exacerbate a subsequent factor that will then confound intentions.
2. Empathize with target system and study the interrelations of forces within the system to overcome frame discrepancies.
3. Analyze one's own cultural biases and assumptions about target system so as to avoid projection.

Overload

1. Follow the procedures listed under "Perverse Diagnosis," but also analyze intervention for ancillary requirements that might be imposed on target system.
2. Determine whether target system has capacity to fulfill ancillary requirements; if not, explore ways of providing such capacity.

Functional Shift

1. Stress orientation to original goals, and plan procedures to maintain alertness to shifts of emphasis to any emergent functions (due to changes in power distribution, etc.).

EXPLOITATION

The major tasks in avoiding the ironic effects of exploitation are (1) to identify all resources of the intervention that might invite exploitation and (2) to locate vulnerabilities in the procedures for expending resources and to consider alternatives, including a totally different intervention. One should also bear in mind that a resource may be either instrumentally or symbolically exploited and that even negative resources (e.g., ostensibly punishing acts) can be converted into positive benefits for certain target populations. Further, some aspects of an intervention (e.g., overly restrictive laws) may be exploited to gain resources that lie outside of the intervention (e.g., payoffs for nonenforcement). Finally, exploitation should not be regarded as inhering only in *illicit* acts but should also be looked for in acts that are *semilicit* and even wholly *licit*. For it is possible, and indeed common, that norms which condemn certain forms of exploitation are not widely shared or enacted in law.

Illustrative Recommendations

Hostile Target Systems

1. Evaluate feasibility of security system before launching a new enterprise that might be exploited by enemy, and assign risk factors to various resource segments.
2. Weigh worst possible scenario of exploitation against intended benefits of the intervention.

Nonhostile Target Systems

1. Diagnose full range and depth of needs in target population, and determine chances of population's being swollen by an influx of nontarget groups with the same needs.
2. Consider alternative strategies for filling needs that do not lend themselves to exploitation, for example, full employment policy instead of welfare measures or training programs for limited employment opportunities.
3. Phase in program gradually by moving from most to least needy.

Agent Exploitation

1. Reduce intermediaries in program to a bare minimum by establishing simple standards of eligibility for assistance to clients.
2. Use paraprofessionals from population being served both as providers and monitors of service.
3. Encourage competition for clients within professional fields by advertising and other measures (with safeguards against false claims).
4. Strive to transfer expertise of agents to the clients themselves, especially with regard to prevention of problems.
5. Provide opportunities to potential trust violators for discrete attention and assistance with financial problems or personal failings.
6. Eliminate laws that are unenforceable so that selective enforcement does not invite corruption.
7. When employing power-equalization model, do not impose innovations on participants, but balance participation and leadership initiatives, and train participants in group problem-solving skills.

GOAL DISPLACEMENT

The main point to bear in mind with respect to goal displacement is that all organized action tends to be self-perpetuating regardless of relevance to or achievement of goals. This disjuncture between means and goals is enlarged by scarcity of resources, ambiguity of goals, status anxiety of agents, cultural emphasis on efficiency and technique, and subcultural emphasis on an exclusive possession of technical skills.

Illustrative Recommendations

1. Analyze consequences for goal orientation of different levels of resources, and either adjust resources to avoid regressive goal displacement or abandon project.

2. Specify terminal goals as clearly as possible within political constraints so that measures of achievement can be devised.
3. Emphasize measures of terminal goal attainment instead of procedures or levels of effort, and provide status security on basis of goal attainment.
4. Incorporate provisions for demolishing and rebuilding agencies or projects on basis of new needs and contingencies in the environment.

PROVOCATION

As with functional disruption, the primary principle for generating policy guidelines to forestall provocation is to develop a thorough, and even empathetic, familiarity with the target system. This is especially important in dealing with implicit threats, which tend to lie below the threshold of an agent's awareness. But it also applies to social control efforts that entail force or the threat thereof. Another principle is the importance of assessing one's own capacity to withstand any reaction that might be prompted by the intervention.

Illustrative Recommendations

Illegitimate Control

1. Analyze *social* capacity of hostile targets for resistance and retaliation.
2. Identify values of target system, and strive to detect any symbolic reasons for deviance; study standards of legitimacy and illegitimacy regarding coercive interventions.
3. Train specialists in violence in the dangers of the provocation effect and in alternatives to force as means of conflict resolution or control.
4. Reward specialists in violence for use of alternatives to violence as a means of social control.

Implicit Threat

1. Identify the sources of status security within organizations subjected to change projects and avoid threats to these sources if possible; if not avoidable, supply compensatory rewards as part of innovation.
2. Employ change agents with backgrounds or values similar to those of the target system, including exemplary members of the system itself.
3. Analyze the values, beliefs, and norms of the target system, and note contrasts with own values, beliefs, and norms so that the two types are not confused (i.e., avoid projection).
4. Avoid delivering message or treatment to wrong target system.

Truncated Therapy

1. Ensure that follow-up will be available for dealing with powerful emotional forces that are released by the intervention.
2. Make preparations for monitoring the casualty rate systematically and objectively.

Enticement

1. Eliminate victimless crime laws that tend to amplify deviance by enticement, and substitute (where necessary for community protection) medical and educational programs.

CLASSIFICATION

Here the critical problems for policy reside in the self-fulfilling potential of objective constraints on personal development and freedom of action (including civil rights) and of subjective constraints on self-images and others' estimates of the subject.

Illustrative Recommendations

1. Eliminate tracking in educational systems, and supplement heterogeneous instruction with para-professionals and other aids to individualized treatment of students.
2. Conduct large-scale experiments with alternatives to incarceration, and eliminate sentences for victimless crimes.
3. Abolish employment restrictions for ex-convicts unless nature of job is directly related to deviant tendencies that remain.
4. Preserve the noninstitutional identities of institutionalized persons by protection of civil rights, rotation between institution and community, and so forth.

OVERCOMMITMENT

The principles to bear in mind with regard to overcommitment are: (1) an underestimation of resource needs, especially for long-term operations, invites disaster, not only to the intervention itself but to related operations; (2) expectations tend to rise in response to implicit as well as explicit promises of an intervention; this fact suggests that they must either be kept within bounds at the outset or satisfied over time with automatic increments in resources.

Illustrative Recommendations

1. Resist political pressures to launch programs without adequate funding and authority.
2. Phase in project activities according to milestones as well as terminal goals, and estimate time required to reach each milestone.
3. Communicate milestones to target population in as clear a manner as possible.

4. Measure scope and depth of needs, and set clear and simple criteria for eligibility to be served.
5. Ensure that long-term resources are adequate before relaxing criteria.
6. When estimating needed resources for the future, add on a "rising expectation" factor.

PLACATION

All action that is nominally addressed to problem solving has a tranquilizing effect, an effect that is especially powerful in dealing with complex issues of deep concern to the public. Thus, authorities are able to retain and expand power independently of goal achievement by exploiting this effect. A collective sense of personal insufficiency is the seedbed of regressive placation. With regard to compromise between contending parties, a basic principle is that alteration in an external prop can invite a renewal of conflict that is all the more intense.

Illustrative Recommendations

1. Increase public accountability of mature programs and agencies.
2. Require disclosure of organized groups expected to be benefited by a new program, and measure and publicize achievements with respect to those groups.
3. Foster competition for clients among professionals, and conduct validity checks on a sample of technical observations and decisions by experts.
4. Assess needs and problems independently of political claims before launching programs.
5. Identify conditions that are required for compromises to be sustained, and build in contingency plans for dealing with alterations in those conditions.
6. Plan evaluation strategies that will measure unantici-

pated consequences of all action programs, and provide means for bringing negative effects to the attention of both agents of intervention and the public.

EVALUATION GUIDELINES

Earlier (Chapter 2) I observed that evaluation research has thus far failed to employ systematic guidelines for measuring unanticipated consequences, with the possible exception of goal-free models that ignore the intended outcomes of programs. This latter solution was criticized on several grounds. Because I was especially critical of evaluation research for lack of serious attention to regressive effects and side effects, it becomes incumbent on me to suggest what guidelines for the study of such effects might look like. This is the purpose of the following discussion.

There are four basic dimensions that must be incorporated into evaluation guidelines. I have referred to these dimensions throughout my analysis. They are

Intended versus unintended outcomes
Prediction versus nonprediction of outcomes
Value of outcomes: positive, null, negative
Relevance of outcome to goal versus relevance only to other aspects of the situation, that is, side effects

The reader will appreciate the fact that a combination of the four dimensions yields a very large number of logical possibilities. Yet, it can safely be said that only two are customarily found in evaluation research: intended achievement of formal goals, regardless of prediction, and unintended failure to achieve goals, again regardless of prediction. This extremely limited perspective ignores the prediction of unintended effects, the nonprediction of intended effects (cynicism), and the prediction and observation of side effects, both intended and unintended. It also ignores the possibility that steps were taken to avoid those negative goal-relevant outcomes and negative side effects that were predicted by means of reflexive monitoring. As Hyman *et al.* (1962, p. 13) have observed: "A program is planned, so to speak, to achieve certain things and avert others." Further, this limited focus overlooks the intriguing idea that goals might be achieved in spite of a prediction of falling short.[1] But perhaps most important, it ignores the fact that side effects are sometimes more important that goal-relevant outcomes. If goals are achieved, the negative side effects might pose too high a cost; if unachieved, the positive side effects might still make the effort worthwhile. This last possibility is often claimed by program participants who are criticized for having failed to achieve formal goals, but such claims are just as often disdainfully dismissed by evaluators because of their fixation on original, formal goals. Then, of course, there is always the possibility that goals not only are unachieved but are confounded by reverse effects that render the situation worse than before. Last but not least, it ignores the realm of personal incentives for participation, presumably on the grounds that the formal goals of the program are uppermost and that private motivations are irrelevant to human action.

The four dimensions call for a particular set of measurements. First, intentions must be ascertained and then rank-ordered in terms of priority, clarity, and consensus. Such intentions should include any personal incentives expected by the actors as well as the formal goals of the program.[2] Second, participants should be asked what results they realistically predict. (No doubt there is variability among participants in the extent to which certain consequences are foreseen; yet, we usually assume that everyone concerned is equally surprised by a particular outcome.) Third, intentions and predictions

---

[1] In fact, goals might be achieved precisely because of the challenges raised by skeptics—a form of self-*non*fulfilling prophecy.

[2] For a comprehensive review of positive and negative incentives and disincentives for participation in educational change projects that suggest a host of side effects, see my synthesis of research for the National Institute of Education (Sieber, 1979).

should be studied to ascertain whether they refer to formal goals or to side effects. Fourth, values should be assigned to the major outcomes: positive, null, negative (regressive). These values should be assigned to predicted and intended outcomes separately with reference to different parts of the target system (including individual participants). Fifth, having identified outcomes according to prediction and intention and having decided whether these are to be regarded as positive, null, or negative from various viewpoints, one must observe the outcomes and compare them with predictions and intentions with different value loadings. Sixth, it is necessary to calculate the net balance of good, bad, and indifferent results, with special attention to negative (regressive) effects because of their tendency to be neglected. Finally the extent to which program managers and local administrators engage in a reflexive monitoring of their action should also be measured, in such a way as to include their awareness of net payoffs and penalties, and their estimations should in turn be compared with the assessments of the evaluators.

Invariably, there will be side effects and perhaps regressive outcomes that were not called to the attention of the evaluator by queries about predictions and intentions. Three procedures will assist in identifying these more elusive outcomes: (1) a search in the literature, especially the *qualitative* literature, for such effects in previous programs; (2) a free-wheeling session of the evaluation team members in which all possible effects are hypothesized; and (3) observation of the program itself. This last approach would benefit from observational and interviewing techniques that listed a number of situational parameters and that explored the influence of the program on each of them. In addition, program participants might be asked general questions such as: "How have things changed around here as a result of the program?" "All in all, how has your life been affected by the program?" "Were there any social or psychological costs of the program that made you wonder if it was worthwhile?" "Were you surprised by any good or bad things that happened as a result of the program?"

"How did the program differ from your (or people's) expectations of it?" Probing of this kind should yield a rich harvest of unanticipated consequences. With respect to direct observation, one should remain alert to any activities or events that do not seem directly relevant to program goals. If it is not clear why these activities or events are taking place, the participants themselves might be able to clarify the issue by reference to their positive functions. Then, of course, there is the time-honored procedure of interviewing the skeptics, the embittered, and the marginal men who have had some experience with the program as a means of learning about nonnormative viewpoints.

CONCLUDING REMARKS

Although I am acutely conscious of the perverse way in which man's best intentions often produce his worst performances, I must ring down the curtain on this inquiry with a recommendation that the same measures be taken to assess the negative outcomes of social interventions as are increasingly being taken to assess the second- and third-order consequences of new technologies. Since a major effort in this direction would probably entail a new bureaucratic layer and a new technical specialty that might produce the very consequences that one hopes to forestall or arrest in other domains of social action, however, I refrain from the usual promise of salvation.

But even the forlornness of a hope should not discourage all hoping when the stakes are staggeringly high. As we move into an era in which social planning and professionalism will loom ever larger, it may be the better part of pessimism to create some organ of assessment to test, monitor, evaluate, and codify not only the unanticipated outcomes of large-scale social interventions, but the organ of assessment *itself*. As Chesterton once said, "All pessimism has a secret optimism for its object."

References

Aeschylus. Seven against Thebes, D. Grene (Trans.). In D. Grene & R. Lattimore, *Aeschylus II*. New York: Simon & Schuster, 1973.

Alford, R. The political economy of health care: Dynamics without change. In I. Katznelson, G. Adams, P. Brenner, & A. Wolfe (Eds.), *The politics and society reader*. New York: David McKay, 1974.

Almony, J. *A synopsis of research on IPI*. New York: Bureau of Applied Social Research, Columbia University, 1970.

Anderson, J. *The Anderson papers*. New York: Random House, 1973.

Anderson, S. B., & Ball, S. *The profession and practice of program evaluation*. San Francisco: Jossey-Bass, 1978.

Arnold, T. *The symbols of government*. New York: Harcourt, Brace & World, 1962.

Back, K. *Beyond words*. New York: Russell Sage Foundation, 1972.

Banfield, E. C. *The unheavenly city*. Boston: Little, Brown, 1974.

Barth, A. *Prophets with honor*. New York: Vintage, Random House, 1975.

Bell, D. *The coming of post-industrial society*. New York: Basic Books, 1973.

Berg, I. *Education and jobs: The great training robbery*. Boston: Beacon, 1971.

Berg, I. Review symposium. *School Review*, 1976, *84*, 283–289.

Berman, P., & McLaughlin, M. W. *Federal programs supporting educational change*. Santa Monica, Calif.: Rand Corp., 1974.

Berman, P., & McLaughlin, M. W. *An exploratory study of school district adaptation*. Santa Monica, Calif.: Rand Corp., 1979.

Bernstein, I. N., & Freeman, H. E. *Academic and entrepreneurial research*. New York: Russell Sage Foundation, 1975.

Blau, P. M., & Scott, W. R. *Formal organizations: A comparative approach*. San Francisco: Chandler, 1962.

Blumberg, A. S. The practice of law as confidence game: Organizational co-optation of a profession. *Law and Society Review*, 1967, *1*, 15–39.

218

Boston Globe. Did counseling 40 years ago harm boys? January 10, 1978.

Boyer, B. D. *Cities destroyed for cash.* Chicago: Follet, 1973.

Brecher, E. M. *et al. Licit and illicit drugs.* Boston: Little, Brown, 1972.

Bridge, G. Citizen choice in public services: Voucher systems. In E. D. Savas (Ed.), *Alternatives for delivering public service: Toward improved performance.* Boulder, Colo.: Westview Press, 1977.

Bridge, G., Blackman, J., & Lopez-Morillas, M. How parents choose schools in multiple option systems. Paper delivered at meetings of the American Educational Research Association, San Francisco, April 22, 1976.

Burke, E. *Reflections on the revolution in France.* New York: Penguin, 1978.

Burns, T., & Stalker, G. M. *The management of innovation.* London: Tavistock, 1961.

Butler, R. N. *Why survive? Being old in America.* New York: Harper and Row, 1975.

Cain, G. G., & Hollister, R. G. The methodology of evaluating social action programs. In P. Rossi & W. Williams (Eds.), *Evaluating social programs: Theory, practice, and politics.* New York: Seminar Press, 1972.

Caplovitz, D. *Consumers in trouble: A study of debtors in default.* New York: Free Press, 1974.

Caplow, T. *Toward social hope.* New York: Basic Books, 1975.

Carter, R. K. Clients' resistance to negative findings. In E. R. House (Ed.), *School evaluation.* Berkeley, Calif.: McCutchan, 1973.

Chadwick, H. *The early church.* Harmondsworth, Middlesex, England: Penguin, 1967.

Chambliss, W. J. *On the take.* Bloomington: Indiana University Press, 1978.

Clark, R. *Crime in America.* New York: Simon and Schuster, 1970.

Clinard, M. B., & Quinney, R. *Crime by government.* In M. D. Ermann & R. J. Lundman (Eds.), *Corporate and governmental deviance.* New York: Oxford University Press, 1978.

Cloward, R. A., & Piven, F. F. *The politics of turmoil: Poverty, race and the urban crisis.* New York: Vintage, Random House, 1975.

Collins, R. Where are educational requirements for employment highest? *Sociology of Education,* 1974, *47,* 419–442.

Corwin, R. G. Militant professionalism, initiative and compliance in public education. *Sociology of Education,* 1965, *38,* 310–331.

Corwin, R. G. *Reform and organizational survival.* New York: Wiley, 1973.

Corwin, R. G. Strategies for organizational innovation. In Y. Hasenfeld & R. A. English (Eds.), *Human service organizations.* Ann Arbor: University of Michigan Press, 1974.

Coser, L. *The functions of social conflict.* Glencoe, Ill.: Free Press, 1956.

Coser, L. A., & Howe, I. (Eds.). *The new conservatives: A critique from the left.* New York: New American Library, 1977.

Cressey, D. R. *Other people's money.* New York: Free Press, 1953.

Czepiel, J. A. The diffusion of major technological innovation in a complex industrial community: An analysis of social processes in the American steel industry. Ph.D. dissertation, Northwestern University, Evanston, Ill., 1972.

Deal, T. E. Alternative schools: An alternative postmortem. In J. V. Baldridge & T. E. Deal (Eds.), *Managing change in educational organizations*. Berkeley, Calif.: McCutchan, 1975.

Deutscher, I. Toward avoiding the goal-trap in evaluation research. In C. C. Abt (Ed.), *The evaluation of social programs*. Beverly Hills, Calif.: Sage, 1976.

Dewey, J. *Human nature and conduct*. New York: Henry Holt, 1922.

Downs, A. Evaluating efficiency and equity in federal urban programs. In R. H. Havemann & R. D. Hamrin (Eds.), *The political economy of federal policy*. New York: Harper and Row, 1973.

Dreeben, R. American schooling: Patterns and processes of stability and change. In B. Barber & A. Inkeles (Eds.), *Stability and social change*. Boston: Little, Brown, 1971.

Dreitzel, H. P. *Recent sociology no. 2*. New York: Macmillan, 1970.

Drug Abuse Council. Survey of marijuana use, state of Oregon. Washington, D.C.: Drug Abuse Council, 1975.

Duncan, O. D.,& Schnore, L. F. Cultural, behavioral, and ecological perspectives in the study of social organization. *American Journal of Sociology*, 1959, 132–146.

Duverger, M. *The study of politics*. New York: Crowell, 1972.

Eckaus, R. S. *Appropriate technologies for developing countries*. Washington, D.C.: National Academy of Sciences, 1977.

Edelman, M. *The symbolic uses of politics*. Urbana, Chicago, and London: University of Illinois Press, 1977.

Ellul, J. *The technological society*. New York: Vintage, Knopf, 1964.

Epstein, E. J. *Agency of fear*. New York: Putnam, 1977.

Farb, P. *Humankind*. Boston: Houghton Mifflin, 1978.

Fitzgerald, F. *Fire in the lake*. New York: Random House, 1973.

Flanagan, S. C. Models and methods of analysis. In G. A. Almond, S. C. Flanagan, & R. J. Mundt (Eds.), *Crisis, choice, and change*. Boston: Little, Brown, 1973.

Forrester, J. W. *Urban dynamics*. Cambridge, Mass.: MIT Press, 1969.

Foucault, M. *Madness and civilization*. New York: Random House, 1965.

Freeman, R. B. Overinvestment in college training? *Journal of Human Resources*, 1975, *10*, 287–311.

Fullan, M., Miles, M. B., & Taylor, G. *OD in schools: The state of the art*. Washington, D.C.: Institute of Education, 1978.

Gans, H. J. *More equality*. New York: Vintage, Random House, 1974.

Gaylin, W. Up the river, but why? *The New York Times*, December 18, 1977.

Gaylin, W., Glasser, I., Marcus, S., & Rothman, D. *Doing good—The limits of benevolence*. New York: Pantheon, 1978.

Geertz, C. After the revolution: The fate of nationalism in the new states. In B.

Barber & A. Inkeles (Eds.), *Stability and social change*. Boston: Little, Brown, 1971.

Geis, G. Avocational crime. In D. Glaser (Ed.), *Handbook of criminology*. Chicago: Rand McNally, 1974.

Giddens, A. *Central problems in social theory*. Berkeley: University of California Press, 1979.

Gilbert, W. S. "Gentle Alice Brown" from *Bab Ballads*. In B. Evans, *Dictionary of quotations*. New York: Avenel Books, 1978.

Ginzberg, E., & Solow, R. M. (Eds.). *The great society*. New York: Basic, 1974.

Glaser, D. *Strategic criminal justice planning*. Washington, D.C.: U.S. Government Printing Office (Crime and Delinquency Issues: A Monograph Series, NIMH), 1975.

Glasser, I. Prisoners of benevolence: Power versus liberty in the welfare state. In W. Gaylin, I. Glasser, S. Marcus, & D. Rothman, *Doing good*. New York: Pantheon, 1978.

Glazer, N. The limits of social policy. *Commentary*, 1971, September.

Glennan, T. K., Jr. Evaluating federal manpower programs: Notes and observations. In P. Rossi & W. Williams (Eds.), *Evaluating social programs: Theory, practice, and politics*. New York: Seminar Press, 1972.

Goffman, E. *Asylums*. Garden City, N.Y.: Doubleday, 1961.

Gold, B. *Change and conflict—A case study of an innovative school*. New York: Center for Policy Research, 1977.

Goldstein, K. *Human nature in the light of psychopathology*. Cambridge, Mass.: Harvard University Press, 1940.

Goode, W. J. *Religion among the primitives*. New York: Free Press, 1951.

Gouldner, A. W. Cosmopolitans and locals. *Administrative Science Quarterly*, 1957–1958, *2*, 281–306, 444–480.

Goulet, D. *The cruel choice*. New York: Atheneum, 1973.

Greer, S. Traffic, transportation, and problems of the metropolis. In R. K. Merton & R. A. Nisbet (Eds.), *Contemporary social problems*. New York: Harcourt, Brace and World, 1961.

Grinspoon, L. *Marihuana reconsidered*. Cambridge, Mass.: Harvard University Press, 1977.

Gusfield, J. R. *Symbolic crusade: Status politics and the American temperance movement*. Urbana: University of Illinois Press, 1963.

Hakeen, M. A critique of the psychiatric approach to crime and correction. *Law and Contemporary Problems*, 1958, *23*, 650–682.

Harrington, M. The welfare state and its neoconservative critics. In L. A. Coser & I. Howe (Eds.), *The new conservatives*. New York: New American Library, 1977.

Harris, M. *Cannibals and kings*. New York: Random House, 1977.

Harris, R. *Justice*. New York: Avon, 1969.

Hasenfeld, Y. Organizational dilemmas in innovating social services: The case of the community action centers. *Journal of Health and Social Behavior*, 1971, 208–216.

Hasenfeld, Y., & English, R. A. (Eds.). *Human service organizations.* Ann Arbor: University of Michigan Press, 1974.

Havelock, R. G. *Planning for innovation through dissemination and utilization of knowledge.* Ann Arbor: University of Michigan Press, 1969.

Henshel, R. L. *Reacting to social problems.* Don Mills, Ontario: Longman Canada, 1976.

Henslin, J. M., & Roesti, P. M. Trends and topics in *Social Problems* 1953–1975: A content analysis and a critique. *Social Problems,* 1976, *24,* 54–68.

Hester, J., Jr. *Systems models of urban growth and development.* Cambridge, Mass.: MIT Press, 1969.

Hill, C. Protestantism and the rise of capitalism. In D. S. Landes (Ed.), *The rise of capitalism.* New York: Macmillan, 1966.

Hintze, O. The state in historical perspective. In R. Bendix *et al.* (Eds.), *State and society.* Berkeley: University of California Press, 1973.

Hobhouse, L. T. *Social evolution and political theory.* New York: Columbia University Press, 1911.

Hofstadter, R. *The age of reform.* New York: Knopf, 1955.

Hook, S. *Pragmatism and the tragic sense of life.* New York: Basic Books, 1974.

House, E. R., Glass, G. V., McLean, L. D., & Walker, D. F. No simple answer: Critique of the follow through evaluation. *Harvard Educational Review,* 1978, *2,* 128–160.

Houston, T. R., Jr. The behavioral sciences impact–effectiveness model. In P. Rossi & W. Williams (Eds.), *Evaluating social programs: Theory, practice, and politics.* New York: Seminar Press, 1972.

Hudson, W. E. The new federalism paradox. *Policy Studies Journal,* 1980, *8,* 900–906.

Huntington, S. The United States. In M. Crozier, S. Huntington, & J. Watanuki. *The crisis of democracy.* New York: New York University Press, 1975.

Hyman, H. H., Wright, C., & Hopkins, T. K. *Applications of methods of evaluation: Four studies of the Encampment for Citizenship.* Berkeley: University of California Press, 1962.

Illich, I. *Medical nemesis.* New York: Bantam, 1976.

Joint Committee on New York Drug Law Evaluation. *The nation's toughest drug law: Evaluating the New York experience.* Washington, D. C.: National Institute of Law Enforcement and Criminal Justice, 1978.

Kerner, O. *Report of the national advisory commission on civil disorders.* New York: Bantam, 1968.

Kerr, N. D. The school board as an agency of legitimation. *Sociology of Education,* 1964, *38,* 35–59.

Killian, L. M. Optimism and pessimism in sociological analysis. *The American Sociologist,* 1971, *6,* 281–286.

Kozol, J. *Death at an early age.* Boston: Houghton Mifflin, 1967.

Kristol, I. About equality. *Commentary,* 1972, November, 41–47.

222REFERENCES

Kuttner, R. *Tax rebellions and hard times*. New York: Simon and Schuster, 1980.

Lampman, R. J. What does it do for the poor? A new test for national policy. In E. Ginzberg & R. M. Solow (Eds.), *The great society*. New York: Basic Books, 1974.

Lamson, R. L., & Crowther, C. *Crime and penalties in California*. Sacramento: State Assembly Committee on Criminal Procedure, 1968.

Lee, E. B., & Lee, A. M. The Society for the Study of Social Problems: Parental recollections and hopes. Paper presented before the Society for the Study of Social Problems, San Francisco, 1975.

Lefebvre, G. *The coming of the French revolution*. Princeton, N.J.: Princeton University Press, 1967.

Levitan, S. A., & Taggart, R. *The promise of greatness*. Cambridge, Mass.: Harvard University Press, 1976.

Lieberman, M.,Yalom, I., & Miles, M. The group experience project: A comparison of ten encounter technologies. In L. Blank, G. Gottsegen, & M. Gottsegen (Eds.), *Encounter: Confrontations in self and interpersonal awareness*. New York: Macmillan, 1971.

Linton, R. *The study of man*. New York: D. Appleton-Century, 1936.

Linton, R., & Kardiner, A. The change from dry to wet rice cultivation in Tanala-Betsileo. In G. E. Swanson (Ed.), *Readings in social psychology*. New York: Henry Holt, 1952.

Loewy, A. H. *Criminal law*. St. Paul, Minn.: West, 1975.

Louis, K. S., & Sieber, S. D. *The dispersed organization*. Norwood, N.J.: Ablex, 1979.

Machiavelli, N. *The prince*. New York: Limited Editions Club, 1954.

Mann, D. *Intervening with convicted serious juvenile offenders*. Santa Monica, Calif.: Rand Corp., 1976.

Marohn, R. C. Trauma and the delinquent. In S. C. Feinstein & P. Gioracchini (Eds.), *Adolescent Psychiatry*, 1974, *3*, 354–361.

Marshall, H. Administrative responsibility and the new science of management decision. In C. S. Wallia (Ed.), *Toward century 21*. New York: Basic Books, 1970.

Marx, G. T. Ironies of social control: Authorities as possible contributors to deviance through non-enforcement, covert facilitation, and escalation. Revision of paper read at International Sociological Association meetings, Toronto, 1974.

Marx, G. T. The new police undercover work. *Urban Life* (forthcoming).

Marx, K. *Marx and Engels: Basic writings on politics and philosophy*. Edited by L. S. Feuer. Garden City, New York: Anchor Books, Doubleday & Co., 1959.

Mayhew, L. Stability and change in legal systems. In B. Barber & A. Inkeles (Eds.), *Stability and social change*. Boston: Little, Brown, 1971.

McGee, R. A. Hope and despair make the scene in crime prevention. In *The change process in criminal justice*. Washington, D.C.: Law Enforcement

Assistance Administration, U.S. Department of Justice, Fourth National Symposium on Law Enforcement Science and Technology, 1973.

Mead, M. (Ed.), *Cultural patterns and technical change*. New York: Mentor, 1955.

Meadows, D., *et al*. *The limits to growth*. New York: Universe Books, 1972.

Melman, S. *The permanent war economy*. New York: Simon and Schuster, 1974.

Merton, R. K. The unanticipated consequences of purposive social action. *American Sociological Review*, 1936, *1*, 894–904.

Merton, R. K. The self-fulfilling prophecy. *Antioch Review*, Summer 1948.

Merton, R. K. *Social theory and social structure*. Glencoe, Ill.: Free Press, 1957.

Merton, R. K. Social problems and sociological theory. In R. K. Merton & R. A. Nisbet (Eds.), *Contemporary social problems*. New York: Harcourt, Brace and World, 1961.

Merton, R. K. Unanticipated consequences and kindred sociological ideas. Paper delivered at the annual meetings of the Society for the Study of Social Problems, San Francisco, 1978.

Merton, R. K., & Barber, E. Sociological ambivalence. In E. A. Tiryakian (Ed.), *Sociological theory, values, and sociocultural change*. New York: Free Press, 1963.

Merton, R. K., & Kendall, P. L. The boomerang response. *Channels*, 1944, *21*, 1–7.

Merton, R. K., & Nisbet, R. A. (Eds.), *Contemporary social problems*. New York: Harcourt, Brace and World, 1961.

Miles, M. B. *Project on social architecture in education. Final report. Part I: Introduction*. New York: Center for Policy Research, 1978.

Miles, M. B. Common properties of schools in context: The backdrop for knowledge utilization and "school improvement." In P. Berman, M. Fullan, E. House, K. Louis, & S. Sieber. (Untitled forthcoming publication.) Beverly Hills, Calif.: Sage, 1981.

Mintz, M., & Cohen, J. S. *Power, Inc*. New York: Viking Press, 1976.

Mitford, J. *Kind and usual punishment*. New York: Vintage, Random House, 1974.

Moore, W. E. Functionalism. In T. Bottomore & R. Nisbet (Eds.), *A history of sociological analysis*. New York: Basic Books, 1978.

Moynihan, P. *The politics of a guaranteed income*. New York: Random House, 1973.

Mulder, M. Power equalization through participation? *Administrative Science Quarterly*, 1971, *16*, 31–38.

Mullen, J., & Carlson, K. *Pre-trial intervention: A program evaluation*. Cambridge, Mass.: Abt Associates, 1974.

National Institute of Law Enforcement and Criminal Justice. *The nation's toughest drug law: Evaluating the New York experience*. Washington, D.C.: Law Enforcement Assistance Administration, 1977.

Neier, A. *Crime and punishment: A radical solution*. New York: Stein and Day, 1976.

Nelson, B. Weber's Protestant ethic: Its origins, wanderings, and foreseeable futures. In C. Y. Glock & P. E. Hammond (Eds.), *Beyond the classics? Essays in the scientific study of religion.* New York: Harper and Row, 1973.

Nevins, A., & Commager, H. S. *A pocket history of the United States* (5th ed.). New York: Pocket Books, 1967.

Niebuhr, R. *Faith and history: A comparison of Christian and modern views of history.* New York: Scribner's, 1949.

Nisbet, R. *Twilight of authority.* New York: Oxford University Press, 1975.

Nisbet, R. *History of the idea of progress.* New York: Basic Books, 1980.

Parsons, T. *Societies—evolutionary and comparative perspectives.* Englewood Cliffs, N.J.: Prentice-Hall, 1966.

Parsons, T. *The system of modern societies.* Englewood Cliffs, N.J.: Prentice-Hall, 1971.

Parsons, T. *The evolution of societies.* Englewood Cliffs, N.J.: Prentice-Hall, 1977.

Persell, C. H. *Education and inequality.* New York: Free Press, 1977.

Piven, F. F., & Cloward, R. A. *Regulating the poor: The functions of public welfare.* New York: Vintage, Random House, 1971.

Pollin, W. Discussion: research allocation strategies. In C. C. Abt (Ed.), *The evaluation of social programs.* Beverly Hills, Calif.: Sage, 1976.

Polybius. *The histories.* New York: Washington Square Press, 1966.

Previté-Orton, C. W. *The shorter Cambridge medieval history.* Cambridge: Cambridge University Press, 1952.

Reedy, G. *The twilight of the presidency.* New York: Mentor, 1970.

Rein, M., & White, S. H. Policy research: Belief and doubt. *Policy Analysis,* Spring, 1977, 239–271.

Rice, A. *The organization and its environment.* London: Tavistock, 1963.

Riess, A. J., Jr., *The police and the public.* New Haven, Conn.: Yale University Press, 1971.

Rogers, D., & Swanson, B. White citizen response to the same integration plan: Comparisons of local school districts in a northern city. *Sociological Inquiry,* 1965, *35,* 107–122.

Rogers, E. M. & Shoemaker, F. F. *Communication of innovations.* New York: Free Press, 1971.

Rossi, P. Testing for success and failure in social action. In P. Rossi & W. Williams (Eds.), *Evaluating social programs: Theory, practice, and politics.* New York: Seminar Press, 1972.

Runkel, R. J., & Bell, W. E. Some conditions affecting a school's readiness to profit from OD training. *Education and Urban Society,* 1976, *8,* 127–144.

Salamon, L. B., & Wamsley, G. L. The federal bureaucracy: Responsive to whom? In L. N. Rieselbach (Ed.), *People vs. government—the responsiveness of American institutions.* Bloomington: Indiana University Press, 1975.

Schacter, S. *The psychology of affiliation.* Stanford, Calif: Stanford University Press, 1959.

Schlesinger, A. M., Jr. *The imperial presidency*. Boston: Houghton Mifflin, 1973.

Schneider, L. *Sociological approach to religion*. New York: Wiley, 1970.

Schneider, L. Unanticipated consequences of social action: Beneficent and maleficent. Paper delivered at the annual meetings of the Society for the Study of Social Problems, San Francisco, 1978.

Schon, D. *Technology and change*. New York: Dell, 1967.

Schrag, C. Theoretical foundations for a social science of correction. In D. Glaser (Ed.), *Handbook of criminology*. Chicago: Rand McNally, 1974.

Schultze, C. L. Perverse incentives and the inefficiency of government. In R. H. Havemann & R. D. Hamrin (Eds.), *The political economy of federal policy*. New York: Harper and Row, 1973.

Schuman, F. L. *The cold war: Retrospect and prospect*. Baton Rouge: Louisiana State University Press, 1962.

Schur, E. M., & Bedau, H. A. *Victimless crimes*. Englewood Cliffs, N.J.: Prentice-Hall, 1974.

Schwartz, R., & Skolnick, J. H. The stigma of "ex-con" and the problem of reintegration. In D. M. Petersen & C. W. Thomas (Eds.), *Corrections—problems and prospects*. Englewood Cliffs, N.J.: Prentice-Hall, 1975.

Schweitzer, A. *Out of my life and thought*. New York: Mentor, 1953.

Scott, R. A. The selection of clients by social welfare agencies: The case of the blind. *Social Problems*, 1967, *14*, 248–257.

Scriven, M. Pros and cons about goal-free evaluation. *Evaluation Comment*, 1972, *3*, 1–8.

Scriven, M. (Personal communication, 1978.)

Sears, R., Maccoby, E., & Levin, H. *Patterns of child rearing*. New York: Harper and Row, 1957.

Selznick, P. *TVA and the grass roots*. Berkeley: University of California Press, 1949.

Sieber, S. D. Toward a theory of role accumulation. *American Sociological Review*, 1974, *39*, 567–578.

Sieber, S. D. *Farewell to innocence: Marijuana and the criminal justice system in America*. (Unpublished, 1977.)

Sieber, S. D. Knowledge utilization. In M. B. Miles, S. D. Sieber, D. E. Wilder, & B. A. Gold, *Final report, conclusions—Project on social architecture in education*. New York: Center for Policy Research, 1978.

Sieber, S. D. *Incentives and disincentives for knowledge utilization in public education*. Washington, D.C.: National Institute of Education, 1979.

Sieber, S. D. Analysis and implications for school administrators. In K. S. Louis, D. Kell, K. J. Chabotar, & S. D. Sieber, *Perspectives on school improvement: A casebook for administrators*. Cambridge, Mass.: Abt Associates, 1980.

Sieber, S. D., Louis, K. S., & Metzger, L. *The use of educational knowledge*. New York: Bureau of Applied Social Research, Columbia University, 1972.

Simmel, G. The triad. In K. H. Wolff (Ed.), *The sociology of Georg Simmel.* Glencoe, Ill.: Free Press, 1950.

Skolnick, J. H. *The politics of protest.* New York: Ballantine, 1969.

Smelser, N. Stability, instability, and the analysis of political corruption. In B. Barber & A. Inkeles (Eds.), *Stability and social change.* Boston: Little, Brown, 1971.

Southern, R. W. *Western society and the church in the middle ages.* Baltimore, Md.: Penguin, 1973.

Spencer, H. *The man versus the state.* Caldwell, Idaho: The Caxton Printers, 1946. (Also, D. Appleton and Co., 1892.)

Starr, P. Medicine and the waning of professional sovereignty. *Daedalus,* 1978, *107,* 175–193.

Steele, S. M. *Contemporary approaches to program evaluation.* Washington, D.C.: Capitol Publishers, 1977.

Steiner, G. Y. Reform follows reality: The growth of welfare. In E. Ginsberg & R. M. Solow (Eds.), *The great society.* New York: Basic Books, 1974.

Suchman, E. A. *Evaluative research.* New York: Russell Sage Foundation, 1967.

Sussman, A. *The rights of young people.* New York: Avon, 1977.

Taylor, I., Walton, P., & Young, J. *The new criminology.* New York: Harper and Row, 1973.

Thurow, L. Education and social policy. *The Public Interest,* 1972, *28.*

Toby, J. The socialization and control of deviant motivation. In D. Glaser (Ed.), *Handbook of criminology.* Chicago: Rand McNally, 1974.

Tocqueville, A. de. *The old regime and the French revolution.* Princeton, N.J.: Princeton University Press, 1955.

Tunney, J. V. *Hearings on reform of the grand jury system.* Subcommittee on Constitutional Rights of the Committee on the Judiciary, September 28, 1976, U.S. Senate.

U.S. Commission on Violence. Washington, D.C.: Government Printing Office, 1968.

van den Berghe, P. L. Dialectic and functionalism: Toward a theoretical synthesis. *American Sociological Review,* 1963, *28,* 695–705.

Vinter, R. D. Analysis of treatment organizations. In Y. Hasenfeld & R. A. English (Eds.), *Human service organizations.* Ann Arbor: University of Michigan Press, 1974.

Warren, C. The magnet school boom: Implications for desegregation. *Equal Opportunity Review.* New York: Teachers College, Columbia University, 1978.

Weiss, C. H. *Evaluation research.* Englewood Cliffs, N.J.: Prentice-Hall, Inc., 1972.

Wicker, T. *A time to die.* New York: Random House, 1975.

Wilson, J. Q. *Thinking about crime.* New York: Basic Books, 1975.

Wing, J. K. Institutionalism in mental hospitals. *British Journal of Clinical Psychology,* 1962, *1,* 38–51.

Wyant, S. Effects of organization development training on intrastaff communication in elementary schools. Doctoral dissertation, University of Oregon, 1974.

Yarmolinsky, A. What future for the professional in American society? *Daedalus*, 1978, *107*, 159–174.

Yin, R. K., *et al. A review of case studies of technological innovations in state and local services.* Santa Monica, Calif.: Rand Corp., 1976.

Young, M. *The rise of the meritocracy.* New York: Random House, 1959.

Zaltman, G., Duncan, R., & Holbek, J. *Innovations and organizations.* New York: Wiley, 1973.

Zander, M. Welfare reform and the urban aged. *Society*, 1978, *15*, 59–67.

Index